The Virilio Dictionary

Edited by John Armitage

EDINBURGH
University Press

Edinburgh University Press Ltd
22 George Square, Edinburgh EH8 9LF

www.euppublishing.com

Typeset in 11/13 Ehrhardt
by Servis Filmsetting Ltd, Stockport, Cheshire, and
printed and bound in Great Britain by
CPI Group (UK) Ltd, Croydon CR0 4YY

A CIP record for this book is available from the British Library

ISBN 978 0 7486 4684 5 (hardback)
ISBN 978 0 7486 4683 8 (paperback)
ISBN 978 0 7486 4685 2 (webready PDF)
ISBN 978 0 7486 8231 7 (epub)

Contents

Acknowledgements

The Virilio Dictionary is the result of extensive collaboration. I want to convey my thanks to: Richard G. Smith, for inviting me to contribute to *The Baudrillard Dictionary* (2010), which he edited, and which subsequently inspired me to edit *The Virilio Dictionary*; each and every contributor to this book for their expert knowledge of Paul Virilio's writings; my good friends at *Cultural Politics*, and above all Ryan Bishop and Mark Featherstone, Joy Garnett and Douglas Kellner for their helpful advice throughout the project; Carol MacDonald and Jenny Daly at Edinburgh University Press, for their receptiveness to the venture, useful editorial comments and organisational support; my partner, Joanne Roberts, without whose love and inordinate tolerance concerning my work on Virilio I would never have been equipped for this particular mission.

Finally, I would like to dedicate this book to Paul Virilio, who first introduced me to the critical investigation of art and technology through my initially stunned discovery of his *Speed and Politics: An Essay on Dromology* (2006 [1977]) in Northumbria University library, and whose later kindness and understanding has continued to motivate my thoughts, reading and writings.

Introduction

John Armitage

Paul Virilio is one of the leading critics of art and technology working today. He has an exceptional scope of investigation, which includes everything from the city to military architecture, from technology to geopolitics, from speed to ecology, aesthetics, cinema and war. This scope, aligned with a potent and piercing critical intellect, comprises the most exciting thing about studying Virilio.

The Virilio Dictionary aspires to offer a compressed yet understandable introduction to Virilio's key concepts and clarify why his ideas are vital to our critical comprehension of contemporary art and technocultural studies. If we want an awareness of why Virilio's notions are significant, and of the effect they are having on critical theory, art and technocultural studies, we must hang onto two important concepts simultaneously: phenomenology and hypermodernism. For many of his fellow critical theorists, Virilio is one of the world's most important interpreters of phenomenological ideas working in the present period; and his writings on hypermodernism are some of the most powerful examinations of that cultural phenomenon (Armitage 2000; James 2007). Anybody writing on these two subjects will most likely find themselves wrestling with 'Virilian' notions.

Phenomenology is a movement rooted in the work of Edmund Husserl (1859–1938) concerned with philosophically examining and methodically enquiring into the argument that reality comprises of objects and events as they are perceived or appreciated in human consciousness and not of anything apart from human consciousness. It has been very prominent in numerous fields of critical, aesthetic and technocultural thought, and has had a specific influence on aesthetic criticism and technocultural studies: a detailed explanation and reflection on phenomenology can be found in the entry on 'Phenomenology'. Hypermodernism, conversely, is the concept I (Armitage 2000) frequently employ to portray Virilio's critical comprehension of the escalated logic of contemporary art and technoculture. It is the manner and the historical era wherein much art and technology is presently being created; a comparable usage of vocabulary sees Postmodernism used to depict the mode of art and technology created throughout the latter part of the twentieth century, or modernism to illustrate the critical works of art and technology created at the end of the nineteenth and the beginning of the twentieth centuries (Jameson 1991; Nicholls 1995). There have not been many efforts to delineate hypermodernism more exactly than this, and the entry on 'Hypermodernism' elucidates these in more detail. In both these important spheres, Virilio's writings have been pivotally and forcefully engaged. His two most well-known books are, arguably, *Speed and Politics: An Essay on Dromology* (2006 [1977]) and *War and Cinema: The Logistics of Perception* (1989 [1984]): the first of these is an influential amplification of phenomenological, aesthetic and political analysis, the second an innovative study of the hypermodern disappearance of war into cinema that established the conditions of a good deal of the discussions about contemporary logistics and perception during the Persian Gulf War of 1990–1 and the Iraq War of 2003. These two emphases of Virilio's writings do not signify any transfer of attention. As we shall discover, Virilio's incisive enquiries into the hypermodern 'sight machine' in *War and Cinema*, for example, are in fact merely the expansion of his enduring phenomenological approaches.

It is as a phenomenologist that Virilio originally came to fame. His insights emanate from and constantly involve a 'hypercritical' viewpoint on art and technoculture, but he is never inflexible, and his allure is not at all confined to those who share his philosophical beliefs. In all that Virilio has worked on, it is the scope and suppleness of his hypercritical methodology, as much as the razor-sharpness of his farsightedness, which continues to gain him so broad a readership. Anyone taken with the aesthetic and technocultural developments of the twenty-first century, with the varied signs of that increasingly valuable idea, hypermodernism, will find his critical analyses of that aesthetic and technocultural logic indispensable reading.

PAUL VIRILIO: AN INTELLECTUAL PROFILE

Virilio's intellectual biography helps to explain the diversity of his concerns. Born in Paris, France, in 1932, he studied German and French phenomenology at the University of Paris Sorbonne in the 1950s, journeying in Germany and France and studying in addition city planning in the 1950s, and military space and the organisation of territory from 1958 onwards. This Franco-German viewpoint intensified Virilio's feeling for his own Breton (mother) Italian (father) inheritance, and gave crucial contexts to his (*Bunker Archeology* 1994a [1975]) interpretations of the 'Atlantic Wall', the name given by Adolf Hitler during the Second World War (1939–45) to the series of Nazi-built fortifications extending some 1,670 miles along the Atlantic coast of Europe from the Netherlands to

Spain. The Atlantic Wall was an important part of the Nazis' defences, but failed to halt the Allied landings in Normandy in June 1944. Virilio took his interest in the city to the French architect Claude Parent, and together they founded, in 1963, the Architecture Principe group and the journal bearing the same title (Virilio and Parent 1996, 1997). Parent and Virilio worked with their phenomenologically inspired theory of the 'oblique function' so as to examine new kinds of architectural and urban orders. Refusing the customary axes of the horizontal and the vertical, they employed oblique planes to produce an architecture of disequilibrium, in an effort to bring the urban environment into a dynamic age of the body in movement. The oblique function resulted in the building of two main architectural works: the Church of Sainte-Bernadette-du-Banlay in 1966 and the Thomson–Houston Centre of aerospace research in Villacoublay in 1969. For Virilio, his pursuit of architecture carried with it in 1969 the appointment to a professorship and workshop director at the École Spéciale d'Architecture (ESA) in Paris Montparnasse, and membership of the editorial board of the review *Esprit* in 1970 before, in 1973, becoming director of studies at the ESA. Few architects, save, perhaps, Virilio's good friend, the late Georges Perec (1997), have attained Virilio's level of hypercritique, though, with many instead surrendering to traditional, infertile concepts of space. This standpoint is vital when contemplating Virilio's intellectual profile: his own unconventional yet strong-minded general directorship of the ESA, his devotion to a phenomenologically motivated philosophy of military architecture in the form of the 'archeology' of military bunkers in a country (France) that has, on occasion, been ashamed of such Nazi impositions, even his distinctive and specific mode of exhibiting at museums, researching into war and peace, and writing on military strategy, technology and cultural space, are all indications of his dedication to contemporary geopolitics and the tricky issue of understanding the world of speed and politics, militarisation and the ongoing revolution in the transportation and transmission capabilities of new information and communications technologies (Virilio, *Speed and Politics* 2006 [1977]). As *The Virilio Dictionary* concentrates on Virilio's key concepts, it will not look into his secondary notions on, for example, popular culture, defence, ecology or struggles against war (which are published in his earlier books such as *Popular Defense & Ecological Struggles* 1990 [1978]). But, one detail worth underlining here is that neither Parent nor architecture are individuals or subjects that direct Virilio's contemporary concerns: both an aesthetic figure and a philosopher of the cultural effects of cinematics in the phenomenological tradition, art, philosophy, the humanities and a hypercritical perspective on cultural space are the major subjects where Virilio currently works (e.g. Virilio 2009a [1980]).

In the 1980s Virilio researched into the crisis in the idea of physical dimension, published in English as *The Lost Dimension* (1991 [1984]), research commenced at the request of the Minister of Equipment and Housing, moving to *War and Cinema*, a book on the deployment of cinematographic methods utilised throughout the First and Second World Wars. From 1984 he worked on *Negative Horizon* (2005a [1984]), which scrutinises the relations of speed to politics, culture and society; and, from 1988, following Virilio's 'National Award for Criticism' for his work en bloc in 1987, he wrote *The Vision Machine* (1994b [1988]), which contends with the 'progress' in computerisation, post-industrial production and human perception. Since then he has been programme director of the International College of Philosophy in Paris (1989) and published numerous book-length treatises, for example *Polar Inertia* (2000a [1990]), which focus on the current developments in remote control technology, the human and the natural worlds, while nearly all of Virilio's writings have been republished and translated into countless languages. Furthermore, he eventually became the president of the ESA and chief advisor to the French Pavilion Commission for the 1990 Universal Exposition in Seville, Spain, in co-operation with the well-known French intellectual, journalist, government official and professor of 'mediology', Régis Debray (2004). However, Virilio's theoretical stress on the aesthetics of military technology and the media must not conceal the truth that during the 1990s he was working on an extremely broad assortment of books and themes, from his *Desert Screen: War at the Speed of Light* (2002a [1991]), an anthology of his reports on the Gulf War of 1990–1 for newspapers, for instance *Libération*, and technoculture, science, war, the city, defence, to architecture. One of the first volumes to earn him an international reputation was *The Art of the Motor* (1995 [1993]), which incorporates in-depth analyses of the multimedia revolution and numerous Continental philosophers in the phenomenological tradition. Virilio was one of the original hypercritics of standing to bring in the currently prominent critical perspectives connected with phenomenological theorists such as Maurice Merleau-Ponty to a younger generation of European, North American and Australian researchers and readers; but *The Art of the Motor* additionally involves a thesis of Virilio's own, that critics should focus on the new advances in nanotechnology and virtual reality as much as on the information, speed and duration that are not simple gear changes but embody, not to say disembody, the third dimension of matter, the accelerated rate of the spread of information, and the disintegration of the extension of the dimension of space and the length of the dimension of time. This powerful contention is discussed in the entry on 'The Art of the Motor'. Two years later, Virilio issued another hypercritical explanation of information technology and the global electronic media, perception and the infantilism of cybernetic misinformation: *Open Sky* (1997 [1995]).

During the 2000s, Virilio published several dazzling books in addition to many substantial interviews. A critique of the new methods of warfare, and its relegation to images on a computer screen, *Strategy of Deception* (2000b [1999]) enlarged on how Virilio could find fascinating and constructive things in the seemingly culpable insincerity that others have understood as terribly corrupted by the way in which the United States and its allies conducted the Kosovo War (1998–9). Here, Virilio makes an incisive condemnation of the Kosovo War's execution; indeed, his is an important critical opinion that heralds the prospect of analysing beyond the façade of the Kosovo War and into the unknown potentialities of theorising the military encounter. This critical outlook was expanded and demonstrated in one of Virilio's most celebrated books, *A Landscape of Events* (2000c [1996]), his sequence of commentaries on the cultural disorder of the 1980s and 1990s, of the time of brutality, urban bewilderment, war machines and the speeding up of the experience of postmodern everyday life. This now landmark work is the focal point of the entry on 'A Landscape of Events'.

If *A Landscape of Events* indicates one of the high spots of Virilio's critical contributions to phenomenological, aesthetic and technocultural theory, and continues to be one of the most influential and extensively cited of his phenomenological aesthetic-theoretical texts, then the 2000s saw him more and more attracted to the phenomena of hypermodernism and hypermodernity. Two books published by the British radical publisher Verso – *The Information Bomb* (2000d [1998]) and *Ground Zero* (2002b [2002]) – are among the most commanding of his declarations on the character of hypermodern human 'advance' and technological 'progress' as ultimately destructive powers. Few critics were astonished by his involvement with this theme, because it was taken for granted by many that a phenomenologist of technoculture would be receptive to thinking through and critiquing many of the things that hypermodernism is thought to signify. But Virilio's writings on hypermodernism, such as his *Art and Fear* (2003a [2000]), which focuses on his vision of the effects of modern technology on the contemporary global state of art and science, politics and warfare, alongside his *Unknown Quantity* (2003b [2002]) catalogue, published to complement the exhibition he created for the Fondation Cartier in Paris, and which considers the philosophical problems elicited by our confrontation with accidents and their influence on our world, develops his rich phenomenological intellectual tradition. Virilio published far and wide on hypermodern phenomena throughout the 2000s, enlarging his reach from his *City of Panic* (2005b [2004]), an exposition on the city as the contemporary target of political and techno-logical dread, the gratuitous erasure of the past, the construction of iden-tikit places, the propagation of gated communities, the ever-widening net of surveillance, and the privatisation of what was public, into *The Original Accident* (2007a [2005]) and other kinds of aesthetic and technocultural production and destruction. *Art as Far as the Eye Can See* (2007b [2005]) is an evaluation of contemporary art and politics, new media technologies, and the general cultural shift into the speed or 'chronopolitics' of mass cultural panic, which Virilio describes as the major characteristics of the twenty-first century. Simultaneously, his concern with and devotion to phenomenological theory and practice has not faded. For instance, a long interview published as *Grey Ecology* (2009) was followed by a study of the phenomenological and philosophical aspects of what he (2010a [2007]) calls *The University of Disaster* or the internment of humanity within the tighter and tighter limits of an accelerating 'dromosphere'.

Since then, Virilio's pioneering intrusions into the debates over hyper-modernity have continued, mixed together with more customary phenom-enological enquiries. Indeed, it is not actually feasible to isolate these two features of his philosophy. *The Futurism of the Instant: Stop-Eject* (2010b [2009]) is his critical account of human displacement by war, of the future of human settlement and of migration considered as a component of the accelerating exodus from the world's major cities. Investigating the crea-tion of a circulating world city of transients on the move that will eventu-ally remove us all from our *Native Land: Stop Eject* (Virilio and Depardon 2008) as we head for the ultimate exile, the exile beyond planet Earth itself, Virilio contends that our departure from planet Earth is a project that the world's crazy technoscientists have been planning for a while. Virilio's hypercritical standpoint has also become more expansive on the city, with interests in the acceleration of uncertainty and history, although some critics, such as the cultural geographer Nigel Thrift (2011), have articu-lated reservations concerning Virilio's writings in this field. *The Great Accelerator* (2012 [2010]) is a complex interpretation of hypermodernism and ideas of insecurity and the past, the fading of privacy, and speed; and *The Administration of Fear* (Virilio and Richard 2012) is a book-length interview on the synchronisation of emotions, the globalisation of affects, real time and the 'propaganda of progress' (Virilio and Armitage 2009).

KEY QUESTIONS CONCERNING VIRILIO'S WORK

As a rule, the problems confronting a reader inexperienced in 'Virilio studies' (Armitage 2011) are twofold: the first is the frequently multifaceted, constantly all-embracing and, from time to time, obscure (at any rate to many English-speaking readers) critical milieu that Virilio occupies. The second problem is the predicament of reading Virilio's own and very 'French', intense, and, to begin with at least, dense writing style.

Any thorough deliberation on Virilio's texts, theories and concepts must be rooted in the settings out of which they have arisen. Certainly, this is vital for any philosopher, but it is especially critical for Virilio since he brings into play so many often avant-garde aesthetic ideas and such complex technocultural theoretical traditions. This is actually one of the many benefits of reading Virilio: in delving into his writings we unavoidably familiarise ourselves with some of the most important critical movements in 'Continental philosophy', that collection of nineteenth, twentieth and twenty-first century European philosophical movements that consider themselves as carrying on the legacy of Georg Wilhelm Friedrich Hegel (Beiser 2005), Husserl (Woodruff-Smith 2009) and Martin Heidegger (1978) and which incorporate phenomenology and existentialism, hermeneutics, structuralism and deconstructionism, particularly as compared with 'analytic philosophy' (West 2010). These movements include critical theory, modernism and postmodernism. In thinking over the key questions concerning Virilio's work, the 100 entries within *The Virilio Dictionary* review the features of these critical traditions that have particular significance for his writings. Entries on the 'Body' and 'Perception' present a number of the important phenomenological notions central to an appreciation of Virilio; and the entry on 'Edmund Husserl' engages with the critical environments of René Descartes and Jean-Paul Sartre.

The first point that countless readers inexpert in Virilio studies make, including the present author on initially stumbling upon Virilio's *Speed and Politics: An Essay on Dromology* (2006 [1977]), is that he is hard to read. This question, of Virilio's idiosyncratic or, better, 'French' and concentrated prose, can set up an obstacle to readers who want a way into his books. Hardly any readers like the Virilian style on first contact, but a lot of them have learned to enjoy his style after several readings: as a fellow phenomenologist, for example, I now find it difficult to conceive that anybody could read Virilio's often at first mystifying, prolifically unsystematic and frequently lengthy sentences without great delight. Virilio's style is hard work but just has to be wrestled with if we are to understand what he has to reveal to us. Detractors have found Virilio's

style monumentally befuddled, unreliable and uninformed; physicists
Alan Sokal and Jean Bricmont have gone so far as to describe Virilio's style
as intoxicated with itself (Sokal and Bricmont 1998: 159–65) while Thrift
argues that, although 'there are some genuine insights' in Virilio's work,
'they are wrapped up in a hyperbolic apparatus that sometimes makes it
very difficult to locate them' or 'win many over who do not already subscribe to Virilio's vision of an all-but-terminal modernity' (Thrift 2011:
147). The understandable question, predominantly for new readers is:
why must Virilio write in such a problematical style?

Virilio proposes two answers that relate to explanation and suggestion. In
reality, these two ideas have a broader significance than simply the matter
of reading Virilio: they are integral to his speculative attitude concerning
reading and writing Continental philosophy. In the 'Fragmentation and
Technology' section of *Pure War* (Virilio and Lotringer 2008), his book-
length interview with the French cultural theorist Sylvère Lotringer,
Virilio defends his problematical style of phenomenological criticism.
He remarks, initially, on his antagonism towards various critical readings
founded on a belief in explanation, on a specific kind of critical writing
style that he assails as blocking out his own faith 'in suggestion, in the
obvious quality of the implicit' (*PW*, 52). Without doubt, declares Virilio,
his work does not obey the rules of transparent, flowing and explanatory
urbane writing taught in Parisian architecture schools. But, he enquires,
what if urbane architectural writing were a deficient mechanism, what if
these notions of lucidity, smoothness and explanation in fact operate as
diversions from the reality of the city, persuading readers to speed read
architectural texts sooner than think intensely regarding them? He contends that:

Being an urbanist and architect, I am too used to constructing clear systems,
machines that work well. I don't believe its writing's job to do the same thing. I
don't like two-and-two-is-four type writing. (*PW*, 52)

In brief, reading about urbanism and architecture ought to be hard: if it
isn't deconstructed, it isn't operational. Whether we assent to the suppositions behind Virilio's philosophical position, which shuns translucent
methods and machines that function properly, is uncertain. We may, for
example, question a phenomenological conviction which implies that
going beyond 'two-and-two-is-four type writing' assures its worth as real
urban or architectural thought; which considers that building transparent
techniques is defective as they are machines that run correctly; that challenging writing is superior because different or even irrational to some
extent.

However, there is another facet to Virilio's understanding of his own prose: the suggestiveness of the 'obvious quality of the implicit'. 'I work in staircases – some people have realized this', he pronounces in the same section of *Pure War*:

I begin a sentence, I work out an idea, and when I consider it suggestive enough, I jump a step to another idea without bothering with the development. Developments are the episodes. I try to reach the tendency. Tendency is the change of level. (*PW*, 52–3)

In this interview with Lotringer, Virilio further discusses his writing in comparable terminology:

In *L'Esthétique de la disparition* [*The Aesthetics of Disappearance*], I had the revelation of the importance of interruption, of accident, of things that are stopped as *productive* [. . .] I handle breaks and absences. The fact of stopping and saying, 'let's go somewhere else' is very important for me. (*PW*, 53)

The inference is that writing in a complex style is a suggestive event. It conveys the implication that complexity is suggestive, that we discover suggestion in the explanatory power of the 'obvious quality of the implicit', in associating ourselves with staircases, rather than in just giving way to 'two-and-two-is-four type writing'. Furthermore, Virilio implies that we are not yet too lost in 'two-and-two-is-four type writing' since we can still set aside spaces for sentences and ideas as evocative jump cuts wherein the laborious development of concepts is shaken off. This is an appeal to a typically Virilian phenomenological notion. For Virilio, we are increasingly disoriented by 'two-and-two-is-four type writing' as a consequence of our ever more regimented yet sporadic lives in the twenty-first century. Virilio envisages touching the 'tendency', the 'change of level'. And his writing precisely exemplifies the tendency. Consider this, Virilio might say, concerning the aesthetics of disappearance: here we are presented with the artistic suggestion, with the visual revelation, of the cultural significance of the interval (see, for instance, Armitage and Bishop 2013). We are then no longer involved with the smooth functioning of well-oiled machines; we no longer find ourselves content with that functioning which 'drives us more and more to even further functioning' until the 'only thing we have left is purely technological relationships' (Heidegger 1998: 105–6); and the productivity we are concerned with no longer has a simple connection to our continuity or presence. In other words, we must liberate ourselves from 'two-and-two-is-four type writing'. Virilio's use of mishaps, of things that are halted as creative, of fractures, non-existence, and of 'two-and-two-is-four type writing' here proposes, without really articulating it, that he is akin to the contemporary street car racer making a handbrake turn: that his prose is unusual, distinctive, it has idiosyncrasies and, above all, the quality of suddenly proclaiming that we need to go 'somewhere else', to an 'elsewhere' that reflects his own significant investment of himself in it. This is set against 'two-and-two-is-four type writing', against the translucent style of writing that eschews suggestion and lacks the 'obvious quality of the implicit'. It is an attractive ideal, but it is not the only means by which we can imagine Virilio's 'staircase' style.

We may, for example, imagine Virilio as an increasingly well respected member of the French critical, social and cultural theory machine, a machine that speculates on everything from architecture and the sociology of the city to the origin of social interaction by theorising empirical evidence obtained from books and newspaper reports, interviews, magazines and survey research (Gane 2003). We may, with Thrift (2011: 146), understand Virilio's works and challenging writing style as ways of deterring real people in favour of 'the idea of people' and of speaking merely 'in the name of a putative humanity'. Equally, just as we are persuaded by the French critical, social and cultural theory machine to appreciate our own academic expertise because we have had to expend many hours on French 'theory', we may be convinced to respect Virilio's theoretical and stylistic complexity as we have had to spend hundreds of hours on the concepts that make it up and which allow us to comprehend them.

Focusing on instances of Virilio's paragraphs can help locate a number of these concerns. Chapter 4 of *The University of Disaster* examines the growth of the mobile phone, and Virilio interprets its complexity to exemplify his argument. Close to the end of the chapter, Virilio remarks:

We can now better understand the development of the mobile phone, its sophistication, while we anticipate some day soon wearing intelligent garments, those future 'electronic straightjackets' that will complete the 'chemical straightjackets' once used on detainees, Soviet or otherwise . . .

It is all about paving the way for a universal remote control that will no longer look so much like the remote control involved in instantaneous telephonic virtuality as like the kind involved in the vitality behind being-there, here and now. In such a remote-controlled existence, the individual will be kept in constant contact, at every moment and at every point in their trajectory, so that they will no longer be left with any spare time. In other words, any free time, time for reflexion, for prolonged introspection. For tomorrow we will all be monopolized by the growing outsourcing of our once immediate sensations; we will all suddenly be collectivized in our affects, in our most intimate emotions, slipping and sliding or, more precisely, 'surfing' as we will then be in a new sort of epidemic of cooperation; the pandemic of a mob once solitary, now plagued with the delirium of a UNANIMISM that the prophets of doom of the twentieth century foretold. (*UD*, 88–9)

What kinds of suggestions can we draw from reading paragraphs such as these concerning our knowledge of the evolution of the mobile phone? Virilio may answer that by obliging us to consider the complexity of the mobile phone he has completed his task; he has made us contemplate the mobile phone not just as a precursor to our wearing of intelligent garments but also as a forerunner to our wearing of electronic straightjackets that will put the last touches on the chemical straightjackets once used on Soviet prisoners. However, there is also a hazard that we may have been too confused even to start this procedure of understanding Virilio's otherwise brilliant characterisation of the mobile phone as an electronic straightjacket, as a form of authoritarian imprisonment, or that we may renounce reading Virilio's paragraphs and turn instead to the propaganda of technological progress he elsewhere disparages as the technique that the mass media employs when presenting new Apple computers and so forth (*TAF*, 16). Philosophising 'otherwise' is not a normal pursuit, as Virilio himself might state.

The paragraphs I have cited above exemplify another trait of Virilio's prose. The second paragraph, with its discourse of control and instantaneity, vitality, individuality, contact, time, sensations, affect and co-operation, ultimately locates itself within the network of another French critical intellectual, his ideas and theories, so much so that we find it problematical to comprehend what Virilio means by 'the pandemic of a mob once solitary, now plagued with the delirium of a UNANIMISM that the prophets of doom of the twentieth century foretold' unless we are also cognisant of Jules Romains (1885–1972) and the Unanimist movement (Norrish 1958). If we think of this as an admirable means of reminding the reader that Virilio cannot be grasped independently of the philosophy and principles of Unanimism, an early twentieth-century movement that takes thoughts of collective consciousness and crowd behaviour and inserts them into art and literature, we also need to deliberate on the ways it transmits a particular inherent avant-gardism. Virilio has reflected on Romains's Unanimism, appreciates Unanimist thought and understands Romains's founding of the Unanimist movement. If his English-speaking readers especially have not studied Romains's twenty-seven-volume (1932–46) series of novels named *Les Hommes de bonne volonté* (*Men of Good Will*) – an extraordinary literary mural portraying the adventurous voyage over twenty-five years of two companions, the author

Jallez and the politician Jerphanion, which offers an illustration in literature of Unanimism – or Romains's theatrical productions, for example,
L'Armee dans la ville (1908–11), *Cromedeyre-le-vieil* (1920) or *Grâce encore
pour la terre!* (1939–40), even those most sympathetic to the avant-garde
may walk away from these paragraphs thinking that both Virilio's theories
and Romains's ideals of Unanimism escape them. This places the reader
effectively not merely as a critic of art or technology but simultaneously
as a critic of the art of French twentieth-century literature and drama,
and Virilio (and his model reader) as scholars of Romains, of French
theatre and literature, and of the Unanimist movement itself. The actual
construction of the second paragraph contributes to this. It begins with
a claim that is clear ('It is all about paving the way for a universal remote
control [. . .]'), but then brings in 'instantaneous telephonic virtuality'
that we have to relate to 'the vitality behind being-there, here and now' in
order that we can understand precisely what has been contended or shown
regarding our increasingly 'remote-controlled existence'. The topic of the
next sentence (the individual, who 'will be kept in constant contact') is
relentlessly assailed with 'information', and this solicits numerous questions (What is individualism? What is the difference between continuous
contact and intermittent contact?), but once more it must be thought
about in terms of time and space, in terms of an arc in the reader's intellect, until the paragraph's ideas of human time and contemplation disclose
themselves. The major futural claim ('tomorrow') involving the coming
totalitarian aspects of the mobile phone ('monopolised') and 'the growing
outsourcing of our once immediate sensations' is an unexpected move that
designates the looming collectivisation of our most personal sensations.
The process of absorbing all this, therefore, entails a prolonged exercise
of dissecting the components, for instance 'surfing' and the 'new sort of
epidemic of cooperation' and then assessing how they affect each other.
The model reader will require an acutely avant-garde or hypermodern
intellect to be capable of embracing all these opinions on pandemics and
mobs, loneliness and pestilence. English-speaking readers in particular
may have lost the plot before they arrive at the delirium of Unanimism;
they will be required to read Romains, that prophet of doom of the twentieth century, and perhaps reread Virilio to take in what he is predicting. If
Virilio is persuading us to read Romains in an attempt to appreciate what
he writes, then he is taking the risk that many readers will become annoyed
with him and just skip over Romains. Conversely, there is the chance that
the 'suggestiveness' of Virilio's paragraph for readers is a kind of 'drama
of the group' that we, the readers of Virilio, have comprehended a few of
the intricacies of researching Unanimism in the writings of Jules Romains.
The next paragraph on the mobile phone reads:

This will happen thanks to the perfect synchronisation of once fleeting emotions that will, if we're not careful, take over from mastery of our feelings and opinions (political or otherwise); for the *freedom of expression* offered by telecommunication companies will suppress the *freedom of impression* of a by then captive audience. (*UD*, 89)

I will not scrutinise this paragraph on the absolute synchronisation wrought by the mobile phone as I did above. However, I will mention a few points concerning it. To begin with, there is Virilio's tendency to incorporate his model reader into his own way of thinking ('if *we're* not careful [. . .]'; '*our* feelings and opinions [. . .]') and to put particular expressions *in italics* ('*freedom of expression*'; '*freedom of impression*'). This has the result of forcing the reader *to pay attention to* the expressions used and introduces a further characteristic of Virilio's prose. As we will see in many of the entries to *The Virilio Dictionary*, it is a vital trait of Virilio's analyses that the assiduous reader must simultaneously consider both the form and the content of his critical texts. Virilio for instance habitually employs wordplay, as in the paragraph above where he plays on the words 'freedom', 'expression' and 'impression'. A blizzard of CAPITAL LETTERS and a sparse referencing convention when compared to the English-speaking academic world are also archetypal Virilian stylistic mannerisms. By intentionally making his work collaborative and italicised, playful, urgent and thinly referenced, Virilio is highlighting the form of his own texts. In fact, he is stating that the form of his texts is not translucent but is a component of their construction of meaning. This is a variant of the 'explanation' interpretation of Virilio that we discussed above. Choosing two or three paragraphs and analysing them as I have done obviously does not communicate the full impact of either reading or 'explaining' Virilio but what it does do is validate his practice of utilising his readers' intelligence.

THE VIRILIO DICTIONARY: ENTRIES, READERSHIP, CROSS-REFERENCING AND BIBLIOGRAPHY

The following entries appraise Virilio's important concepts. They are organised alphabetically to provide a transparent idea of how he has expanded a fertile philosophical tradition. *The Virilio Dictionary* comprises 100 entries of either approximately 1,000 words for major philosophers, themes and movements, or about 500 words for minor theorists, subjects and movements. As editor, I made the most of the expert understanding of the commissioned contributors in producing the final list of specialised terms, on the basis that the bringing together of many Virilio authorities would be much better than my lone capacity to create such a catalogue of Virilian concepts.

As well as thinkers evidently linked with Virilio's philosophy, for example, Edmund Husserl, *The Virilio Dictionary* also considers: sociologists and philosophers such as Jean Baudrillard and Gilles Deleuze, who, while not figures discussed in detail in Virilio's writings, have influenced his theoretical point of view; Franco-German thinkers or philosophical movements, for instance, Maurice Merleau-Ponty and Friedrich A. Kittler, or Modernism and Postmodernism, where there are substantial echoes with Virilio's thought; subjects and movements, for example, Cybernetics and Futurism, which, while not crucial to Virilio's philosophy, are intimately connected to his thinking; and areas and movements such as the city and grey ecology, space-time and theory, which have been shaped to some degree by Virilio's ideas.

The Virilio Dictionary is not merely intended for expert Virilian theorists, who would perhaps recognise themselves as 'Virilians', but also for those students embarking on Virilian thinking and other critical, aesthetic and technological humanities, arts and social science fields, for specialist thinkers in the Continental tradition and for non-academic readers. *The Virilio Dictionary* aspires to be a benchmark reference book for all these readers. It offers reliable and precise, impartial, sensitive and critical reflections on Virilio's thought, associated philosophers, issues and technical terms in comprehensible language. Given that one of the primary problems of Virilio's philosophy is its occasionally esoteric vocabulary and his difficult prose style that I talked about earlier, the entries in *The Virilio Dictionary* seek to present an inspiring overture to the realm of 'Virilio studies' (Armitage 2011) for those initially unsettled by its intricacies. Nevertheless, in offering this assistance, the entries also concurrently try to make clear what critical, aesthetic and technological motivations directed Virilio's thought processes to take on those philosophical concepts and methods at the outset. Reliability, exactness, summary and straightforwardness free of ostentation or gullibility have been my guiding editorial principles.

The Virilio Dictionary supplies 'See also' cross-references at the conclusion of major 1,000-word entries only on philosophers, areas and movements to identify entries dedicated to other thinkers, themes, movements and professional terms related to Virilio's writings or to point out where they are considered in entries on theorists, issues, movements or other domains. It does not do so in the opposite way, namely, from minor 500-word specialist conceptual entries to major 1,000-word expert conceptual entries. As a rule, *The Virilio Dictionary* does not offer extensive references to philosophers referred to in an entry on a movement or subject.

The 'Entries A–Z' section is followed by a 'Bibliography' which lists Virilio's books in English, selected books by Virilio in French, other Virilian texts, books on Virilio in English and other texts cited in *The Virilio Dictionary* that exemplify the influence Virilio has had on the spheres of criticism, art theory and the philosophy of technology in particular. Throughout *The Virilio Dictionary* contributors signify Virilio's writings by means of abbreviations, for example, *BA* for *Bunker Archeology*. A complete inventory of these abbreviations is found in the first part of the Bibliography section, 'Paul Virilio: Books in English', which lists all of Virilio's own works published at the time of writing. The second part of this section lists a selection of Virilio's books in French, which may be helpful to readers. Where contributors cite Virilio, his books in English, other Virilian-related texts in English or a fellow critic, their name and the date of the work appears following the quotation, and comprehensive particulars of these works can be found in the sections that precede the Notes on Contributors.

Reading Virilio is always invigorating. He is one of the most refreshing and incisive critics of art and technology alive today. Indeed, Virilio's ideas are some of the most inspired developments in the traditions of phenomenological critique, and his perception of the nature and significance of hypermodern cultural events, often before they have occurred, is nothing short of breathtaking.

A

ACCIDENT

Paul Crosthwaite

The accident, in Virilio's philosophy, is the negative potentiality inherent in every technological system. If the history of technoscientific innovation is conventionally understood as a progressive lineage, in which human capacities are incrementally augmented, enhanced and extended, then Virilio is determined to highlight the fact that every such advance necessarily brings into existence, as its ineradicable shadow, new risks, dangers and threats. As he puts it in conversation with Sylvère Lotringer in *Pure War* (2008):

Every technology produces, provokes, programs a specific accident. For example: when they invented the railroad, what did they invent? An object that allowed you to go fast, which allowed you to progress – a vision *à la* Jules Verne, positivism, evolutionism. But at the same time they invented the railway catastrophe. (*PW*, 46)

The accident, then, is central to Virilio's sceptical approach to technology.

The roots of Virilio's notion of the accident lie in the philosophy of Aristotle. Whereas in Aristotelian metaphysics, however, ideas of the accident concern that which is secondary, relative, contingent or – precisely – *accidental*, in Virilio's ontology the potential for the accident is a necessary and essential property of any object or process. Similarly, Virilio fully mobilises the term's connotation of a destructive malfunctioning – a malfunctioning that is also, at the same time, the realisation of the phenomenon's true character:

The word accident, derived from the Latin *accidens*, signals the unanticipated, *that which unexpectedly befalls* the mechanism, system, or product, *its surprise failure* or destruction. As if the 'failure' were not programmed into the product from the moment of its production or implementation. (Virilio 1993 [1982]: 211–12; emphases in original)

More idiosyncratically and contentiously, perhaps, Virilio's conception of the accident also draws on his 'Judeo-Christian religious background' (he is a practising Catholic): 'it is obvious to me', he remarks, 'that one must link any definition of the accident to the idea of original sin [. . .] [T]his idea of original sin, which materialist philosophy rejects so forcefully, comes back to us through technology: the accident is the original sin of the technical object' (Virilio 1998b: par. 8).

While '[e]very technical object contains its own negativity' (1998b: par. 8), however, its destructive potential may be anything from negligible to cataclysmic. One of Virilio's key claims is that the scale of the accident has vastly expanded in the period since the Second World War. Earlier accidents, such as those spawned by the 'transportation revolution' of the nineteenth and early twentieth centuries, while often devastating, nonetheless remained 'localized in space and time: a train derailment took place, say, in Paris or Berlin; and when a plane crashed, it did so in London or wherever in the world' (Virilio 1996b: par. 2). In a radical break, however, the advent of the atomic age at Los Alamos and then – catastrophically – at Hiroshima and Nagasaki materialised on the horizon as the prospect of an 'integral', 'generalised' or 'global' accident that would '[take] place somewhere' but 'might destroy everything' (Virilio and Armitage 2001a: 32), for the horror of radioactive fallout lies in its unfurling of a shroud of sickness and death across vast expanses of terrain. It is not only the development of atomic and nuclear energy and weaponry that 'makes the accident global', however, but also 'the revolution of instantaneous transmissions brought about by telecommunications' (Virilio 1998b: par. 2). 'To invent the electronic superhighway or the Internet,' Virilio claims, 'is to invent a major risk which is not easily spotted because it does not produce fatalities like a shipwreck or a mid-air explosion. The information accident is, sadly, not very visible. It is immaterial like the waves that carry information' (Virilio 1999: par. 6). The 'information accident' or 'information bomb' is no less destructive for its invisibility and immateriality, however, as contemporary phenomena ranging from computer viruses to stock market crashes abundantly demonstrate. Similarly, as Steve Redhead notes, the new communication technologies such as satellite television mean that a disaster such as the collapse of the World Trade Center in New York in September 2011 'was not simply a local, catastrophic event but a global "accident" shown "live" [. . .] around the world at the same moment' (Redhead 2004a: 4).

Virilio has proposed several responses to the pervasive presence of the accident in modern life. First, as a self-professed 'critic of the art of technology', he argues that the accident should simply be confronted and acknowledged as an integral dimension of technological modernity, rather than occluded, marginalised or dismissed, as it is in progressivist narratives of technoscientific change. Second – and more pointedly and provocatively – he has called for the institutionalised examination 'of the havoc wreaked by progress' (*OA*, 25) in a university, laboratory or (most often) museum of the accident, a vision at least partly realised by the exhibition 'Ce Qui Arrive', which Virilio (*UQ*) co-curated at the Fondation Cartier pour l'art contemporain in Paris in 2002. As Virilio explains in *The Original Accident*:

in order to avoid shortly inhabiting the planetary dimensions of an integral accident, one capable of integrating a whole heap of incidents and disasters through chain reactions, we must start right now building, inhabiting, and planning a laboratory of cataclysms, the museum of the accident of technological progress. (*OA*, 24)

Finally, in a more pragmatic and interventionist vein, Virilio urges scientists and policymakers to strive at least to mitigate the dangers of the accident by learning the lessons of 'the previous development of transport technologies'. Whereas 'engineers of the 19th century [. . .] invented the block system [. . .] a method to regulate traffic so that trains are speeded up without risk of railway catastrophes', 'traffic control engineering on the information (super)highways is conspicuous by its absence' (Virilio 1995: par. 11). While the actual and potential accidents that face us today might be curbed, however, the logic of Virilio's work makes it clear that – inherent as they are to our technological way of life – we will not rid ourselves of such accidents without relinquishing that way of life itself.

See also: Accident of Art; Accident Museum; Propaganda of Progress

ACCIDENT OF ART

Shannon Bell

For Virilio, the accident of art is a shift from representation to presentation; a shift that in *The Accident of Art* he terms visual, phenomenological and affective (Virilio and Lotringer 2005: 46). Instead of modern representations, which occupied space, what defines the latter half of the twentieth and twenty-first centuries are Postmodern presentations or performances, which occupy time, thereby compressing the time of the past and of the future into today's instantaneity.

'Art is the casualty of war' (*AA*, 17) is Virilio's theory of the accident of art in a nutshell, and contemporary art is both 'terrorist' and 'terrorised' (*AA*, 14). According to Virilio, there are three stages of 'terrorist' and 'terrorised' art: art after the First World War, art after the Second World War and the art of the present or of the instant. After the First World War, Otto Dix (German Expressionist) and Georges Braque (Cubist Surrealist) collected smithereened reality into disfigurative representations wherein the face disappeared. Virilio claims that one 'can't understand Dada or Surrealism without World War I' (*AA*, 14), just as one cannot understand Joseph Beuys without awareness that he was a Stuka pilot, a bombardier in the Second World War (*AA*, 16). Virilio contends that 'contemporary art has been a war victim through Surrealism, Expressionism, Viennese Actionism and terrorism today' (*AA*, 16–17). And it is this shift in the early 1960s from disfigured representation to Actionism, performance art, body art and event art that, in conjunction with new technological capabilities, by the last decade of the twentieth century, gave rise to what Virilio terms the 'new terrorism' in art in *The Art of the Motor* (1995 [1993]: 20).

This 'new terrorism' brings into the gallery, into the exhibition space, a new form of art brut, a technologically enhanced art both amateur and professional and in some cases displaying no distinction between a live event and a presentation. Virilio cites as an amateur example the inclusion in the 1993 Biennale at the Whitney Museum of American Art in New York 'the famous video of Rodney King being beaten up [. . .] this time presented and signed with the name of the "auteur", one George Hollyday, the video amateur who witnessed the police violence and also indirectly caused the riots, murder and looting in Los Angeles in April 1992' (*AM*, 20). Perhaps more effectively chilling is the Egyptian Pavilion installation for the 54th Venice Biennale in 2011, which consisted of video documentation of Ahmed Basiony's live performance piece *30 Days of Running in the Space*, in which the artist ran for an hour a day wearing a sensor-fused plastic suit that measured his sweat and counted his steps, juxtaposed with a set of screens showing Basiony's raw footage of the revolts on the streets of Cairo filmed from 25 to 27 January. Basiony was killed filming on 28 January. The sounds of Basiony's body art and the Egyptian revolution blend into what Virilio (2011: 235) terms the 'MAGMA' of audiovisual spectacle that removes any distinction between reality and art, life and live art, terror and aesthetics.

As professional examples, Virilio references 'Orlan and my friend Stelarc, the two best known body artists, the duo' (*AA*, 16); Dr Günther von Hagens, the plastination body-corpse artist creator of *Body Worlds* showing worldwide; and what Ars Electronica now calls hybrid art. Hybrid art includes artists such as Oron Cates and Ionat Zurr who culture human and other animal cells into semi-living art objects capable of life in a bioreactor; Stelarc's recent *Partial Head*, a digital transplant of his face onto a hominid skull seeded with ovine smooth muscle cells and grown in a bioreactor, and his surgically implanted multifunctional *Ear on Arm* prosthesis; Eduardo Kac's transgenic petunia flower, the *Edunia*, that expresses the artist's DNA sequenced from his blood; and Marion Laval-Jeantet's injection of horse blood plasma into her body in the live documented performance entitled *May the Horse Live in Me*. These artists' practices are precisely what Virilio terms 'extreme art' and which he identifies in *Art and Fear* (2003a [2000]: 51) as manifestations of the accident of art: 'transgenic practices [that] aim at nothing less than to embark BIOLOGY on the road to a kind of "expressionism"'. For Virilio, extreme art is a continuation of what he terms in his *Art as Far as the Eye Can See* (2007b [2005]: 70) art as war, an 'expressionism of terror'. While Virilio might well appreciate some of the works of 'extreme art' and other contemporary artworks, his philosophical critique goes to the very foundation of contemporary art: it came into being as a response to war and to its spectacle of terror and shock value, which has only increased in speed and intensity.

Virilio sets the new figurative painting of Peter Klasen apart from other contemporary artists from the 1960s and those of the present day. In *Klasen-Virilio. Impact Inspections* (1999), Virilio praises Klasen's painting as a representation of the human situation under the occupation of time and as a resistance to such occupation: 'a warning light for everything threatening the visual field and the optical depth of appearances' (*KV*, 43). Klasen is not a collaborator in the accident of art. Rather, his is an 'art of the accident' (*KV*, 114) where a sense of 'threat is omnipresent [. . .] [and where] Klasen sees his work as an act of insistent resistance to the delirium of acceleration' (*KV*, 114).

From Virilio's standpoint, the contemporary phenomenology of perception is a digitally induced blindness, 'a gazeless vision' (*KV*, 30) where machine optics replace the human eye as organ of perception (*AA*, 78), where high-definition imagery captures and makes visible what humans cannot see or hear, and does so according to the specifics of its operating system. As Virilio states: 'As for the mass culture of the century of audio-visual illuminism, it makes you deaf and dumb in the face of any heretical opposition to its conformism' (*AFE*, 93); 'Everything is seen, déjà vu already seen – and instantly forgotten' (*AFE*, 121).

The absence of emotion and pity solicited by 'the iconoclasm of presentation' (*AA*, 25), by the increasing spectacle of the terror of actually existing reality, is presented in order to shock and thus to seize the viewer's attention, thereby provoking an emotional condition of intensity in the viewer that Virilio identifies as 'expectation of the unexpected' (*AFE*, 5) an inattentive fear, 'cold panic' (*AFE*, 4) or an emotion in standing reserve ever ready both to resurface and to disappear.

See also: Accident; Aesthetics of Disappearance; Art

ACCIDENT MUSEUM

Nicholas Michelson

A mechanism for revealing the accident to human consciousness; an exhibition of industrial and technological failures, breakdowns and natural disasters; and a problematic associated with new media.

Virilio observes in his *Unknown Quantity* (2003b [2002]) that technical damage now massively outweighs the costs of natural disasters to insurers: there are many more, and more destructive, man-made accidents than there are natural ones (*UQ*, 41). Indeed, for Virilio, the growth of scientific thought integrally includes its own negativity, in the form of specific accidents that attend any innovation (car crash, rail-derailment, electricity-electrocution). As a consequence, it should not surprise us that accelerating progress leads to accelerating accidents. This insight is suppressed by the propaganda of progress, but finds manifestation in modern industrial techniques, which develop simulation technologies to test the accidents of specific inventions (for example, the crash-test dummy). The Accident Museum seeks the exposure of the accident per se as integral to progress, and in this sense has an ontological relationship to crash simulation. It aims, however, for a broader reversal of the trend towards our escalating exposure to accidents, by revealing the accident as the major enigma of modern progress.

This project found concrete expression in Virilio's exhibition held at Paris's Fondation Cartier pour l'art contemporain in November 2002, entitled 'Ce Qui Arrive', the catalogue of which is translated into English as *Unknown Quantity*. Virilio described the event as 'a pilot project' for the Accident Museum (*UQ*, 8) and the exhibition mobilised a range of media-form artworks. The catalogue contains a wide range of extraordinary images of accidents and disasters from September 11 to nuclear tests, train crashes, wildfires, demolitions, volcanoes and oil spills, attended by Virilio's commentaries on the nature and problem of the accident, and an interview with, and excerpts from, Svetlana Aleksievich's Chernobyl diary recording the 'experiences and feelings that people underwent in the first days and first months after the catastrophe' (*UQ*, 207).

The Accident Museum is in an important sense 'an anti-museum'. Rather than exhibiting inventions, it seeks to unmask industries' 'other face', its hidden side, which is the simultaneously unlikely and inevitable breakdown or accident as Virilio puts it in his *Landscape of Events* (2000c [1996]: 56). The Accident Museum reveals the accident in technology, and thereby tells the untold story of a progress that exposes us to a kaleidoscope of hazards. The Accident Museum reveals the importance of the 'mishap or the beneficial mistake', thus disrupting the ideological assumption of linear technoscientific advance (*LE*, 56).

We must, Virilio argues in *The Original Accident* (2007a [2005]), disrupt the Panglossian myth of progress so that we can reverse its inducement of the trend towards ever more catastrophic disasters. The Accident Museum seeks to make us aware of the accident, not for the sake of fear or mass alarm, but to 'make room in the realm of public information for fallibilism' (*LE*, 56). This allows the legitimate concerns of the green ecology movement to be 'supplemented by an eschatological approach to technical progress' (*OA*, 24). The Accident Museum seeks to prevent history from constructing its own catastrophic finale.

The Accident Museum is a visual prosthesis, or media, for consciousness, unconcealing the accident. The concept thus engages directly with a paradox associated with modern media. Media, Virilio argues, has increasingly promoted the 'ultra-short time span' (*OA*, 25). This mediatised temporal compression onto the now, onto the instantaneous, marks our entire civilisation with a systematic, if unwitting, privileging of accidents. Global television turns any catastrophe into 'a scoop', a spectacle for consumption – and so becomes a 'museum of horrors' (*OA*, 27). The digital display, the television or screen, is thus already an accidentological milieu. Virilio argues explicitly that 'the accident museum exists, I've come across it: it is a TV screen' (*LE*, 60).

As Steve Redhead (2004a: 102) has observed, Virilio deems TV to be a largely passé cultural form, increasingly overtaken by interactive media. Yet the televisual recording of accidents has already had fundamental significance for human society. It allowed the simultaneous obviation and 'overexposure' of the accident, which remains conceptually unrecognised as an eschatological problem, while obsessive forms of morbid curiosity or romanticisation of disasters proliferate. Accidents are perpetuated and globally amplified through televisual repetition, as September 11 demonstrated, even as their broader significance for technological and scientific progress is ignored.

Given global scale by global media, accidents threaten to cripple and pollute human society, synchronising our anxieties, panic and grief into a catastrophism of insecurity that renders traditional politics obsolete. The televisual Accident Museum has displaced politics and replaced it with the logistical management of our fears, giving birth to an era of psycho-politics. Virilio's answer is to exhibit the accident as an eschatological problem, and thereby give cognitive organisation to our present condition.

Virilio's exhibition at the Fondation Cartier aimed to visually embody a landscape of events; 'screening the phases of the accidents' which beset modern progress (*LE*, 59). This exposes the wall of progress that we miss only because we are presently crashing into it. Virilio's work on the Accident Museum is peppered with enjoinders to slow down. A disparate sense of nostalgia seems to animate him; nostalgia for a politics of dura-tion, territory, space and time which Virilio warns we must regain if we are to avoid a generalised accident. The Accident Museum embodies that warning in the face of the 'Time accident' wrought by modern progress (*UQ*, 26).

The Accident Museum will allow us to face up to the reality of the accident. Doing so, Virilio writes in *The University of Disaster* (2010a [2007]: 66), will reveal the urgent need 'to sing the praises of inertia'. Technological speed, he declares in *Pure War* (Virilio and Lotringer 2008: 203), has become a 'god-machine' which is in direct conflict with the 'transcendent god'. For Virilio, we must resist that god-machine of tech-noscientific progress, rather than collaborate through apathy in its suicidal trajectory. The Accident Museum is thus Virilio's practical contribution to the strategy of resistance, by which he remains a soldier of God.

See also: Accident; Landscape of Events; Media; Overexposed City; Polar Inertia; Propaganda of Progress

ACCIDENT OF SCIENCE

Nicholas Michelson

The integral negativity of scientific and technological progress. Virilio's late works, *The Original Accident* (2007a [2005]) and *The University of Disaster* (2010a [2007]) in particular, are concerned with the 'acciden-tological' problematisation of modern society. He argues in these texts, and elsewhere, that every invention of modern science – the train, the automobile or the nuclear power station – entails the invention of a specific accident – the train derailment, the car crash, or the meltdown. Scientific innovation is inseparable from its accidents. These 'indirect inventions' are nothing less than the sacrifice that must be agreed if we are to enjoy the gains of scientific progress (*OA*, 5, 93).

Science has always exposed us to hazards, but, as Virilio quotes Albert Camus to observe, the accidents that attend recent scientific advances seem to cancel out their benefits, inasmuch as they 'threaten the entire world with destruction' (*UD*, 127). The Accident in Science identifies scientific and technological advance as increasingly becoming a global catastrophism. Given this state of affairs, says Virilio in *Politics of the Very Worst* (Virilio and Petit 1999 [1996]: 33), we must subject scientific progress itself to critical evaluation and perhaps query our own orientation ('collaboration or resistance') in relationship to it.

The accident of science is reflexive, that is to say, it finds manifestation in a refusal to recognise its own integral defectivity. This refusal is 'the accident in knowledge', which leads to 'technophilia'; a hubristic attitude that embraces outrageous scientific excesses under the banner of the propaganda of progress (*UD*, 26, 120). The positivist methodology of falsification, Virilio argues, is structurally unable to recognise its accident.

Virilio recognises that scientific techniques have always exceeded the scientists who deploy them, but what he terms 'technoscience' fully unburdens technique of human constraint. In this way, science is stripped of not only conscience but also fundamental meaning, and becomes consumed by a faith in its own inexorable motion. Science, Virilio argues, has allowed itself to be corrupted by technoscience; a totalitarian impulse whereby rationality commits suicide by frenzied over-extension. In this movement unto excess, the very biological existence of humanity is at issue (*OA*, 37).

This process is evident in modern attempts to achieve mastery of the future through the science of prediction (risk analysis). The rise of a purely operative or logistical thought defines a 'new reason', based on estimate, and is designed to technologically counter the uncertainty which itself follows from technological progress (*UD*, 16). The logistics of futurity cannot but remain oblivious to their accident, and thus, convinced of their own infallibility, they lead inevitably to catastrophic results. As a creature born of risk-management techniques, the economic crisis of 2008 provides some confirmation of Virilio's argument as to the disastrous consequences of technoscientific 'faith'.

Science's contamination by technoscience is mirrored by, and embedded in, the corruption of politics by military logistics. Military science privileges the accident in search of ever more destructive armaments. With the invention of the atomic bomb this method reached its absolute limit. In the process, the spirit of science was corrupted, 'dragged along by the absurd perspective of the supremacy of the death principle' (*OA*, 80). The corruption of science, Virilio notes, is the very essence of *Pure War* (Virilio and Lotringer 2008: 187). Technoscience is science become an 'extreme sport'; enraptured by a delirious, and fundamentally military, embrace of its own accident.

The Accident in Science refers to positivistic rationality's seduction by the totalitarian promise of technoscience; defined by a refusal to acknowledge the accident of progress. Hubris and excess are thus integral to the scientific techniques that in turn drive the headlong rush of contemporary society.

AESTHETICS OF DISAPPEARANCE

Eric Wilson

A seminal notion in Virilio's work, the term is deployed in two distinct manners. The first is as the title of *The Aesthetics of Disappearance* (2009a [1980]), a neo-phenomenological meditation on the interrelationships among consciousness, perception, speed and film: 'Cinema is the end in which the dominant philosophies and arts have come to confuse and lose themselves, a sort of primordial mixing of the human soul and the languages of the motor-soul' (i.e. the film projector) (*AD*, 115). The entire work operates as an extended gloss on an earlier remark of the sixteenth–seventeenth century French mystic Jeanne Guyon: 'The idea of time can be reduced to a point of view: duration is made of transitory instants just as a straight line is made of points without depth' (*AD*, 114). Virilio posits 'the duration of mind' – the subjective experience of time – as the phenomenological basis of reality: 'the first product of consciousness would be its own speed in its distance of time, speed would be the causal idea, the idea before the idea' (*AD*, 32). The psyche is metaphorically reconstituted as a movie reel, consciousness as a series of 'freeze frames' ('transitory instants') separated by a multitude of micro-absences of (self-) awareness, a condition denoted as 'picnolepsy'; 'However, for the picnoleptic, nothing really has happened, the missing time never existed. At each [picnoleptic] crisis, without realizing it, a little of his or her life simply escaped' (*AD*, 19). Yet picnolepsy also doubles as a conceit that allows Virilio to advance his most challenging analysis of the phenomenological significance of cinema: as with film, the 'reality' of the subject-spectator is guaranteed through the underlying discontinuity of both motion and perception. The 'reality' or 'truth' of the human body in Virilio's *Polar Inertia* (2000a [1990]: 45) is that it can only be preserved at a perceptual rate of low velocity: '*to save phenomena is to save their rate of apperception*'. The construction or 'aesthetics' of reality is grounded upon a series of temporally recurrent micro-disappearances that collectively act to slow down the rate of apperception. The individual is, quite literally, a 'cinematic self', with the cinematic 'flicker' becoming the sign of the reality of both film and the human subject. The abolition of this temporally slow discontinuity, or, conversely, the speeding up of perception, which is tantamount to the continuity of that straight line which is without depth, results in the accidental loss of phenomenological reality; speed 'ostensibly perverts the illusory order of normal perception, the order of arrival of information' (*AD*, 110). The hegemony of the depthless straight line, Virilio argues in *Open Sky* (1997 [1995]: 28) yields an 'infinitesimal lack of duration without which the spectacle of the visible world would quite simply not take place'.

The second manner of deployment is as the nexus between art and both the *Pure War* (Virilio and Lotringer 2008) and the 'Pure State', seminal topics of Virilio's later work. Here, Virilio's concept is inextricable from the parallel phenomenon of *Negative Horizon*'s (2005a [1984]: 109) 'dromoscopy', wherein 'the consistency of [. . .] places has disappeared in the aesthetics of speed'. The universalisation of the 'logistics of perception' is a traumatic historical event that radically accelerates the phenomenological 'decomposition' of reality: 'movement governs the event; in making transparency active, speed metamorphoses appearance' (*NH*, 113). As optics reduces the meta-body of the Earth to a straight line of points without depth, reality, paradoxically, becomes '*the first victim of speed* [. . .] what happens more and more quickly is perceived less and less distinctly' (*NH*, 116, 118). Virilio's more technocentric works thus mark a partial turn towards materialism, albeit one strictly governed by the phenomenological concerns of his overall project. Although Marx proclaims 'the annihilation of space through time' (Harvey 2006: 100), for Virilio, speed is not a mode of production but a factor of production that has acquired sovereignty over the mode in the form of velocity: '[T]he transportation revolution,' Virilio (*NH*, 118) maintains, 'also sets off the industrialization of the traditional enterprise of images, *a factory for speed*, and, therefore, also for light and images', which 'suddenly becomes *a cinematic projection of reality*, the fabrication of the world, of a world of artificial images, *a montage of dromoscopic sequences where the optic of mobile illusion renews optical illusion*'.

Ironically, the autonomy of speed creates the grounds for a 'double disappearance', both phenomenological and political. The universalisation of the commodity fetishism of optics creates the 'ultimate traffic accident where, at the speed of light, the apparent reality of the visible world comes

to an end, implosion, dimensional collapsing [*telescopage*] that would see
the disappearance of appearances in the dazzling speed of light' (*NH*,
118). Simultaneously, speed-politics reduces the being of the state to
the panoptical effect of an unlimited transparency that is ultimately self-
consuming: 'The state's only original existence', Virilio (1989 [1984]: 33)
argues in *War and Cinema: The Logistics of Perception*, is as a visual hallucination akin to dreaming. Politics disappears into aesthetics precisely
through its inability to successfully uphold the reality principle, which is
premised upon conventional representational demarcations between the
real, the visual and the virtual.

Virilio denotes this ontological and political loss of reality, of speed-
politics, as 'kinematic optics', which effectively dissolves substance through
the acceleration of perception; time supplants space, which 'deletes' Being
through an ontological substitution of the straight line without depth for
the duration of transitory instants. The final outcome for the Virilio of *The
Vision Machine* (1994b [1988]: 49) is a total 'virtualizing' of reality arising
from 'the unprecedented limits imposed on subjective perception by the
instrumental splitting of modes of perception and representation'. This
optical and ontological collapse of politics into speed underlines the key
Virilian notion of *Pure War*, a military metaphor that signifies the centrality of the panoptical to the contemporary mode of combat: 'The primacy
of speed is simultaneously the primacy of the military' (*PW*, 51); *Pure
War* is the master-sign of a Postmodern world-system that is governed by
absolute speed, signifying the total reversibility among the political, the
military and the economic. The state, the key referent of orthodox political discourse, disappears into a tripartite logistics of perception – military,
tele-cinematic and technoscientific – signifying the fatal subjugation of
politics to the decomposing formlessness of contemporary aesthetics.

See also: Cinema; Dromoscopy; Logistics of Perception; Optics; Picnolepsy

ARCHITECTURE

John Armitage

Architecture has always been a theme of passionate concern in Virilio's
cultural theory. This is for a multiplicity of reasons: its location on a shifting architectural agenda, including a reworked interest in 'the function
of the oblique' concerning the architecture and archaeology of military
bunkers; a fervent involvement with the city and with 'critical space'; a
broad interest both inside and outside of his academic life in issues regard-

ing events and accidents; his self-reflexive thoughts and contentions about the problems associated with the 'city of panic'; the effect of urban theory upon ideas of the city; and his present consideration of architecture as a military space shaped by war, and developments in new information and communications technologies.

Architecture Principe (Virilio and Parent 1997), the architectural group and review that Virilio founded with the French architect Claude Parent in 1963 (disbanded 1968), was always marked by differences of orientation and arguments over the idea of a critical architecture, turning Architecture Principe into a place of genuine discussion concerning the identity of the urban order, and varied perspectives on 'habitable circulation' (Virilio 1997b), which, in the early 1960s, looked to the emerging 'media city' (Virilio 1997c; see also McQuire 2010) as a key cultural category. This denoted that the architecture of power and of the imagination was essential to urban construction, along with notions of disorientation and dislocation. A supplementary repositioning, linked with Parent especially, sought to redraft normative descriptions of architecture by turning to it as motivation for an oppositional discourse of singularity and discontinuity and an architectural imaginary of clouds (Prix and Swiczinsky (Himmelb[l]au) 1997: 154–6) to dispute the modern architectural manifestos, narratives and aesthetics of le Corbusier and Mies van der Rohe. Modern architectural philosophy was seen as problematical by Parent and Virilio in not conceding agency to a disoriented, avant-garde, conception of architecture 'where not only the forms and materials of construction but also the techniques of the body are called into question, thereby putting an end to the postural schema of the classical age, the static state equilibrium that is imposed on human movements' (Virilio 1997a: 7).

Additional discussions have related to 'the function of the oblique', Architecture Principe and the critique of modern architecture. Virilio and Parent's architectural projects, such as their realised Church of Sainte-Bernadette du Banlay at Nevers (1966) and their unrealised Charleville Cultural Centre, were signalled as important topics by Pamela Johnson (Virilio and Parent 1996: 1) and the lobby for a complete reassessment of Virilio and Parent's oblique architectural style remains vociferous, particularly in France. These and succeeding debates over the definition of a critical architecture and the continuing influence of Architecture Principe have exposed profound differences between radical, mainstream and other, mostly avant-garde, alliances in contemporary architecture. Meanwhile, a number of Architecture Principe's texts from its manifestos, again chiefly in France, have been reconsidered and the previous resistance to its 'aim of investigating a new kind of architectural and urban order' (Lucan 1996: 5) has been loosened for a readiness to re-examine 'the end of the vertical as the axis of elevation' and 'the end of the horizontal as the permanent plane' (Virilio and Parent cited in Lucan 1996: 5). While often causing a grin when elucidating their architectural beliefs in the 1960s, for example, Jacques Lucan (1996: 5 and 9) maintains that, today, Virilio and Parent's refusal of 'the two fundamental directions of Euclidean space' has inspired many contemporary architects, among them Jean Nouvel and Bernard Tschumi.

A more recent perspective on military space is adopted by Virilio in his *Bunker Archeology* (1994a [1975]), with Virilio here developing rather than disclaiming his former 'oblique' views as a member of Architecture Principe. Indeed, *Bunker Archeology* recognises how the architecture of the bunker – far from being merely a given physical space – is actually a military space that is moulded consistently with the model of the stronghold, of the monolith, under the force of the Second World War and widespread militarised cartographical and chronological ideas of the perfect war landscape. Anthropomorphy and zoomorphy have consequently become architectural subjects as has that shrine to danger, the military bunker, in conjunction with its 'concrete ambivalence' (Beck 2011) and temporalities, transformative capacities, aesthetics of disappearance, and role in war and 'peacetime' (*BA*).

On a different front, Virilio's *The Lost Dimension* (1991 [1984]) points to the increasingly mediated Postmodern city and its morphology, and, in a compelling essay, 'Improbable Architecture' (*LD*, 69–100), Virilio combines technocultural insights and a critique of current philosophical thought on space in an academic analysis that traverses a host of diverse subjects from film studies to fine art. His investigation delves into the similarities between architecture and cinema in discourses on art, while evaluating the 'sudden confusion between the reception of images from a film projector and the perception of architectonic forms', and seeks to pinpoint the significance of the transformation in our notions of 'surface' and of the 'face-to-face', which are presently giving way to 'the appearance of the interface' (*LD*, 69).

The multifaceted importance of architecture under the sign of *A Landscape of Events* (Virilio 2000c [1996]) was made obvious by Virilio's influential text on contemporary history, and this has been much explored by him since. His architectural theory has alerted readers to an extended history of temporal and spatial events enforcing contemporary ways of thinking. This has been concentrated upon the concept of 'trans-history' (the landscape of time) and upon the 'architecture' of events that 'suddenly take the place of relief, of vegetation; in which the past and the present loom up together in all their obvious simultaneity' (*LE*, x); in myths of space and disjointed time, and the presence, for example, in the advanced countries today, of a lack of time where 'the perpetual present' limits 'the cycle of history and its repetitions' (*LE*, x). At present, his focus upon 'the long chain of historical facts and events' – frequently experienced by people as a telluric disturbance or as a kind of avalanche – spotlights the obliteration of truth and meaning in the contemporary city. In the interim, some people, criminals and terrorists for instance, have been differently responsible for the brutality of our era through their sometimes literal attacks on the architecture of daily life, such as the attacks on the World Trade Center in New York City in 1993 and 2001.

In all of these examples, the architecture of everyday life has been embattled not only by the lawless but also by technoscientists without a conscience (occasionally intersected with media representations of the 'wonders' of technology and science or what Virilio calls 'the propaganda of progress') whose aim is to 'rationalise' normative technoscientific arrangements. The fundamental question for Virilio (from technoscientific invention to museology to the future of planet Earth) is one of accidents – the means whereby architecture is implicated in the 'progressive spread of catastrophic events' – which 'do not just affect current reality, but produce anxiety and anguish for coming generations' (*UQ*, 5). Virilio's architectural theories speak to this issue in diverse ways: in terms of the historical appearance of the architecture of the accident, marked by 'catastrophes and cataclysms, in which we are endlessly running up against the unexpected' (*CP*, 5); or of the judicious management not just of architecture but also of 'what is impending', of 'those events coming upon us inopportunely, if not indeed simultaneously' (*CP*, 5).

Virilio helpfully sums up his critique of contemporary architectural theory in *City of Panic* (2005b [2004]) and in *The Futurism of the Instant: Stop-Eject* (2010b [2009]). He calls for a fuller acknowledgement of architecture as a military space formed and informed by war (*CP*, 1–24, 47–62); a military space that is worked upon within technoscientific discourses and predominant ideologies of accelerated temporality. Virilio's focus on military space, allied with his concern for the city, and despite its pervasive apparatuses of explicit and implicit terror, has, nevertheless, also produced his theory of 'The Twilight of Place' (*CP*, 113–50). Also pertinent here is the development of new information and communications technologies from the Internet to the iPhone, which, for Virilio, raise the issue of the 'sedentary man' being 'at home everywhere, and the nomad nowhere, beyond the provisional accommodation offered by a pointless transhumance' (*FI*, 3). Certainly, the theme of transhumance is currently Virilio's way of contemplating the technologies and ethics of placeless identities both in theoretical works (e.g. *FI*) and assorted interviews (e.g. Virilio and Richard 2012).

See also: *Bunker Archeology; Church of Sainte-Bernadette du Banlay; City of Panic; Critical Space; Events; Military Space; War*

ART

Eric Wilson

Virilio provides no formal theory of aesthetics. Consistent with his self-proclaimed identity as a phenomenologist, he deploys art as the site of a series of intertextual meditations on the political and cultural meanings of an aestheticised phenomenology of perception: optics, perspective, depth, televisual culture, virtual reality and the abolition of the sensory.

In terms of art history, Virilio politically radicalises the development of depth perspective in the Renaissance, linking it to the military revolution of the sixteenth century. With parallel transformations in both artistic perspective and optical technology, a quantum leap in military affairs is achieved, in which, according to Virilio's *War and Cinema: The Logistics of Perception* (1989 [1984]: 2), 'winning is keeping the target in constant sight'. Art and war merge through the enhancement of the visual fields of perception, which render the revealed enemy helpless: 'The engine of war,' suggests Virilio in *Negative Horizon* (2005a [1984]: 80) 'is first and foremost an "engine of surveillance" and then an engine of assault'. The aesthetic fusion between photography and impressionistic painting in the late nineteenth century that Virilio describes in *Art and Fear* (2003a [2000]: 26) is followed by a parallel convergence between aerial reconnaissance photography and cinematic art during the First World War (*WC*, 70–2), which serve as the immediate historical background to the catastrophic and phenomenologically annihilating aesthetics of disappearance, the master-sign of *Pure War* (Virilio and Lotringer 2008). 'The art of war pertains to an aesthetic of disappearance that is probably the whole issue [. . .]' of the artistic history of the twentieth century (*NH*, 80).

In Virilio's *The Vision Machine* (1994b [1988]: 70) the 'vision of annihilation' attained in the First World War equates with a more wide-ranging annihilation of vision, in which the continuity of the phenomenology of form is abolished by the ubiquity of a 'will to universalized illumination: a scientific permutation on the eye of God which would forever rule out the surprise, the accident, the irruption of the unforeseen'. Totalising and overlapping fields of perception, the Virilian equivalent of Michel Foucault's labyrinthine systems of incarceration constitute a void that is both optical and ontological: universal perception suspends all classical aesthetic theories of depth, violently reducing the Earth to a unidimensional plane of a dehumanising 'logistics of perception': 'One no longer knows who is who, or rather, by a transformation of sight, one can become whoever, wherever' (*NH*, 86). The simultaneous rise of both telematic 'real time' and 'the freeze frame' that Virilio explains in *Open Sky* (1997 [1995]: 25) yields an 'infinitesimal lack of duration without which the spectacle of the visible world would quite simply not take place' (*OS*, 28). Not surprisingly, it is the cultural awareness of this perceptually induced sense of 'nothingness' or 'absence' that is the unifying principle of twentieth-century aesthetics (*NH*, 27–8).

The implicit cultural logic of the aesthetics of disappearance correlates with the explicit imaginary of a 'terror art', which, paradoxically, aestheticises terrorism. A parodic inversion of the mimesis that historically governed the relationship between art and both religion and the sacred, twentieth-century aesthetic reproduction, or 'PROFANED ART' (*AF*, 48) self-consciously privileges barbarism and the horrific. Virilio approvingly quotes Andy Warhol, the signifier of 'the end of the man of art', who declares: 'The reason why I'm painting this way is because I want to be a machine' (*AF*, 47). Historically, 'the role of art was to announce prophetically what was in the offing', Virilio argues in *Crepuscular Dawn* (Virilio and Lotringer 2002: 100); with Warhol, as Virilio writes in *City of Panic* (2005b [2004]: 57), 'the "creator" disappears along with his work in mass suicide terrorism, the self-mutilation of a social body that takes the sadistic rituals of the Viennese Actionism of the 1960s to their logical extreme'. A continuation of the decomposition of the body by other means, the 'pitiless' art of the late twentieth-century replicates within the dissemination of its 'images of the annihilated corpses of tyranny' (*AF*, 48) the omnipresence of the equally annihilating 'logistics of perception'. 'There is no abstraction, everything presents a figure; the formless is an innovation in the West' (*NH*, 27). And it is within the First World War, the birthplace of both *Pure War* and the Pure State, that art becomes pitiless. As with Jean Baudrillard, the 'terror' of art lies not solely within its imagery but within its infinite and nihilistically designifying circulation.

This pitiless art, this modern art of the 'impitoyable', was born after all in 1914. It was born in the atrocity of Verdun, in the atrocity documented by Otto Dix, just as Breton's Surrealism emerged directly from the First World War. These are people who saw Verdun and Auschwitz, and who, if they play with all of this, do so in full awareness of this kind of horror and abomination. By contrast, artists today seem unable to register this dimension of horror. Horror has simply become another effect, a seduction effect like any other, despite the fact that we are still confronting this dimension of horror in the recent massacres in Srebrenica and in Rwanda.

Needless to say, Virilio's favourite film, and one that he alludes to constantly throughout his work, is Alain Resnais's *Hiroshima, mon amour* (1959) in which the 'atomic disappearance' of the Japanese city is constantly relooped, both literally and metaphorically, throughout the film; an uncannily precise cinematic mimesis of the original 'terror act/art' of the dropping of the Bomb, both film and weapon governed by optics, the physics of light and, therefore, of sight (*CP*, 48).

Art and Fear is Virilio's most extended and radical meditation on the relationship between pitiless art and the political logic of the Pure State; 'Hasn't the universality of the extermination of bodies as well as the environment, from AUSCHWITZ to CHERNOBYL, succeeded in dehumanizing us from without by shattering our ethic and aesthetic perceptions of our surroundings?' (*AF*, 16). Although ostensibly about terror art and the decomposition of the social and animal body by the infinite density of globalising speed-politics, *Art and Fear* is really a meditation on the relevance of pitiless art to 'endo-colonisation', to the 'highest stage' of *Pure War*, specifically the cyborgian and nanotechnological penetration and conquest of phenomenological interiority. Along with Warhol, Virilio's bête noire of contemporary art is the Australian cyborgian performance artist Stelarc, who pursues the aesthetic logic of pitiless art to its ultimate end: terminal art or the reduction of aesthetics to 'clinical voyeurism', in which artistic production requires nothing more than 'a showdown between a tortured body and an automatic camera' (*AF*, 23). A passionate critic of all forms of body modification, both cosmetic and performative, Virilio's apparent cultural conservatism makes perfect sense within the phenomenological terms of his discourse: the physical impenetrability of the body as the final and indispensable line of defence against the annihilating logic of an aesthetics of phenomenological terror that is nothing less than the somatic reconstitution of the sacredness of the soul.

See also: Accident of Art; Aesthetics of Disappearance; Baudrillard, Jean; Perception, Perspective; Pitiless Art

ART OF THE MOTOR

Ryan Bishop

The Art of the Motor (1995 [1993]) is both a book and a key Virilian concept. However, as with many of Virilio's ideas, this concept appears in several of his works and is modified and connected to a host of other related issues and analytical positions. One could argue, in fact, that Virilio's corpus is but a set of volumes of the same larger book, making him the philosophical equivalent of Proust but with movement rather than memory as the primary site for reflection and engagement.

The Art of the Motor shifts Virilio's emphasis on 'dromology' or the logic of speed toward 'dromoscopy' or the logic of accelerated seeing, away from the logos (word or thought) of speed to the scopic (visual) qualities produced by speed, though with mutual influence between thought and vision underlining the relationship. The motorisation of the image found in the technological developments that birth cinema serve as the entry point for this shift toward speed's influences on vision, a moment captured by the French cinematic term to start the cameras rolling – 'Moteur!' (which is 'Action!' in English). The motorisation of the image is but part of a larger 'dromological' domain, in which all parts of life become motorised and, more to the point, accelerated. Painting and even the photograph undergo change, he argues, once the latter in particular is made animate by machinery. Further, this motorisation influences other branches of art, including theatre, dance, sculpture and music. And the motorisation of art results in the various crises that have afflicted modern and contemporary art. We lose something in the general motorisation, Virilio asserts, but we gain as well: what is gained is speed, which is what modern society and culture seems to value above all else.

Yet for Virilio the art of the motor becomes also the motor of art, in that art largely participates in this acceleration and rarely resists it, though occasionally it provides the illusion of doing so. Virilio can be, and often is, read as nostalgic for times less tainted by acceleration. However, such a reading ignores his long historical trajectories of humanity's desire to literally harness speed (e.g. in the case of the soldier on horseback). It also ignores insights such as the one proffered in *The Art of the Motor*, in which he states that 'the plastic arts will come to immobilize movement, thereby *offering the illusion of seeing, of having the time to see*' (*AM*, 69). This statement undermines claims of nostalgic yearning on Virilio's part, for he asserts that painting and photography will be interpreted as resisting the headlong embrace of acceleration and providing viewers who turn to these art forms not with the ability to see and to repossess time but merely with the illusion of doing so.

The Art of the Motor, then, becomes a way of understanding that dromoscopy has always been our fate and that speed as a relationship between phenomena, and not a phenomenon in and of itself, throws us back onto the underlying import of sensory experience. Nevertheless, powerful and influential as empirical experience is, it is also inherently flawed and open to the delusion of establishing objective reality. Within a larger set of related concerns for Virilio, the idea of the art of the motor thus becomes one historical and genealogical means for understanding the intensification of accelerative technologies that alter time and space and bring us to maximum velocity: to a point where information and historical time encounter the speed of light.

$$B$$

BAUDRILLARD, JEAN

Mike Gane

Jean Baudrillard's (1929–2007) name is often linked with that of Virilio's. There are certain similarities in their philosophies and they have co-operated together. All this despite the fact that their backgrounds are very different: Baudrillard's in literature, sociology and anthropology; Virilio's in theology, craftwork and architecture. There might be a common background in Catholicism but this was never explicitly stated by either of them. They share points of view concerning the critique of modern consumer society, materialistic culture, from the standpoint of a set of symbolic values – with Virilio this is mainly but not exclusively Catholicism, with Baudrillard (1993) it is the anthropological idea of symbolic exchange. Virilio theorised modern society from the viewpoint of the war machine, whereas this plays almost no role in Baudrillard's thinking. Indeed, Catholicism is one of the principal sources of modern simulacra for Baudrillard whose later thinking finds its support in pagan pre-Christian cultures. Baudrillard famously critiqued the collapse of the social, whereas Virilio has sought in the social the very basis of opposition to the alienated features of modern mass society.

Baudrillard once said of Virilio:

We have worked together [...] without any problem [...] His analysis of the cyberworld is intransigent, inexorable, fatal I might dare say, and I find it beautiful and remarkable [...] [but] He puts himself in the position of the anti-apocalypse prophet, having been persuaded that the worst can come about. On this point we have ended up going our separate ways. I do not believe in his real apocalypse [...] it is the coming of the virtual itself which is our apocalypse, and this deprives us of the real apocalypse. (1996: 46–7)

The most significant agreement between them is perhaps their very rapid perception of the way society and the world changed after 1968. The old stasis of bourgeois society was fading, and the new neo-liberal capital-ism had transformed space and time, through hyper-communication. The very terrain of class struggle had gone. The old communism equated progress with speed, but for Virilio and Baudrillard, things had been reversed: the new total peace was in fact absolute war. Whereas Virilio believes that the new technologies can induce an apocalypse, Baudrillard's analysis of the new media of virtualisation concluded otherwise. So the two theorists parted and went their separate ways, but on the basis of an agreement that the old world as analysed by Marx was passing away.

The two paths of these writers then continued to drift apart, as Virilio retrenched into the social as a means of defence against the new capitalism. He saw that the social had been weakened by social change, such as the rise of feminism and terrorism. Baudrillard, on the other hand, saw the new capitalism as more radical in its destruction of the social, as exempli-fied in his famous declaration concerning the 'end of the social' and his thesis that the power of the silent majorities embraces a fatal logic. Virilio dislikes this theoretical move, thinking it a form of neo-nihilism. He also dislikes Baudrillard's (1983) radical theses on the displacement of forms of the real in modern cultures by simulations which produce the real and its variations. Virilio's 'simulations', by contrast, are representations of the real world, representations which are substituted for one another as technology develops. Yet the central concept for Baudrillard is an anthro-pologically rooted idea of symbolic exchange, modelled on the idea of the gift. Modern cultures go through phases of structural reorganisation realised in the economy – for example, phases of commodity exchange – and technological change also follows this ordering. Christianity for Baudrillard passed from a symbolic order into a simulational order with the Jesuits who contributed decisively to modern simulacra. For Virilio, there is more an appeal to the determinant role of technology itself. Watching television, for example, according to Virilio, introduces inertia, a form of dead time. His critique is earnest and humourless, and derives from his conception of the relentless nature of accumulative 'dromocracy'. It does not become a technological determinism, however, since Virilio interposes the concept of the war machine at crucial points in the explana-tory logic. The decisive effects of the war machine concern the new levels of rapidity of communication between interlocutors: the violence induced by speed is not a simple technological phenomenon. The motor has been war, with industrial civilisation its transformed effect. Baudrillard, in contrast, is interested in reversibility and collapse: not a 'dromology' but a 'palindromology' (2001: 122). Rather than analysis of content, Baudrillard is more interested in form, and his analysis of the media is more complex, introducing the notions of hyper and virtual reality as a way of analysing the disappearance of conventional war. But, in fact, there are passages in Virilio that appear to develop a position not unlike that of Baudrillard's. One such is the idea that war and peace are not opposite states but transformed into each other: the priest transforms war into peace; the warrior transforms peace into war. The priest plays a role in this reversion. So Virilio proposes a defence of the real, of social resistance, of the role of the peacemaker and preparation for the great apocalypse. Baudrillard, conversely, proposes a defence of symbolic cultures in a context where the apocalypse of the virtual has already occurred. As the concept of the symbolic order is one that includes the great religions it might be thought that Virilio and Baudrillard both see them as bulwarks against the destructive power of neo-liberal culture. But Baudrillard sees this as already out of date and that Virilio's 'attempt to escape the apocalypse of the virtual, is [. . .] the last of our utopian desires' (2001: 117).

See also: Speed; Technology; War

BODY

Eric Wilson

The centrality of the body to Virilio's work is all-pervasive. Whether discussing dromology, subjectivity or human consciousness, the body is the master-sign of Virilio's discourse on everything from war and technology to philosophy, politics and desire.

However, Virilio posits three different types of bodies: the territorial body; the social body (*socius*); and the individual human or animal body.

The territorial body is primary: the 'first body is the world', Virilio explains in *Crepuscular Dawn* (Virilio and Lotringer 2002: 102): 'without the world proper, the social body and the [human] body proper don't exist [. . .] The territorial body is more important than the socius or the animal body. If there is no land there are no humans'. The primal grounding provided by the frame of the territorial body thus sets the scene for Virilio's manifold discussions of accidents and selfhood, being, alienation, speed, politics, mortality, history, globalisation, time-space compression and, especially, technology. Nevertheless, Virilio is chiefly preoccupied by the disappearance or deterritorialisation of the territorial body brought about by the uncoupling of the social and individual human bodies from the territorial body of the Earth. In *Polar Inertia* (2000a [1990]: 83), for example, Virilio stresses that human activities are 'no longer limited by extension or duration' and that the human body's real presence in the world is increasingly dislocated in space and time:

> Not only is the 'full body' of the earth vanishing before our eyes, but our own body is becoming blurred and afflicting us with an unprecedented 'disorder', a paralysis (or autism) which leaves us still where we are, with an imposing ponderous mass, while the loss of the full body of being is carrying us towards the void. (*PI*, 83)

Traversed by the ever more accelerated teletechnologies of so-called 'telepresence', the Earth becomes the setting for humanity's self-imposed imprisonment while its individual human bodies are more and more subject to those damaging and disorienting techniques associated with the speed-induced disappearance of humanity into the technological abyss.

The continuing disappearance of both the territorial and the individual human body not only has implications for the social body, because everybody is influenced by humanity's presently distorted relationship to reality, but also for the stability of a world wherein bodies of all kinds are 'subjected to the threat of chaos' (*CD*, 164). Territorial, social and individual human bodies experience this chaos in two primary ways: the first as endo-colonisation, the second as decomposition.

For Virilio, to articulate the endo-colonisation of bodies is principally to convey the interiority of technologised human bodies, of their claustrophobia, incarceration and, critically, of their internalisation of technology. Indeed, for him:

> technology is becoming something physically assimilable, it is a kind of nourishment for the human race, through dynamic inserts [and] implants [. . .] like additional memory storage. What we see here is that science and technology aim for miniaturization in order to invade the human body [. . .] Here is an icon of the transplant revolution, of the human body being eaten up, being possessed by technology. Technology no longer spreads over the body of the territory, as with railways, motorways, bridges, and large factories, but now enters the innards of the human body [. . .] (Virilio and Armitage 2001a: 42)

It could be argued that Virilio's position on the microscopic technologisation of the internal spaces of the human body is a profoundly nostalgic or conservative moral and aesthetic reaction, not so much against science and technology, or even miniaturisation, but against internal body modifications of all sorts. Yet, for Virilio, the transplant revolution is not merely a technological revolution but, crucially, a political revolution. This last is perhaps best exemplified by way of Virilio's critical engagement in *The*

Art of the Motor (1995 [1993]) with the Australian performance artist
Stelarc, whose art expands the human body's abilities through technology, medical techniques, sound systems, robotics, electronic sensors and
computer programs. Certainly, for Virilio, Stelarc serves as the template
for the disappearance of the territorial, individual human and, ultimately,
of the social body into technology: 'Bristling with electrodes and antennae
and sporting two *laser eyes*', Virilio (*AM*, 111) writes, Stelarc, a 'willing
mutant' on the road to disappearance, takes the individual human body
particularly to its 'rational' technological conclusion: from here on in,
'man lurks inside the android'.

   As Virilio's technological discourse indicates, Stelarc's fervent endo-
colonisation of himself signifies a futural wider decomposition of the
individual human body. For the technologised individual human body
is forerunner to the final decomposition of both the territorial and the
social body, of, in fact, all geographical, psychophysical and psychophysiological space (*CD*, 165).

*See also: Aesthetics of Disappearance; Decomposition; Endo-Colonisation;
Technology*

BUNKER ARCHEOLOGY

John Beck

Virilio began investigating the remains of the German-built Atlantic
Wall fortifications along the French coast in 1958. A seven-year period of
exploration and documentation resulted in an exhibition of photographs
and texts at the Museum of Decorative Arts in Paris in 1975–6 and the
book *Bunker Archeology* (1994a [1975]). In addition to the photographs
of the bunkers, the book offers a series of historical, architectural and
phenomenological ruminations on the structures, along with maps, dia-
grams providing a typology of the fortifications and a chronology that runs
from the publication of Adolf Hitler's *Mein Kampf* (2007 [1929]) to the
launch of the first V2 rocket in September 1944. The project is at once
archaeological and historical in its desire to record and provide accurate
documentation of the bunkers and their significance, and also architectural in its concern to place the buildings within the context of European
Modernism and post-war Brutalism. There is, too, a powerful aesthetic
dimension to *Bunker Archeology* that suggests something of the work of the
influential Düsseldorf-based artists Bernd and Hilla Becher, who began
their own typological documentation of industrial structures around the

same time that Virilio became interested in the bunkers. The muteness of the bunkers is reproduced in the affectless seriality of the images, a style of photography that emerged alongside minimalist and conceptual art in the 1960s and is characteristic of the Düsseldorf School in Germany and the New Topographics photographers in the United States.

In a short early article, also called 'Bunker Archeologie', written in 1958 and published in *Architecture Principe* in 1966, Virilio describes the bunkers, stripped of context and function, as a set of found remnants from a lost world that 'bespeak of an unknown meaning' (Virilio and Parent 1997: xvii). From this archaeological perspective, the bunker blueprint for Virilio is reminiscent of Aztec temples and recalls Egyptian and Etruscan tombs. Because they are unsecured by foundations, the concrete shells have often moved and shifted due to the passage of time. As a result, the skewed geometry gives form to what Virilio and the French architect Claude Parent called during the 1960s the 'oblique', a dynamic and organic form that speaks to the violence of history.

The bunker explorations, then, were a process of rediscovery and of recovery of a recent past that appeared much further away in time, another era not so much lost to history as made to seem ancient because its forms have come to stand in prehistoric relation to the present. For Virilio, the excavation of the bunker served to reattach military architecture to the history of modernism, but also functioned as a form of personal and social archaeology, motivated, as he (1996a: 11) has said, 'by the desire to uncover the geostrategic and geopolitical foundations of total war I had lived through as a young boy in Nantes, not far from the submarine base of Saint-Nazaire'. This personal observation reveals the extent to which the bunker has come to stand for the restructuring of everyday life in the aftermath of the Second World War, the material embodiment of a world governed not just by the cataclysms of total war but by the subsequent Cold War. 'The bunker,' Virilio (*BA*, 46) writes, 'has become a myth, present and absent at the same time: present as an object of disgust instead of a transparent and open civilian architecture, absent insofar as the essence of the new fortress is elsewhere, underfoot, invisible from here on in'. What is clear from Virilio's remarks is that an interest in bunkers is never entirely a matter of historical curiosity or architectural concern. The bunker is evidence of a power that has moved on; the visibility of the historical bunker asserts the invisibility of power's current location. The immobility and solidity of the carapace only confirms the fluidity of the object it is designed to preserve, which has gone to ground somewhere else. The complex set of associations the bunker embodies – security and terror, solidity and vulnerability, past conflicts as warnings of future devastation – and which is held in tension in Virilio's work, is what has made *Bunker Archeology* such an influential project.

Part of what fascinates Virilio about the bunkers is the way their very obvious physical presence has been deliberately ignored: 'why would these extraordinary constructions, compared to seaside villas, not be perceived or even recognized?' (*BA*, 11). The answer is obvious and Virilio gives an account of post-war attempts to destroy some of the bunkers; how others are covered in graffiti and filled with litter; how they bring back bad memories and still generate fear and hatred, of 'lurking danger' (*BA*, 14). This haunting of the landscape by traces of war has, in recent years, become a dominant theme for a range of artists, photographers, archaeologists and heritage professionals in the emerging field of 'combat archaeology' (Schofield 2005) and given rise to the term 'bunkerology' to describe the inventorial gathering of locations, data and photographic records of bunkers and other fortifications around Europe and beyond.

See also: Architecture

CATASTROPHE

Hugh Davies

Since the 1990s Virilio has identified catastrophe as both an inevitable side effect and the true nature of rapid technological progress. The concept first appears in *Open Sky* (1997 [1995]), then in *Polar Inertia* (2000a [1990]), but becomes a central concern in *The Information Bomb* (2000d [1998]), *Unknown Quantity* (2003b [2002]), *The Original Accident* (2007a [2005]) and *The University of Disaster* (2010a [2007]), all works in which Virilio develops and extends his theory of the integral accident and unpacks the role of catastrophe as a potential redeeming force.

Virilio laments the widely held perception of technological accidents as an exception, subversion, contamination or deviation to an otherwise functional norm. In contrast, he repeatedly points out that accidents are not unforeseeable faults in otherwise perfect operations but that they are integral aspects of the technological devices and scientific systems produced by modernity's drive for progress. Virilio explores the accidents associated with the heroic products of the twentieth century, observing how each new invention also brings about its accompanying catastrophe: the ship has introduced the shipwreck; the jet plane has brought about the air disaster; the automobile has ushered in the car crash; and electricity combined with modern technology has brought forth nuclear meltdown. Yet the hubris of modernity is such that it continues to foolishly embrace the positive side of technology while ignoring its implicit dangers. As a joint result of this ignorance and modernity's accelerating 'progress', industrial design and manufacturing processes have ensured the large-scale production and distribution of new technologies, and, in turn, their corresponding accidents have become more numerous, globally widespread and mass produced.

Yet it is not individual accidents that occupy Virilio so much as rapid innovation, which, he believes, is increasingly producing all-encompassing catastrophes or accidents so total that they obscure the individual disasters that occur within them. This unfolding wreckage, a result of the velocity of 'progress', particularly towards virtualisation, is not impending; it is already here. Crashes of cars, planes, stock markets and computers, disasters and catastrophes of all types have become so commonplace and 'naturalised' that it is no longer possible to tell genuine accidents, simulated crash tests and acts of war apart. Meanwhile, the drive of so-called 'progress' continues.

Virilio believes that this state of hurtling 'progress' cannot continue. Its methodologies have reached their limit, global society has hit a 'wall of acceleration' (Virilio and Armitage 2001a: 17), and we are beginning to fall upwards toward a new and likely unsurvivable impact. Society has accelerated forward so quickly that in some strange realisation of Albert Einstein's theory of relativity it has begun to move backwards and against itself. This is evidenced not only in spectacular, famous disasters of mobility such as the sinking of the *Titanic* or the fire aboard the airship *The Hindenburg*, and more recently September 11 and the 2008 global financial crisis, but also in the recent explosions of immobility manifested in walls, borders, prisons, office cubicles and other restricted spaces whose logic of bunkerisation is the antithesis of modernity's velocity of movement. Torn between technologies of acceleration and the static, contorted positions the human body is being forced into, the world is becoming uninhabitable for the human subject outside of virtual spaces.

Virilio's ideas on accidents and catastrophes have led to repeated accusations of pessimistic technological determinism and Luddism, yet he emphasises that he is not opposed to technologies per se, but, rather, against the present logic of reckless technoscientific fetishism that drives their uncritical invention, production, distribution and consumption. Without the ability to critique, he argues, there can be no room for either improvement or praise and the dangerously imperfect underside of technology remains denied. Even when accidents, disasters and catastrophes occur, there is rarely any consideration of the capacity for the undoing of the technology involved. Virilio steadfastly believes that accidents and catastrophes should not be experienced as unmitigated woes but that the underside they reveal should be approached as pregnant with potential. In this way, Virilio's conception of catastrophe parallels Hannah Arendt's (1973) view: that progress and catastrophe are two sides of the same coin. Both writers follow the Greek etymology of the word *katastrophe*, which means an overturning or reversal of the expected, a down (*kata*) turn (*strephein*) or a sudden end.

While embracing neither overall chaos nor individual accidents, Virilio steadfastly believes that catastrophes should not simply be experienced as wretched incidents but should also be recognised as loaded with the possibility of offering a more holistic understanding of the substances of technologies. Here Virilio follows Aristotle's (2002) view in *The Metaphysics*: that the accident reveals the substance and that the substance of accidents must be investigated. Such a recognition and resulting reinterpretation, he believes, might enable humanity to eventually uncover new ways of living more harmoniously with technology. But, until such time as we can critically approach our own inventions, expose the accidents they bring about and recognise the knowledge contained in their catastrophes, we will continue to experience only apocalyptic (yet revelatory) disasters without realising that which they reveal to us, just as in our present situation where we feel helplessly surrounded by the disastrous side effects of our own 'progress'.

In order to address both individual accidents and total catastrophe, Virilio proposes institutionalising the recognition of the negative aspects of technology by deploying such proposals as the Accident Museum. Virilio's *Unknown Quantity* exhibition at Paris's Fondation Cartier in 2002–3 served as an illustration of the destructive capacity of progress and sought to overturn received ways of seeing and to create new forms of vision. Recognising that the Accident Museum already exists in the form of television, a device which constantly exposes the spectacle of catastrophes as 'disaster-tainment', ultimately producing a self-reflexive desire for catastrophe rather than educational critique, Virilio believes that more fertile ground is found in the decisive gesture of art, a medium he sees as both critical and engaging that might yet productively expose catastrophe and reveal its potential for creation.

See also: Accident; Accident Museum; Propaganda of Progress; Speed; Technology

CHRONOPOLITICS

Eric Wilson

Chronopolitics, according to Virilio, is the political space of today. Technically, it is 'the geography of time', or '*azimuthal equidistant perception*' (Virilio and Lotringer 2008: 21). Poetically, it is 'the Apolitics of the worst' (*PW*, 119): 'Apolitics' because it signifies the disappearance of the classical state and notions of governance; 'the worst' because it is the expression, through political calculation and anti-humanistic urban planning, of the ascendancy of *Pure War* (*PW*).

An aphorist like Nietzsche ('I don't believe in explanations. I believe in suggestion, in the obvious quality of the implicit' (*PW*, 52)), Virilio's notion of chronopolitics only makes sense when placed within a wider arena of numerous other and, more or less, 'free floating' series of associations: 'I have no global answer or unifying vision of what must be done. I only have questions, clips, glimpses. Always fractals' (*PW*, 124). Understood and deployed aphoristically, the hegemony of chronopolitics is the political sign of a much wider cultural and aesthetic shift from geography, the master-sign of territoriality and the demarcation of the state, to the counterveiling sign of deterritorialisation and the borderless world of endo-colonisation: 'All that remains is the single individual and his deterritorialization' (*PW*, 121). Through the picnoleptic effects of that aesthetics of disappearance – the absolute and universal acceleration of speed – 'space-distances', which are the discursive objects of all orthodox forms of political speech, are supplanted by 'time-distances'. All of the standard units of measurements of Virilian political ontology are chronological, not spatial: 'Politics is less in physical space than in the time systems administered by various technologies [. . .] There is a movement from geo- to chrono-politics: The distribution of territory becomes the distribution of time. The distribution of territory is outdated, minimal' (*PW*, 126). Constituting in some fundamental way an attempt by Virilio to aphoristically articulate a theory of governance ('Organization, prohibitions, interruptions, orders, powers, structuring, subjections are now in the realm of temporality' [*PW*, 127]), chronopolitics is the discourse of a contemporary post-statist political ontology in which space has been rendered null and void through time.

Although it would be technically incorrect to attribute to Virilio the impulse to locate a material(ist) 'base' for chronopolitics, he repeatedly 'loops' the para-Foucauldian phenomenon of governance-through-time, 'the realm of temporality', with the parallel emergence of pure war. This is the central discursive ploy of Chapter 10 of *Pure War* (*PW*, 115–28),

'The Production of Destruction'. It is, of course, perfectly consistent with Virilio's *oeuvre* as a whole, having been described by Sylvère Lotringer as 'one of the few French thinkers to have abandoned the language of philosophy or sociology in favor of war discourse' (*PW*, 17). From the application of war discourse to the question of political sociology, Virilio (*PW*, 125) is able to conclude that the 'weapon is always an alibi'. The twin doctrines of nuclear deterrence and Mutually Assured Destruction (MAD) are terror techniques deployed by the neo-militarised state to hold its own civilian populations hostage, governed by the diffuse mechanisms of endo-colonisation. The 'true' City, or *polis*, is the antithesis of endo-colonisation, which is the displacement of *Pure War* towards the interior; therefore, the City must undergo a co-ordinated elimination via 'de-urbanisation', rationalised by and through the means of civilian defence, most illustratively through the construction of the anti-humanist 'mega-suburb' (*PW*, 125). The contemporary urbanist nightmare of the mega-suburb reveals the nexus between endo-colonisation and chronopolitics: logistics. Any state that is premised upon nuclear deterrence and civilian defence must reconfigure the entirety of its being to accommodate in full the absolute speed of nuclear warfare, the apotheosis of post-humanism. Following former US President Dwight D. Eisenhower's 'Logistics is the procedure following which a nation's potential is transferred to its armed forces in times of peace as in times of war' (*PW*, 32), Virilio hypothesises that logistics is 'the beginning of the economy of war, which will then become simply economy, to the point of replacing political economy' (*PW*, 20). And since the *polis* is the 'space' (that is, 'not time') of subject-centred political discourse calibrated to the true scale of the human, for the chronopolitical manager the City will 'have to die' (*PW*, 125). Under the aegis of chronopolitics, the 'city of the beyond is the City of Dead Time' (*PW*, 22). Chronopolitics is a thanatalogical phenomenon.

Paradoxically, it is the selfsame 'realm of temporality' that also serves as the possible future site of new forms of political resistance and liberation. It is the discursive link that Virilio establishes between urbanism and humanism that permits him to undertake this double movement: 'Cities correspond to a civil status, to citizenship, to the appearance of politics in a space which opposes endo-colonization' (*PW*, 125). The key to rescuing the *polis* from the thanatalogical time of chronopolitics is, in fact, to aesthetically highlight and re-present the centrality of death to contemporary social and cultural discourse: 'We must get inside *Pure War*, we must cover ourselves with blood and terror. We mustn't turn away. *That* is political and civil virtue' (*PW*, 120). Akin to Karl Marx's (1987) seminal concept of ideological mystification, *Pure War* and its urbanist manifestation of chronopolitics operates hegemonically precisely through its success in reconstituting the artificial as the natural; the paradigmatic figure of chronopolitics is Howard Hughes, who had 'managed to foreshadow a *mass situation*, the quest for the progress of speed without the knowledge of the engine's exterminating character' (*PW*, 87). The governance mechanisms of chronopolitics, uncannily like Foucault's (2010) notion of bio–power, are premised upon the abolition of death through the collectively induced disappearance of both time and history. Accordingly, the reversal of chronopolitics is the authentic recovery of the phenomenological realities of extensivity and duration, the necessary preconditions for all successful meditations upon the absolute limit(s) of finitude. Hence, Virilio is able to conclude that 'we're really in civilian life when we confront the question of death' (*PW*, 120).

See also: City; Politics; Space–Time; War

CHURCH OF SAINT-BERNADETTE DU BANLAY

John Beck

The church of Saint-Bernadette du Banlay was designed by Virilio and the architect Claude Parent and completed in 1966 in the French city of Nevers. Saint Bernadette experienced childhood visions of the Virgin Mary at the Grotto of Massabielle near Lourdes in 1858 and joined the Sisters of Charity in Nevers in 1866. The church draws heavily on the vocabulary of military architectural forms evident in the German bunkers of Hitler's Atlantic Wall, though the bunker forms, according to Parent, were a late addition to the design and introduced mainly in order to 'play up the drama of the exterior' of the building while 'stripping' the military vocabulary 'of its lethal functions' (Virilio and Parent 1996: 19). The project was Parent and Virilio's first venture in what they called 'the function of the oblique' and preceded the theories they developed in the *Architecture Principe* magazine. Drawing on Gestalt theory and Merleau-Ponty's phenomenology, Virilio and Parent were seeking to produce a dynamic spatial environment created through the deployment of the inclined plane. In a rejection of the horizontal and vertical, the oblique plane of the floor compelled the body to move and adjust to instability. As such, the relationship between the body and building becomes active and circulatory rather than static and inhibiting. To an extent this investigation of the fluidity of the oblique seems in opposition to the stubborn concrete weight of the bunker and Parent has claimed that the convergence of oblique structure and bunker form came together only because he and Virilio approached the project with two different sets of design ideas they wanted to explore. Nevertheless, the combination of bunker concrete and dynamic, fractured space does embody the disturbing and contradictory energies of immense power and anxious stalemate characteristic of the Cold War. Indeed, while Second World War bunkers may have provided a grammar of forms for the church, Virilio has said that the building had more in common with the fallout shelter than the military bunker (Virilio and Armitage 2001b: 175). Despite the rough concrete and hostile blankness of the structure, it does offer the protection and security of the more conventional religious building. As Parent explains, 'The church has a menacing appearance: its opaque concrete carapace is defensive, even deliberately "repulsive" in its relation to its surroundings, but at the same time it forms a protective enclosure for the interior, which has been conceived as a grotto, in homage to the life of the church's patron saint' (*FO*, 19).

CINEMA

Tom Conley

The core of Virilio's reflections on the history and theory of cinema is found in his *War and Cinema: The Logistics of Perception* (1989 [1984]), a monograph informing much of his later writing on subjectivity, politics and societal control. Key are two observations he draws from close study of war films from the silent era up to now: first, the causes and effects of the Wars of 1914–18 and 1939–45 were intimately related to the development of cinema. The 'war movie' became a strategic apparatus vital to the programming and execution of local and global conflict. In its growth in the genre, extending from *The Birth of a Nation* (dir. D. W. Griffith, 1914), *The Big Parade* (dir. King Vidor, 1925), *What Price, Glory?* (dir. Raoul Walsh, 1926) and other features up to *Wings* (dir. William Wellman, 1927) and *Hell's Angels* (dir. Howard Hughes, 1930), it is said to represent the toils and spoils of war. Second, from the conception, production and marketing of such feature films, Virilio concludes that from its inception the seventh art is harnessed to shape and control perception itself. The medium discovered how it would tell its spectators who and why they happen to be living in the world into which they were born, and, further, how it could determine the nature of perception and human experience.

For Virilio, cinema is a medium of perception built to construct events. An event, according to Gilles Deleuze (1990), is a nexus of 'prehensions' or perceptions (including the perception itself) that shapes subjectivity and symbolic life in general. Because they are marketed on an international scale, cinematic events quickly become a tool vital for social control. Producing a common register of 'experience' through what its adepts have called its 'universal language', cinema programs the conscious and unconscious register of life. Virilio (*WC*, 11–12) adheres to Griffith's precocious intuition that cinema was a vitally strategic instrument for the construction of history and the shaping of diplomacy. The fear, pathos and fascination that its narratives elicited could be yoked to pattern collective behaviour. Virilio observes that later generations of directors and studios mobilised Griffith's views: in the field of perception the melodrama would show viewers how to control their emotions; the western would offer vistas of imaginary space and romantic escape to palliate social immobility; for a duration of eighty-plus minutes the screwball comedy would let poor spectators become rich; the gangster film would allow spectators to act out fantasies of revenge on unjust political leaders; the war film would offer blueprints for future conflict and elicit sympathy for military policy.

Through his work on the management of perception Virilio draws attention to the ways that cinema affects ideology, understood not as a collection of conscious beliefs but the unconscious relation the imagination holds with real modes of production. Montage made its visual effects exceed and even contradict a film's ostensive meaning or message. For Virilio, these effects are the 'captures' or double binds that constitute the perception and experience of cinema. Drawing attention to the sensory register of film, he studies areas where emotive purchase is made on the spectator. He observes, for example, first, that after the First World War the logo with which Twentieth Century Fox prefaced its features was constructed to elicit a mix of fear and marvel. The nature of its sculpted characters extending across the frame was accompanied by an array of beacons shooting flickering shafts of light about and around the monument. What the viewer senses to be a 'spectacle' is in fact related to traumatising memory-images from the First World War where, as a sequence of *Hell's Angels* reminds us, anti-aircraft gunners projected beacons of light into the sky to catch sight of enemy Zeppelins carrying payloads of bombs. Traumatic reminder of the deadly effects of air power becomes integral to the promotion of the medium.

Second, and correlatively, he notes the German war machine had found inspiration in what cinema had wrought: the success of the blitzkrieg in the years 1939–40 was owed to co-ordination of aerial attack and deployment of parachuting 'shock' troops landing in advance of fast-moving tanks rolling ahead of heavily armed infantry. For optimum effect the Luftwaffe equipped its Stuka dive bomber (a slow-moving aircraft lacking retractable landing gear) with sirens that screamed when it zoomed downward to release its payload. It was felt that in the field of perception, prior to the detonation of the bombs, the shrill whistle would elicit collective fear and trembling in both reality and in the newsreels that followed. Orchestrated events of this sort were cinematic and, historians have noted, gruesomely effective. Similarly (but by then in utter futility) when the Allied invasion of Europe had begun, Adolf Hitler insisted that the inventions of the Messerschmitt 262, the first jet plane, an interceptor, could be used in the same way. In cinematic delusion the Führer felt that by swooshing overhead while strafing troops on beachheads on the coast of Normandy the aircraft's mesmerising effects would defeat the soldiers who had taken the beachhead and captured the bunkers.

A homage to Virilio's work is found in the first hour of Jean-Luc Godard's televisual *Histoire(s) du cinéma* (1989), a melancholy mosaic of flickering snippets of film, music, sound, printed characters and words in which the director studies how cinematic control of perception scripted much of the Second World War and the Holocaust. Godard decries what cinema had wrought while suggesting that nonetheless traumatic images (from Auschwitz) and their soppy counterparts (in Hollywood cinema) must be recalled and revived for the world to be aware of the power of the medium. Godard cites Virilio through the clips of Stukas and sirens in synchrony with quotation of the logo of Twentieth Century Fox. The brilliance of Godard's film owes to the technology of fear that Virilio had developed in *War and Cinema*. Virilio's later writings that deal with the devastating effects of the rapid circulation of unsettling images and the production of accidental events in cinema and televisual media are based on the same foundations. Like Godard's epic film, his reflections on cinema are born of what he (2007a [2005]: 8) calls in *The Original Accident* the historian's preventive intelligence.

See also: Bunker Archeology; Logistics of Perception; War

CITY

Richard G. Smith

One of the defining concepts of urban studies is that of centrality; the clustering or agglomeration of activities in central places is the de facto geographical definition of any settlement. Ironically, the defining feature of Virilio's urbanism, and a theme that links together much of his *oeuvre*, is his lament that the centrality and axiality of the city is not so much declining as disappearing altogether into a full-blown structuralist nightmare whereby 'one can no longer understand cities in terms of separate entities, defined by some kind of specific location, but only as a global network, because all these once separate cities are now in a constant state of exchange with each other' (Virilio and Ruby 2001: 64).

Virilio's urbanism is above all an account of the decentralisation and disurbanisation of post-industrial societies: '[u]rban agglomeration has lost its reason for being' he declares in *The Lost Dimension* (1991 [1984]: 122). A lost centrality that is not because cities are shrinking (e.g. be it from the infamous anti-city policies of the Khmer Rouge in Cambodia or because of the devastation of de-industrialisation on, and consequent exodus from, North American centres such as Detroit and Cleveland), or because cities are expanding (e.g. the hyper-concentration of populations in Mexico City, Shanghai and São Paulo), which Virilio interprets as cataclysmic evidence for the 'quickly approaching disintegration of the historic town, of traditional urban development, and of the State' (*LD*, 120), but rather because the central has been replaced by the nodal as the city has become 'overexposed' through its integration in networks of transfer, transport, transit, transmigration and transmission.

Such is the immediacy, simultaneity, instantaneity and ubiquity of interactivity afforded by advances in information and communications technologies that the city for Virilio is now a 'phantom landscape' because it has lost its long-held essence as a sedentary and centralised place:

If the metropolis is still a place, a geographic site, it no longer has anything to do with the classical oppositions of city / country nor center / periphery. The city is no longer organized into a localized and axial estate. While the suburbs contributed to this dissolution, in fact the intramural–extramural opposition collapsed with the transport revolutions and the development of communication and telecommunications technologies. These promoted the merger of disconnected metropolitan fringes into a single urban mass. (*LD*, 12)

In other words, in an age where acceleration is the primal dimension cities are no longer separate bounded and unified places of face-to-face encounters because through neo-liberal globalisation and the 'transmission revolution' they have come to be networked together under a unity of time – 'a chronopolitics of intensitivity and interactivity' (*LD*, 124–5) – which reduces them to be merely 'instantaneous interfaces': 'The screen abruptly became the city square, the crossroads of all mass media' (*LD*, 25).

Through the means of mass communication, transportation and robotisation the city has 'dissipated and withered down to a nub' to be nowadays no more than 'a memory, a recollection of the unity that was a neighborhood' contends Virilio (*LD*, 29). The most elementary reference points of urbanity – symbolic, historic, architectonic and geometric – have disappeared:

> Where once the *polis* inaugurated a political theater, with its *agora* and its *forum*, now there is only a cathode-ray screen, where the shadows and spectres of a community dance amid their processes of disappearance, where cinematism broadcasts the last appearance of urbanism, the last image of an urbanism without urbanity. (*LD*, 19)

That is to say that the elimination of temporal diversity, with everything now being played out in the real instant of ubiquitous hyperrealist globalisation, inaugurates the 'twilight of places' in Virilio's *City of Panic* (2005b [2004]) whereby the city has lost its centrality and unity because it has been subsumed by the 'virtual world–city' where 'from now on every *real* city is only ever the remote periphery, the great urban wasteland of this *virtual* city that rules over it totally' (Virilio 1997 [1995]: 144).

Most recently, in *The Futurism of the Instant: Stop-Eject* (2010b [2009]), Virilio has moved further on from his critiques of decentralisation, disurbanisation and panic urbanism to criticise what he sees as the emerging trend of 'exurbanism'. Virilio's contention is that the geopolitics of settlement in the age of globalisation is now being overturned by the dawning of a new era of exodus or 'habitable circulation'. Virilio describes the emerging trend of 'exurbanism' as having two key consequences for the city. First, that the persistence of urban sites is becoming blurred through the global mobilisation of populations. The forced exile of populations and the resettlement of nations has created a 'worldwide circulating city' of transients who are 'adrift from their moorings in urbanity' (*FI*, 3) and without 'hope of returning to the sedentariness of the semi-autonomous city' (*FI*, 5) of their origins. Second, that '[t]he original town is giving way to the *ultracity* produced by an exurbanism that is not so much metropolitan as omnipolitan' (*FI*, 36–7). An ultracity because the axis of the city has been tilted from the horizontal to the vertical; 'upwardness' has taken over from a 'downtown' centrality surrounded by an urban sprawl to become the dominant and menacing logic now shaping the contemporary urban form(ation):

> What is in play is an actual reversal in metropolitan centrality, with the static vehicle of the very high tower today carrying the day [. . .] with the axiality that extended the old urban centre making way for a rising axiality. The 'superficial' primacy of the centre over the periphery disappears in aid of an axis now vertical, where the high dominates the low. The primacy of 'upwardness' thereby takes over from the primacy of the formerly privileged city centre, 'downtown', where

the horizontal axis of the expanse of land, and ownership of land, once held sway. (*FI*, 49–50)

See also: *Aesthetics of Disappearance; Landscape of Events; Media; Overexposed City; Ultracity*

CITY OF PANIC

Richard G. Smith

Under the satellites that orbit the world of neo-liberal globalisation Virilio's *City of Panic* (2005b [2004]) has, bombarded by 'weapons of mass communication' (*CP*, 87), become overexposed to the 'black holes' of globalised interconnectivity. Besieged by tools of mass communication, cities are becoming unrecognisable as they are repeatedly reimagined and reconstructed for viewers as quailing epicentres of anxiety, devastation, disaster, distrust, emergency, fear, paranoia and vulnerability; transformed to be no more than civilisation's 'lost citadels' (*CP*, 103) by 'the *looping* of terrorizing images' (*CP*, 85). *In nuce*, the *idée fixe* of Virilio's sermons on the urban condition is that while *all* modern metropolises and their civilian populations have always been targets for terror they are, nowadays, in the mass telecommunications age, so gripped by an apocalyptic 'state of siege', by surveillance and the management of public fear in the wake of the *total war* of the attacks on the World Trade Center (see Virilio 2002b [2002]), that they are increasingly being made to appear as if they have stepped straight out of a dystopian movie like *Blade Runner* (dir. Ridley Scott, 1982), *Code 46* (dir. Michael Winterbottom, 2003), or *District 13* (dir. Pierre Morel, 2004).

'[A] target for all terrors, domestic or strategic' (*CP*, 95) cities are the loci of perpetual accidents, alienation, attack, cataclysm, catastrophe, density, despair, division, and insularity. Through a process of what Virilio calls 'bunkerisation', an urban social geography of retreat, apartheid, and prevention has been produced so that the modern metropolis is no longer a cosmopolis but rather a 'claustropolis' of 'people cloistered in their private communities, on the pretext of social insecurity [. . .]' (*CP*, 93). As targets and territories for conflict and war, urban forms have come to follow fear, to be shaped as landscapes of defence and exclusion that are designed to militate against all scales and forms of violence and mixture. This new aesthetic of security, privatised spaces and fortified enclaves is most visibly manifest through the ubiquitous gated communities and militaristic and fortress architectures that increasingly shape and segregate the world's metropolises from São Paulo and Cape Town to Los Angeles, Moscow and the 'deluxe gulag' of Dubai. In short, cities are becoming, says Virilio, increasingly nightmarish, analogous to 'concentration camps' and 'torture chambers' as 'the *social body* gradually disintegrates' (*CP*, 125).

The transformation of the cityscape and the direction of city life have reached an inflection point, swerving toward a common urban destiny that is a warped version of the age-old adage: *si vis pacem, para bellum* (if you wish for peace, prepare for war). To cut Virilio's *tour d'horizon* short, *City of Panic* is his requiem to the city as civilisation: '*the greatest catastrophe of the twentieth century has been the city*' (*CP*, 90). A counterpoint to Panglossian accounts of the modern metropolis, Virilio's portrayal of a post-humanist panic urbanism is the most Cassandra-like account and definition of the modern and future metropolis available, not least because there is no *deus ex machina* end to his *City of Panic*, a city that cannot be saved because it will always be doomed as a target 'for firestorms!' (*CP*, 103).

CLAUSTROPOLIS

Mark Featherstone

Virilio introduces the notion of the claustropolis in his *City of Panic* (2005b [2004]). According to Virilio, the claustropolis emerges when the ideology of speed, which for him characterises contemporary society, collides with the urban principle of communal living. While the former foregrounds the importance of unimpeded freedom, movement and mobility, the latter requires people to live together in society, a social form that necessarily involves the limitation of individualism. In this respect, Virilio's concept implies a conflict between liberal individualistic ideology and the city as the classic space of community and sociability that we find expressed in the works of authors such as Lewis Mumford (1968). Here, the city is a container, which offers people security in exchange for the surrender of freedom, and a place where Thomas Hobbes's (2002 [1651]) original social contract between the individual and society is sealed.

However, Virilio's city replays the original Hobbesian problem, which was that limitation does not sit well with people who desire freedom, but at an advanced stage of technological development, where the need for light speed and constant mobility is an ideological imperative that cannot tolerate the social principle deeply rooted in the idea of the urban. The result of this collision of the principles of speed and community is that the city becomes a space where people feel claustrophobic and anxious about the proximity of other people who appear to be invading their personal space and limiting their freedom to move. Moreover, this sense of claustrophobia is exacerbated by the problem of light speed in contemporary society where there is nowhere else to go and people cannot move any faster. In Virilio's view, then, the claustropolis is an effect of the light speeds of a contemporary society collapsing in on itself, towards a state of immobility or flat-line inertia. This last produces enormous anxiety in people conditioned to pursue mobility as an ideologically defined goal. Virilio's *The University of Disaster* (2010a [2007]) in particular defines the modern form of subjectivity organised around the need for speed through reference to the term 'dromomania' and the claustrophobic city of panic is in many ways the city of the 'dromomaniac' forced to live in confined space.

In this respect, it is possible to trace the origins of Virilio's theory of the claustropolis back to urban theorists, such as the German sociologist Georg Simmel (1969), who introduced the problem of social relations in the modern city in the early twentieth century and who also linked this issue to the emergence of pathological psychology. In Simmel's work, the central effect of the new technological city was to create an urban condition defined by speed and movement, which created particular psychopathological effects in the modern metropolis. For Simmel, these psychopathological effects included revulsion towards other people, anxiety about proximity and emotional hardness, and it is possible to see how much of this psychological language, crucially inflected by Gestalt psychology, survives in Virilio's account of the city as claustropolis. Although Virilio is famously critical of psychoanalysis, his notion of claustropolis clearly employs the use of psychoanalytic thought and introduces Freudian (1977) psychoanalytic concepts such as anxiety and phobia through a lens comparable to that of Simmel, who first spatialised Freud's psychological theory.

CRITICAL SPACE

Verena Andermatt Conley

Space, a term that generally refers to the physical and mental milieus in which humans find themselves, mobilises many of Virilio's reflections on the condition of our world. In his view, what Cartesian philosophy had called *res extensa* does not apply to contemporary life. Determined by displacement, space is discernible both through and *as* movement. Space is a product of acceleration or even inertia of motion. It is a vector, the *resultant* movement of an object on which a variety of forces are being exerted.

It is driven electronically and perceived in the relation of the passage and illumination of light that 'exposes' the world to its perceivers.

In *Bunker Archeology* (1994a [1975]), Virilio draws on childhood memories of the Second World War to explain a shift in spatial consciousness he intuited when seeing Allied planes flying over the Atlantic Wall the Axis had constructed along the coastline of Normandy. Aerial bombardment of the railway, of roads and of civilian populations behind the fortifications effaced the formerly indelible borderlines that had been established on the northern front in the First World War. Battles waged in the air in the years 1939–45, especially with the advent of the atom bomb, made clear that all war would hereafter spread across and over the globe.

Drawing on his knowledge in architecture, Virilio soon used his training in phenomenology under philosopher Maurice Merleau-Ponty to focus on telluric space, that is, areas populated by human subjects who make sense of it through their existential relation with their milieu. Yet, at the same time, this very notion of space that Merleau-Ponty (2002 [1945]) had developed in his *Phenomenology of Perception*, Virilio laments in *The Aesthetics of Disappearance* (2009a [1980]) and elsewhere, was already in a state of evanescence. The relation that humans keep with space is to a strong degree marked by military technology. Since the bombardment of civilian populations, a logistics of speed spreads fear and is cause for a new condition of worldwide displacement. In *Speed and Politics* (2006 [1977]) Virilio traces the history of speed that, far from being simply added to Western time-space co-ordinates, entirely alters them. Speed, under the dictate that the fastest wins, introduces a new dimension. From the 'metabolic vehicle', such as a person or a horse to the car, the plane, and, today, the electronic transmission of information, speed has caused traditional space to shrink and indeed become eradicated.

In 1984 Virilio (1991 [1984]) published his decisive essay, *L'Espace critique* in a series of the same name that he continues to direct at the Éditions Galilée in Paris. The equivocal French title implies that space becomes (1) critical and (2) a critical concept. The fate of space is a decisive issue, and even more so is the need to reflect on what is happening to it and why. Translated into English in 1991 as *The Lost Dimension*, the English title loses the political dimension where space is alloyed with critical theory. In the opening essay, 'The Overexposed City', Virilio (*LD*, 9–28) announces what he will reiterate throughout his writings, namely, that *here begins elsewhere*. When no line of demarcation marks an urban form, and all phenomena are put under the sign of programmed time, humans can no longer be physically located in a place. Humans are conveyed in an ever-accelerating movement that calls into question the idea of 'departure' and turns everything into an arrival. If space was that which prevents everything from being in the same place, humans are henceforth brought back to a place without a place. The exhaustion of natural contours and of temporal distances undoes all possibilities of positioning.

In his writings Virilio deals with different kinds of spaces: telluric, maritime, virtual and cybernetic. Not surprisingly given his life-long affinity with architecture – his collaboration with Claude Parent goes back to the 1960s – he focuses on urban spaces and the urbanisation of the planet. Time and again, he discusses the changes that (read 'European') city spaces have been undergoing since the Renaissance and, especially, since the Second World War. Traditional cities were spatial (and temporal) constructions defined by *centres* and peripheries that allowed inhabitants to locate themselves. The gate that used to mark the division between city and country has disappeared under a rampant urban sprawl that has neither beginning nor end. Identification of a city-dweller with monuments and place names is superseded by another with a technical duration that knows neither a calendar of activity nor a shared collective memory. As he argues in *L'Insécurité du territoire* (1993), humans lose the security they once acquired by occupying a mental *and* physical topography or 'territory'.

Writing at the frontier of a tendency, Virilio (*LD*) claimed in 1984 that North American cities in particular are dying. Because they teeter-totter on the edge of financial collapse, such cities are the scene of a massive exodus. Today, however, many of these cities have become playgrounds of the super-rich. What Virilio found in a condition of global urban exodus turned out to be an impending redistribution of wealth and a new class structure that electronic technologies that are functions of speed have helped to set in place. In cognisance of this development, Virilio constructs the spatial diagram of a new social pyramid, at whose apex are media people, CEOs and administrators, who are all adepts of speed, while consumers settle more slowly at the bottom. The great majority of the inhabitants of this Earth, however, are parked outside this pyramid, in a worldwide *banlieue*.

Far from glorifying the loss of a phenomenological sense of space and territory, Virilio criticises what he calls a generalised 'derealisation'. In consonance with his idea of *critical space*, he urges readers to think through the consequences of the world as it is now moving. He focuses on what he sees as a confrontation between a geodesic faculty to define a unity of time and place for human activities, in contrast to another that consists of structural capacities of means of mass communication. Without opposing electronic modes of communication, Virilio criticises the new 'space' that military technologies have imposed to 'globalise' the world economy.

From *The Lost Dimension* to *Open Sky* (1997 [1995]) and beyond,

Virilio argues that what is local today is already global. If architecture had functioned in relation with geology, with natural reliefs and structures – from pyramids to Gothic towers – it is now measured by cutting-edge technologies that exile humans from all terrestrial folds. A territorial crisis affects nations, places, people, justice and rights. The transformation of space affects cities *and* democracy since it eradicates the spatial dimension upon which the latter were founded. Democracy becomes emotive: people are manipulated by means of images and mass communications that instil fear of terrorism (Virilio 2005b [2004]). The future of human settlements and migrations can be read through the evolution of a city that has been reduced to the circulation of transients (Virilio 2010b [2009]). Politics have to be reinvented along with the city and a notion of space that valorises a sensory experience and extension (*OS*).

For all its seeming excesses, Virilio's pronouncements on space are timely provocations that introduce a critical wedge into the idea, inherited from the Enlightenment, that new technologies are signs of progress in a digital humanity.

See also: City; Overexposed City; Place; Space-Time; Speed-Space; Territory

CYBERNETIC

Hugh Davies

The realm of the cybernetic presents an insidious peril for Virilio. Throughout his *oeuvre*, he relentlessly critiques technological mediation and systematisation, the very antithesis of his cherished embodied experience. While his scrutiny of cybernetic concepts can be traced back to his writing from the 1970s and 1980s, in which he excavates the military origins of civilian technologies, he does not begin to employ the term 'cybernetic' to describe technological phenomena until the late 1990s.

The first published use appears in his *Open Sky* (1997 [1995]), in which Virilio dedicates a chapter to examining the cybernetic monopolisation of sensual pleasure. In 1999, Virilio's *Politics of the Very Worst* rolls out his constellation of thought concerning the contemporary world in which cybernetics begins to feature significantly. But the term becomes a key concern for Virilio in *The Information Bomb* (2000d [1998]), a volume made up of his articles from the European press from 1996 to 1998. Variations of the term proliferate throughout the book: cyberterrorism, cybercrime, cybersects, cyber acceleration, cybersex, with each used to describe the multifarious tendencies of a dreaded cyber age. Virilio deplores what he sees as Western societies' complete domination by cybernetic technologies and their willing submission to the dogma of the 'totalitarian techno-cult'. The cyberworld, he claims (*IB*, 27), is an entirely new continent, a duplicated reality construct of the information age, towards which all rational criticism has ceased. By *Crepuscular Dawn* (2002), Virilio is using the term cyber bomb interchangeably with the term information bomb (*CD*, 35, 136, 142).

Virilio's aversion to the cybernetic is that it represents the subordination of politics, society, the human body and mind to technological enhancement and regulation. The epitome of this cybernetic invasion is so-called human enhancement through technological intervention. Even the ramparts of the body have been breached. Nowhere is this more evident than in the creative practice of Virilio's close friend, the Australian performance artist Stelarc, who willingly invites the infiltration of experimental science into his own body, celebrating a transhumanism that, for Virilio, is barely human at all. Virilio divides such bodily invasions into two battle fronts. First, genetic engineering, which he derides as a politically correct term for a cybernetic eugenicism driven by science's artificial selection of the human species and the commercial privatisation of our genetic code (*IB*, 136). Second, the prosthetic augmentation that he claims comes at the cost of atrophy both of the sensual experience of the body as well as of the body itself, rendering, for example, the able-bodied person the equivalent of the mechanically wired disabled person (*OS*, 11). Whether through bionic prosthetics or genetic tampering, Virilio claims that the intrusions of experimental science have turned the body into a testing ground. He argues that the sole aim of innovation is to render all exchanges cybernetic. As such, cybernetic exchanges convey the prospect of a united humanity, but also of humanity reduced to a uniformity, the eventual outcome of which Virilio fears will be the ultimate disappearance of the human subject altogether.

CYBERSPACE

Ronald E. Purser

In less than a millennium, our socio-cultural perception has shifted from the geometric optics of Alberti's real-space window of linear perspectival vision, developed artistically during the Renaissance, to gazing at the flat screen physical optics of Gates's Microsoft 'Windows' (Virilio, 2002b [2002]: 7). Whether it is a PC, Macintosh, iPad or the latest smartphone, the world of cyberspace has become a ubiquitous everyday reality for billions of people. In his seminal work, *The Art of the Motor*, Virilio (1995 [1993]: 151) traces how the real-space perspective of the painters during the Renaissance (quattrocento) has been 'motorised' by information and communications technologies, resulting in a 'loss of reality' of 'space-time-matter'. Classical linear perspective, which mapped the landscape and physical space through geometric co-ordinates against an apparent horizon, was based on a perception of distance and relief between the observer and the observed. Cyberspace collapses the sense of distance on the one hand (by creating instantaneous connections), while maintaining the phenomenological sense of a distanced subject that 'interacts' with informational objects. In cyberspace, it is no coincidence that movement across surfaces of information objects is metaphorically referred to as 'surfing the net'. In *Open Sky*'s (1997 [1995]: 35–48) 'Optics on a Grand Scale', Virilio articulates how spatial distance and temporal relief collapse within cyberspace. Such hyper-perspectivity is now apparent as the time it takes to traverse space appears to have remarkably shrunk, creating popularised images of the 'global village', 'spaceship earth' and the 'Worldwide Web'.

The hegemonic global temporality that Virilio anticipated is a digitised extension of the perspectival conquest of space. Conquest of space would not have been possible without the 'small optics' – accurate maps and representations of the actual terrain, which allowed the observer to occupy an externalised perspective in which the globe could be viewed as a knowable totality. An apparent and visible horizon serves as a key point of perceptual orientation for making sense of scale and perspective, and a deeper horizon grounded in our collective imagination is instrumental in deriving meaning from our situated experience. For some thing or object to exist, it literally must stand out against the background of a horizon. The depth of field in small optics is based on the preservation of spatial distance, giving rise to such distinctions as 'near vs far', 'here vs there'.

Cyberspace, however, introduces a new global vision and fundamentally different sensibility, where the cartographic image of the globe no longer needs to stand in for or represent the 'real world' because in cyberspace the image has become 'the world'. Virilio points out that spatial depth is now represented for us by a highly abstract, mathematically conceived, information-energy. In fact, Virilio equates cyberspace with the fusion of information-matter-energy, or what he (*OS*, 22) refers to as 'cybernetic space-time'. Cyberspace is governed by surfaces without true insides; it is flattened out, superficial and depthless. In contrast, with real-time and large-scale optics, time moves at the speed of light, erasing distinctions based on spatial distance. Having instantaneous access from any point in space to virtually any other point in a 'real-time instant' renders such spatial notions as 'near vs far', 'here vs there', meaningless. The result for Virilio is a distortion of our depth of field and fundamental disorientation.

DECOMPOSITION

Eric Wilson

Consistent with Virilio's authorial strategy of employing phenomenology as a source of political and aesthetic metaphor, decomposition serves as the nexus of a series of intertextual references on globalisation, catastrophe and the post-humanist 'de-centring' of the self. Following Paul Valéry's comments reproduced in Virilio's *Open Sky* (1997 [1995]: 144) that the 'individual of the scientific age is losing his capacity to experience himself as a centre of energy', Virilio asserts in his seminal later text *Crepuscular Dawn* (Virilio and Lotringer 2002: 161) that 'the rapidity of a phenomenon liquidates you'. In no other work does Virilio so display his credentials as a phenomenologist; the entirety of this text serves as an extended commentary on Merleau-Ponty's observation that 'Our own body is in the world as the heart is in the organism: it keeps the visible spectacle constantly alive, it breathes life into it and sustains it inwardly, and with it forms a system' (*OS*, 28). With globalisation and dromoscopy as a catastrophic collapse towards an infinitely dense and claustrophobic centre of spatial and temporal instan-taneity, the ontological annihilation of temporal duration, Virilio metaphori-cally redeploys speed-politics as psychosomatic trauma: 'Decomposition is everywhere, everywhere. What is decomposing is the geographical space, the psychophysical and psychophysiological space of being. It affects at once the big territorial body, the small animal body and the social body' (*CD*, 165).

Virilio divides the speed-traumatised decomposing body into three forms: the territorial (which equates to the classical notion of the state), the social (*socius*) and the 'animal', or the phenomenological. The analysis is framed in a descending order, from the higher modern political construct of the nation-state as the signifier of Enlightenment politics downwards towards the pre-Cartesian realm of unreconstituted bodily sensation:

The first body is the world. Without the world proper, the social body and the body proper don't exist [. . .] The territorial body is more important than the

socius or the animal body. The first mortality occurs when the relation between
the body proper and the world is cut off [. . .] (*CD*, 102)

Beginning with the Roman Empire, the process of political formation is
governed by an interconnectivity regulated by speed, yielding a surplus of
temporal compression. With the revolutionary transformation of speed-
politics that erupts as globalisation, however, a catastrophic 'tipping
point' is reached: 'For the first time in history, the [spatio-temporal]
contraction occurred at a meta-geophysical level, and not at a sociologi-
cal, or socio-physical level. And this is unheard of [. . .] Therefore we're
in front of a situation without reference [. . .]' (*CD*, 102). On the level of
socius, the proliferation of the telematic signs of globalisation, information
technology and an aggressively imperialistic computational reasoning,
have replaced our collective means of perception and the traditional body-
spatial grounding of social reality: 'We are faced with the reconstruction
of the phenomenology of perception according to the machine. And this
is a catastrophic event' (*CD*, 141). Finally, and most vitally, the animal
body-self undergoes a parallel process of dissolution and final extermination. Virilio cites Husserl: 'Does not optical flesh, qua body, then have its
place in the space of bodies, as well as the property of being unable to go
further in space, in a direction where another body blocks its way?' (2000a
[1990]: 83). Here, Virilio's *Polar Inertia* (2000a [1990]) identifies the universalisation of the telematic as the ultimate source of the loss of bodily
sensation and, therefore, of the body-self. The simultaneous conjunction
of temporal compression with the (illusory) unbounded space of virtual
reality effectively dis-places the 'real presence' of the subject into a post-
phenomenological 'no-where:'

Not only is the 'full body' of the earth vanishing before our eyes, but our own
body is becoming blurred and afflicting us with an unprecedented 'disorder', a
paralysis (or autism) which leaves us still *where we are*, with an imposing ponder-
ous mass, while the loss of the full body of being is carrying us towards the void.
(*PI*, 83)

Even worse, this fatal 'void' is neither ontological nor existential, but
irretrievably social, the annihilating contamination of the decomposed
socius. Speed-politics mediated through the logistics of perception has,
in Virilio's beautifully phenomenological metaphor, 'exploded the philo-
physical nucleus':

So we could say that speed is aging the world. Speed is wearing out the world.
Speed is the exhaustion of the world. We are coming back to confinement. We

are coming back to enclosure and incarceration. And also exclusion. Whence the escape velocity which offers the way out, but *a way out to nothing*. To emptiness and the black hole. There is no light outside the atmosphere. (*CD*, 150)

Decomposition is the discursive key to Virilio's increasingly pessimistic critique of globalisation, and *Crepuscular Dawn* is, arguably, his most radically anti-globalisation work: 'Globalization is the world becoming too small, and not too big [. . .] Not only too small because of overpopulation, but because we have reduced the world to nothing' (*CD*, 89). The tripartite division of the decomposing 'body' illuminates the multilevel operation of catastrophic temporal compression, a rhetorical move that complements Virilio's 'double movement' between exo- and endo-colonisation:

Trying to keep decomposition at a distance is a misunderstanding of how chaos works. No one can remain immune from chaos, globalization being chaos extended to the totality of the world, including America, including each of us. Each one of us as a person, as a body, is subjected to the threat of chaos, or to real chaos. (*CD*, 164)

Decomposition is an aphoristic continuation of the same strategy of cultural critique that underlines the 'wall of history' and 'the aesthetics of disappearance': the post-humanist abolition of all possible grounds of future becoming. 'But when we are in a decomposing world, when every-thing decomposes because of the acceleration of exchange, the deconstruc-tion of instances and institutions, then there is no future [. . .]' (*CD*, 164). Even the singularly unipolar nature of the American territorial body fails to render it immune from the catastrophic processes of decomposition unleashed by the plenitude of temporal compression, yielding a total, and permanent, loss of faith in the political and historical certitudes of democracy as the guarantor of the classic liberal body-self. In a manner strikingly reminiscent of Baudrillard's theory of the eternal loss of the ref-erent through simulacra and simulation, the United States, as the paragon liberal and democratic 'body', loses all capacity to act as a discursive refer-ent through its collective vacating of phenomenological being. 'America is done for. When I say America is done for, I mean that the world is done for. Globalization is a phenomenon that surpasses America [. . .] Globalization, this is the end of America' (*CD*, 166).

See also: Body; Globalisation; Phenomenology; Speed

DELEUZE, GILLES

George Katsonis

The late philosopher Gilles Deleuze (1925–95) rose to academic renown
with the publication of his doctoral dissertation and career-defining work
Difference and Repetition (2004 [1968]). The coincidence of his vision of
anarchic ontological difference with the revolutionary events in Paris in
May 1968 spawned a series of ramifications for the future of his *oeuvre* and
of philosophy at large, foreseeable by Michel Foucault (2000 [1970]: 343)
in his light-hearted yet much-cited quote: 'perhaps, one day, this century
will be known as Deleuzian'. All through the 1970s, Deleuze's collaboration with the psychoanalyst and political activist Félix Guattari for the two
volumes of *Capitalism and Schizophrenia – Anti-Oedipus* (2004 [1972]) and
A Thousand Plateaus (2004 [1980]) – reoriented his thought towards politics, mass movements and microsociology, and established strategic alliances with the works of fellow philosophers such as Foucault and Virilio.

In particular, Deleuze and Guattari's collaborative works linked the
problem of the 'image of thought' Deleuze had previously articulated
in relation to Platonism, phenomenology, psychoanalysis and to the
problem of power, by constructing a 'desiring' discourse of production that queers and conflates the well-established and well-separated
Kantian, Marxian and Freudian milieus (transcendental, social, libidinal).
Here, Deleuze and Guattari are keen to demonstrate desiring-production
as a molecular plane of immanent causality populated by contingent
'becomings' (-woman, -animal, -music, -imperceptible) that materialise
in intensive relations among 'partial objects, flows, and bodies' (Deleuze
and Guattari 2004 [1972]: 28). Power is presented, on the other hand, in a
number of transhistorical modalities, ranging from the affirmative model
of nomadic life – nomadology, or the 'war machine' – to repressive 'molar'
organisations (primitive, despotic and capitalist) that deal differently with
the fundamental social problems of flows, territory, the state apparatus
and the war machine.

The war machine is, arguably, the apex of Deleuze's collaboration with
Guattari, but also of his entire *oeuvre*, managing to sensibly associate his
seemingly disparate interests towards vitalist materialism, a metaphysics
of difference, transcendental aesthetics, practical ethics and revolutionary
politics. But the war machine marks also the beginning of a close encounter with the works of Virilio. At this 'plateau', their works intersect at
many levels: thematically, in discussion of war, speed, geometry, topology,
the body and the phenomenology of matter; metahistorically, where both
privilege a concept and logic of the 'event' over substance; historically

and strategically, in view of fascism, totalitarianism and capitalism; and, finally, intellectually, on the form of post-Second World War philosophical expression, where both advocate a philosophy that imparts elements from science and literature and produces graphic concepts. On the whole, these intersections entail convergences as well as divergences, reservations and departures, which are often revisited in later works, and still reverberate in Virilio's continuing *oeuvre*.

Beginning with *A Thousand Plateaus* (2004 [1980]), Deleuze and Guattari draw heavily on Virilio's war model and political geography, concurring with his idea that the war machine originates from hunting whence 'the idea of the motor' appears (Deleuze and Guattari 2004 [1980]: 437), his notions of 'smooth space' and 'fleet in being' (Deleuze and Guattari 2004 [1980]: 529–30) and his thesis on 'the geometrical or linear reason of State' that dictates 'the management of the public ways, or the control of movement' (Deleuze and Guattari 2004 [1980]: 233, 425–6). Furthermore, their critique of the post-Second World War 'capitalist axiomatic' through 'a macropolitics of society by and for a micropolitics of insecurity' (Deleuze and Guattari 2004 [1980]: 237) resonates with Virilio's idiosyncratic 'apocalyptic or millenarian' convictions that by bringing in 'an absolute peace of terror or deterrence' technoscientific progress has established 'a new conception of security as materialized war, as organized insecurity or molecularized, distributed, programmed catastrophe' (Deleuze and Guattari 2004 [1980]: 516).

These themes are later refined by Deleuze in his 'Postscript on the Societies of Control' (1995 [1990]: 177–82), where the relation between post-Second World War schizoid materialisms and a politics of insecurity is subsumed under the formal notion of 'control', which he introduces in view of the accelerating developments in consumer capitalism, state and corporate institutions, and the rise of new information and communications technologies. Heralding the impending obsolescence of Foucault's (1991) enclosed disciplines – factory, prison, hospital, school, family – societies of control celebrate capitalism as mannerism or 'modulation' and, as such, establish 'ultra-rapid' and 'free-floating' (Deleuze 1995 [1990]: 178) modalities of domination (and insecurity) like mass debt, marketing, lifestyle, as well as, at an institutional level, perpetual training, apprenticeships, flexible salaries and bonuses, prison and healthcare reform, and outsourcing in the police and the army. The central tenet of Deleuze's thesis on control, which resembles Virilio's notion of the depopulation effect of mobility, is his view of the 'dividual' (Deleuze 1995 [1990]: 180) replacing the individual under the digital language of passwords operating through computers.

While confessedly stepping onto Virilio's persistent scrutiny of the issue, which notably goes as far back as his *Speed and Politics* (2006 [1977]), and where mass control is held as 'primordial' as urban defence (*SP*, 15), Deleuze's 'Postscript' follows along the lines set in *A Thousand Plateaus* and repeats and represents at once a convergence and a departure from Virilio's thought. The dystopian tonality of Deleuze's text could arguably suggest a closer proximity. However, a departure from Virilio was predetermined all along and arose from Deleuze's particular ontology and epistemology.

In *A Thousand Plateaus*, for example, Deleuze and Guattari explain that their difficulty with Virilio is that he has a tendency to assimilate all the groups of speed he after all made possible to distinguish (i.e. nomadic, state, planetary) under 'a general case for the "fascist" character of speed' (Deleuze and Guattari 2004 [1980]: 623–4). Yet, all in all, the issue at play here is the rift between Virilio's phenomenological background and Deleuze's profound 'Nietzscheanism', which pre-dates and outlasts his collaborations with Guattari. In view of speed and its deterritorialising effects, whereas Virilio discerns a 'physically repulsive' (Virilio and Armitage 2001a: 25) pseudo-metaphysics of the void, or at the very best (i.e. outside of state geometry or planetary control) an ambiguous, potentially 'energising', bodily experience, Deleuze invests the nomadic war machine with a metaphysics of intensive becomings, and a corresponding concept of power, which, in the end, allows Deleuze and Guattari to assess speeding bodies according to immanent ethical criteria (e.g. joy/sadness). Deleuze's investment in the nomadic war machine is, then, quite different from Virilio's metaphysical approach to speed, grounded as it is in war, science and relativity, and altogether outside of a phenomenological image of sensible reality.

See also: Phenomenology; Speed; State; War

DESERT SCREEN

John Beck

The Gulf War of 1990–1 confirmed for Virilio the convergence of media and military technologies that he had been writing about since *War and Cinema: The Logistics of Perception* (1989 [1984]). The Gulf War decisively marked the end of Cold War deterrence strategy and, for Virilio, signalled the onset of information war. The instantaneous electronic control of combat operations opened up, as Virilio saw it, a 'fourth front' of real-time communications into which collapsed the conventional fronts of land, sea and air. CNN's 24-hour news network provided a televisual theatre of real time through which the image war could be witnessed by a global audience as it happens. Virilio's newspaper and magazine work on the Gulf War was published as *L'Écran du désert: chroniques de guerre* in 1991. Michael Degener's English translation – *Desert Screen: War at the Speed of Light* (2002a [1991]) – appeared in 2002 with a preface and new interview with Virilio by James Der Derian. The book itself has a tripartite structure. The first two sections are named after the operational codenames used by US forces during the Gulf War and dated accordingly: 'August 1990: Desert Shield' and 'January 1991: Desert Storm'. The third part introduces Virilio's term: 'June 1991: Desert Screen'. The movement here, from the accumulation of hardware and intelligence (Desert Shield) through the deployment of air and ground forces (Desert Storm) to the triumph of dematerialised, deterritorialised, televisual theatre (Desert Screen), follows both the unfolding of events and the development of Virilio's thinking. Each bulletin within the three sections is also dated, making the book, as the French subtitle indicates, literally, a chronicle of war. This is important because what Virilio wants the book to document is the experience of what he calls the 'tele-spectator of a world war in miniature' (*DS*, 1) that is spatially local but temporally global. The collapse of space and time into the lightning flash of the perpetual instant means that room for reflection and analysis has been eliminated. All the spectator can do is register a series of momentary observations as they happen upon the screen. By maintaining a clear temporal chronology, Virilio turns these instants into an accumulating interrogation of what it is like to deal with the information war in real time. As such, the early part of the book is preoccupied with the emerging threat from Saddam Hussein of chemical weapons and tactical nuclear strikes. As the likelihood of these events recedes, the discussion moves deeper into the ramifications of a CNN-driven media war and the ways technologies of surveillance are increasingly shaping the form of weapons themselves: in this first postmodern war, Virilio notes, the form of the stealth bomber is linked less to the requirements of movement in space and more to the requirements of its remote representation on the screen. Virilio concludes that the Gulf War subordinated economic and political issues to experimental and promotional technological concerns. In many ways, Virilio's analysis in *Desert Screen* has provided the vocabulary and the conceptual framework for an understanding of post-September 11 conflicts in Afghanistan and Iraq.

DETERRITORIALISATION

Eftychia Mikelli

The term whereby Virilio refers to the displacement experienced at our contemporary moment, as conventional perceptions of space and territorial geopolitics give way to the extermination of distances in the new chronopolitics that speed has introduced. Virilio argues that accelerated motion contracts distances and upsets traditional conceptions of territory, leading to feelings of disorientation and loss of identity. A far cry from feudal societies which sustained a close bond between land and the individual, contemporary urban structures have encouraged and facilitated mass mobility, to the point that territory-based embedding has become exceptionally difficult. The disruption of the close association with one's native soil leads not only to geographical, but also to mental confusion, as high mobility impacts upon identity formation and dismantles any sense of stability and security.

Virilio sees decolonisation as a heightened expression of this displacement, and in *Negative Horizon* (2005a [1984]) he describes it as the liquidation of territory. Exo- and endo-colonisation deprive the individual of fixed points of territorial reference, and the new type of nomad that emerges is deterritorialised, rapidly moving through depersonalised urban conglomerations.

The experience of deterritorialisation becomes further intensified by contemporary military technologies. In *The Original Accident* (2007a [2005]), Virilio argues that the balance of terror between East and West, engendering the threat of the destruction of the Earth, leads to a panic deterritorialisation which even becomes de-terrestrialised, with orbiting space travel a clear indication of this trend. Contemporary warfare is similarly deterritorialised. In *Bunker Archaeology* (1994a [1975]), Virilio foresees the loss of firm ground in military operations. Virilio's *Speed and Politics: An Essay on Dromology* (2006 [1977]) is particularly interested in the concept of 'the fleet in being', which constantly engenders the possibility of attack and destruction. Unseen and untraceable, 'the fleet in being' advances a new conception of warfare, its power resting on the fear and anxiety it can arouse. Territorial space and individual effort give way to a new model of warfare which, in its contemporary manifestations, is no longer conducted from the sea but from orbital space, as, for example, in the Kosovo War, or even becomes a cyberwar, as Virilio believes to be the case with the Asian financial crisis of 1997–8.

Virilio extends his discussion of deterritorialisation to the field of contemporary art, which he also sees as deterritorialised. In *The Accident of Art* (Virilio and Lotringer 2005), he argues that art has lost its ground, and goes on to explain that he rejects the loss of bodies and the practice of elimination that he feels contemporary visual art advocates.

As the individual becomes increasingly deterritorialised, popular resistance is numbed. When people lose their ground, it becomes particularly problematic for them to advance opposition. Geographical and, in turn, conceptual disorientation diminish the prospect of defiance and conflict. In *Pure War* (Virilio and Lotringer 2008), Virilio proclaims deterritorialisation to be the pressing question for the end of the twentieth century; in our current context of acceleration, contraction of territory, loss of identity, and war of information, this question remains exceptionally poignant.

DROMOLOGY

John David Ebert

From the Greek word *dromos* for 'race' or 'racetrack', dromology is a science invented by Virilio for the study of speed and its impacts upon human cultural and technological systems. Speed, according to Virilio, exerts a number of transformative effects upon human culture, sometimes in very subtle ways, such as, for instance, the phenomenon of the gradual enclosure of the human individual inside the automobile as it moves ever faster, first with goggles, then with the windscreen and finally the complete enclosure of the body within the sedan.

Indeed, for Virilio, speed is the decisive factor in human technological evolution. In *Negative Horizon* (2005a [1984]), he surveys the course of technological development, noting that there has been a gradual increase in speed throughout history, beginning with woman as the first pack animal to the mounted horse to the chariot and the road, and then onward to the automobile and the aeroplane. He points out that in the nineteenth century, a transportation revolution occurred which developed from the railroad to the automobile to the aeroplane, and that these technologies of relative speed tended to support industrial democracy. The absolute speed achieved by the communications revolution, on the other hand, with the advent of electromagnetic technologies such as the telegraph, telephone, radio and TV tended to abolish the necessity for human physical movement and to reverse into the stasis of inertia of human individuals in their homes surrounded by the gadgets of their smart houses that provide so many services for them that they no longer have any need even to leave the house. Virilio often points out the paradox of stasis resulting from the gradual increase in speed, as in the case of Howard Hughes, whom he discusses primarily in *The Aesthetics of Disappearance* (2009a [1980]), who spent the first half of his life rushing about the planet in his aeroplanes, only to end, in the second half, isolating himself in his hotel room from which he rarely ventured forth at all.

The effects of the transport revolution on military technologies, Virilio insists, have led to the gradual disappearance of the geostrategic battlefield, so that the front is no longer to be found at the boundary of the territory, but wherever the vectors of mechanised transport are found. Where the mechanised vehicles are, there we find the state, for the country has today disappeared in the non-place of the state of emergency in which territorial space vanishes and only time remains. Whereas in conventional warfare we could still talk about manoeuvres of armies in the field, today there is no field, since the speed of reaction time is so fast and the invasion of the instant now succeeds the invasion of the territory. The countdown becomes the scene of battle now. Reaction time and the time for political decision are reduced to nothing by nuclear deliverance. Today, speed *is* war.

In *Speed and Politics: An Essay on Dromology* (2006 [1977]), where Virilio first developed the idea of dromology, he points out that the reason the West was able, through colonial genocide and ethnocide, to conquer other populations was because of its speed. It moved faster than these other societies because of its ever-increasing mastery first of the sea, then the rail, then the sky, etc. In *Negative Horizon*, he insists, furthermore, that because the Spaniards had the horse and the Maya had no pack animals other than women, this gave the Spaniards a dromocratic superiority which allowed them to conquer the Maya simply by their ability to manoeuvre much more quickly.

In *Speed and Politics*, he also points out how the increase in military speed has given preference to movement itself over the strategics of place, which has led to the disappearance of places themselves in what he calls 'vehicular extermination'. The strike power of the navy in the 1940s, for instance, in which power was spoken of in *knots* gave way in the 1960s to *machs* with the advent of jet power. Geographic localisation has therefore given way to the speed of the moving body and the undetectability of its path.

Furthermore, according to Virilio, it matters little whether what is sped up is information or physical objects, since in both cases it is the message of movement itself that is at issue. Acceleration, moreover, tends to produce accidents, since the faster a technology moves, the greater the likelihood that a crash of some sort will result. Dromological speed-up has affected both the realms of transport and of human data communications equally, for after the crashes attending the speed-up of rail and maritime accelerations comes the crashes of planes and cars, while after them, in turn, come the electromagnetic wave trains with their mediatic crashes of video and radio signals, in which news functions as what Virilio calls *The Information Bomb* (2000d [1998]).

Dromology is also tied in with Virilio's concept of the aesthetics of disappearance, since excess speed tends to correspond to a loss of information content. With the speed-up of war, as we have seen, the geostrategic front disappears, while the soldier himself disappears with camouflage. With the stealth bomber, the speed-up in flight has resulted in the actual disappearance into invisibility of the aeroplane off the radar screen. The increasing speed of the automobile leads, via the phenomenon of dromoscopy, to the impoverishment of the information content of its immediate milieu, which speeds past the observer and tends to take on a certain flatness in the process. Cities, too, are disappearing with mobile architecture and the rapidity of demolition of buildings that are not built to last for more than a dozen or so years.

The speed-up in media, in addition, has led to the disappearance of deferred time, a kind of mental space in which thought could move about slowly enough to reflect upon the significance of events, into the advent of real time, in which events take place so fast that the mind cannot keep up with them, and written media, correspondingly, suffer a diminishment of information content.

See also: Aesthetics of Disappearance; Speed; Technology

DROMOECONOMICS

Phil Graham

Virilio has long identified the need for 'a political economy of speed' (Virilio and Armitage 2001b: 185). Despite denying his role as economist in *Politics of the Very Worst* (1999 [1996]: 107), from at least one perspective, the entirety of Virilio's dromology can be seen as containing all the necessary elements for such a formulation. Tentative steps have been made to integrate the theories of Virilio and Marx into a dromoeconomics (Armitage and Graham 2001: 111–23), yet questions about the shape and constitution of a Virilian political economy remain largely unanswered (Kjøsen 2010). Other analyses of the role of speed in contemporary political economies include Armitage's (2001: 131–48) 'Hypermodern(organ) ization', Graham's neo-Marxist *Hypercapitalism* (2006) and Kjøsen's (2010) more formalist approach to exchange theory in the formulation of a political economy of digital music markets. Popular references to a political economy of speed are beginning to emerge daily in the concept of a 'two-speed economy' following the 2008 global financial collapse (Martin 2011), indicating that the concept of a dromoeconomic formulation is entering general consciousness.

If political economy is (a) the science that investigates links between the production of values and the production of power and (b) the science that links the workings of the city (*polis*) with the functioning of the 'household' (*oikos*), and we divide this science into its necessary analytical and conceptual components, then Virilio has already provided a framework within which we might proceed to develop a sophisticated and useful dromoeconomics.

Using speed as heuristic, Virilio has developed dromologies of labour and the family, land, value and accumulation in *Negative Horizon* (2005a [1984]); the nation-state, circulation, power, politics, wealth, technology, distribution and exchange in *Speed and Politics: An Essay on Dromology* (2006 [1977]), all of which amounts to nothing less than political economy when seen *tout ensemble*. At the most abstract level, Virilio supplies a cultural theory of time and space, which is essential to a political economy that cannot (because entirely concerned with vector and velocity) be criticised for being what Marx would call a *dingliche* (thing-like) approach.

Virilio thus provides what can be read as a historical materialist analysis of how speed became the generative core of current technomilitaristic civilisations. It begins with woman specialising as familial beast of burden, freeing up a small surplus of time for man to become a more systematic and specialised hunter. It is a theory of family (patriarchy), sex and gender as dromoeconomic determinants of the urban and post-urban civilisations that followed. With such a view in place, it is possible to see a historical development of the division of labour framed in terms of the overproduction of speed. More so, and more centrally to political economy, Virilio presents a basic and hitherto untheorised division of labour based on speed as an advantage deriving from cultural organisation (the first technology) that is plausible as the historical basis for our collective and ongoing obsession with the conquest of time and space.

Given the rise of 'new economy' discourses, and of their fruitlessness in terms of delivering new understandings of the kinds of things we are experiencing on a planetary basis, the need for a dromoeconomics based on what already exists in Virilio's work can be both fruitful and predictive at the most practical levels and its elements are there waiting to be assembled.

DROMOMANIA, DROMOMANIACS

Mark Featherstone

Virilio introduces the notions of dromomania and the idea of dromomaniacs in his *Speed and Politics: An Essay on Dromology* (2006 [1977]). There he explains modernity as a historical period defined by constant change, recalling Karl Marx and Friedrich Engels's famous definition of the modern condition, 'all that is solid melts into air', from their *The Communist Manifesto* (2004 [1848]). On this view, modernity is characterised by constant technological development and endless social and political upheaval. However, what are central to this idea of interminable social and political change in both Marx's and Virilio's accounts of modernity are the principles of contest, competition and, ultimately, struggle. But, whereas in Marx's account of the development of capitalism the idea of constant upheaval as conflict is rendered as economic competition, in Virilio's version of modernity as a period of turbulence conflict is rethought as a *dromocratic* contest characterised by the obsession to win the race into the future. Thus Virilio understands modernity, which is defined by notions of change but also, importantly, progress and development, as a form of society organised around the rule of the race. If this is the literal meaning of dromocracy, from *dromos*, 'race' and *kratos*, 'rule', then dromomania is the condition of being addicted to the race, and the dromomaniac is the person who is possessed or obsessed by the idea of the race.

It is important that Virilio's idea of modernity emphasises not simply change but, crucially, change motivated and possessed by direction. This last is significant because it enables Virilio to think about social and political turmoil and conflict as progressive competition. His modernity is then not simply about struggle but struggle *towards* an *end*, even though this end may not be defined, but, rather, resides somewhere beyond the horizon of the future. However, it is this motivated and directional element which allows him to consider society as a race and link the psychological condition of mania, which appears in Sigmund Freud's works and specifically his (2005) essay *On Murder, Mourning and Melancholia*, to a form of society geared around the pursuit of the future. In *Speed and Politics*, Virilio specifically links the condition of dromomania, which we may now contemplate as a kind of manic pursuit of the future, to the French Revolutionaries, and especially to the Jacobins, who were obsessed with the realisation of the pure society of reason. The competitive element of this struggle to realise a new properly modern society was founded in the need to destroy the remainders of the old regime and the leftovers of the past, which persisted in the form of counter-revolutionaries and subversives. Here, the other was conceived as an opponent, or competitor, who would stop the dromomaniac's progress into the utopian future.

In this way, it is possible to see how Virilio's French Revolutionary dromomaniacs who turned to terror in order to win the race to the new society were possessed by a competitive militaristic psychology which transformed them into 'projectiles' (Armitage 2001, 'Projectiles': 131–48) or perhaps 'subjectiles', fired into the future. However, Virilio's notions of dromomania and the dromomaniac have wider application beyond the example of French Revolutionary and could equally be related to the Nazi and Soviet totalitarians, who Hannah Arendt (1973) tells us in *The Origins of Totalitarianism* were obsessed by movement and dynamism, and also to the contemporary neo-liberal hegemony and even the mobile phone, which Virilio talks about in *The University of Disaster* (2010a [2007]) in terms of the 'globalitarian' system. In the case of the neo-liberal, globalitarian system, dromomania is definitive of the principle of obligatory mobility, whereby the dromomaniac who is possessed by the need to win the race into the future can see no alternative but movement and the endless pursuit of the future.

DROMOSCOPY

John David Ebert

A term which Virilio opposes to stroboscopy, in which cyclical objects are made to look as though their motion was slowed down or completely arrested, whereas dromoscopy is concerned with the effects of speed on human perception, especially insofar as objects upon the horizon, when perceived from an accelerating vehicle, appear to be in violent motion (i.e. houses appear suddenly, trees pass abruptly, etc.). In *Negative Horizon* (2005a [1984]), Virilio compares the windscreen to a kind of cinematic screen upon which the phenomenologically distorted objects of the landscape appear, only it is the driver and his passenger who are projected through a countryside that appears to exhibit optical distortions as a by-product of the process of acceleration of the vehicle.

What appears through the windscreen, Virilio points out, is actually a simulated landscape, for the distortions do not belong as properties to the objects themselves, but only to one's perceptions of them. Speed changes perception: it flattens the approaching horizon, for one thing, by eliminating lateral vision. The different gears and their corresponding speeds, furthermore, dromoscopically alter the environment of what one sees through the windscreen, each gear shifting one, in linear sequence, into a different plane of temporality. The driver of the speeding vehicle, meanwhile, is always on the lookout for objects that can become potential hazards for his vehicle (images, but also birds, insects, etc.), and in the case of collisions, the simulation is brought to a halt. It is only the seatbelt that prevents the passenger from being hurled into the theatre, as it were, thus changing modes from that of spectator to actor.

The driver corresponds to a sort of artist, with the passenger in the traditional role of the spectator. The two are surrounded by four windows – a quadriptych, as Virilio puts it – through which the phenomenological display unfolds around them. One of the illusory effects that such accelerations convey is that of the shrinking of the world, for speed actually makes it appear as though it were smaller.

The phenomenon is analogous to the dromoscopic illusion of the heavenly bodies, which *appear* to rise and set, but this is due only to the speed of the Earth's rotation on its axis and its orbit around the sun. Virilio analogises the Earth to a speeding vehicle, and the panoramic display of astronomical bodies through its atmosphere to the display of distorted objects upon the windscreen.

The art of the dashboard, he says, is therefore a sort of seventh art.

Thus, truth, the real, is the first victim of speed, since dromoscopy conceals reality behind a simulacrum of phenomenologically distorted objects. The faster we go, the more distortions reality seems to take on, and as a result, truth disappears behind the screen of special effects that is exhibited by the display of ever-accelerating vehicles in motion.

DROMOSPHERE

Drew S. Burk

Coming from the Greek word *dromos* meaning 'race', the dromosphere is the term coined by Virilio for the sphere of the acceleration of reality by technologies of instantaneous transmission and transportation of bodies, images, communication and perception. His self-proclaimed title of dromologist is meant to reflect the person who studies this sphere of reality based no longer on space or place or concrete conceptions of time, but the acceleration of exchanges and movements that strive to obliterate these elements. While we still live and are used to concepts of night and day, of here and there, our daily movement and interactions are continually being restructured within a sphere predicated on achieving instantaneous transmission and transportation whether it is through real-time instant messaging technologies or high-speed trains and aeroplanes. For Virilio, this realm of the acceleration of reality, this dromosphere, has built into it as one of its essential elements, the integral accident. With every so-called innovation of 'progress', there is also the innovation of a novel accident. With the invention of the high speed train, there is the invention of the speed train accident; with the invention of the aeroplane, the potential for appalling air accidents. Virilio's project of dromology to study this sphere based on acceleration focuses its attention on how the dromosphere has come to supersede all previous conceptions of time. Because of this, he envisions the necessity to view all social interactions today, whether they are political or economical, as suffering from this dromospheric accelera- tion of reality. The example of the recent economic crashes where stock- traders gave the decision of trading over to the calculations of machines programmed to trade at the speed of light is one such interaction. Indeed, the crash led to an unheard of accident of acceleration. For Virilio, this is precisely the sort of disaster that we must have the courage today to analyse in order to slow down and to take a step back. Otherwise, the elusive and tempting desire to continue within a sphere where due to the instantaneous nature of transmission the accident happens before we know it has happened will be our fate.

E

ENDO-COLONISATION

Mark Featherstone

Virilio outlines the idea of endo-colonisation in *Pure War* (Virilio and Lotringer 2008) to explain the shift from traditional forms of external or 'exo-colonisation', whereby the state invades other territories, to a new form of intensive or endo-colonisation, where the state progressively attacks its own territory. In Virilio's thought, this shift takes place against the backdrop of processes of globalisation, which have seen modernity run up against the limit of terrestrial space, so that there is nowhere else for the modern state to go, but to turn back upon itself and start to march into its own territory. Apart from this statist interpretation of endo-colonisation, Virilio also offers a more general notion of the process of intensive colo- nisation related to the ways in which science and technology have run up against their external limit in processes of globalisation and have now started to occupy the human body itself. As Virilio argues in a conversation

with John Armitage, the endo-colonisation of the human body by technology is an invasion and an attempted control of the body by technology
(Virilio and Armitage 2001a: 42). However, the primary meaning of the
idea of endo-colonisation remains the state's assault on its own territory
and its own population. To explain this process, Virilio starts by describing the idea of deterrence and the way this relates to the notion of total
peace. In his view, deterrence enables total peace through the creation of a
permanent threat of war. The danger of war is always there and the population lives in a state of fear of the enemy. For Virilio, this is the military
society, which entails the control of the population through the creation
of fear and state intervention into their everyday lives. Virilio (*PW*, 106)
points to 1970s' Cambodia and Pol Pot's Khmer Rouge regime, which
waged war on its own population. In his view, Khmer Rouge Cambodia
represented the suicide state par excellence and was a perfect example of
what endo-colonisation means: the translation of external colonisation into
a new internal form of colonisation, which involves the insinuation of state
power into the everyday lives of the population.

    Apart from Cambodia, however, the notion of endo-colonisation clearly
has other applications. For example, Virilio calls attention to Latin
America, including countries such as Brazil, where state and society are
militarised as laboratories of endo-colonisation. Here, Virilio's endo-
colonisation resonates with Mike Davis's (2006) concept of the militarised
society from his book on Los Angeles, *City of Quartz*, where military
police power is deemed necessary to hold society together and to prevent
complete chaos from breaking out. Indeed, in much the same way that
Davis draws links between violence and economy in his work, Virilio also
shows that deregulation leads to the creation of an armed state, which
has to control the unruly masses. Thus, the term 'deregulation' not only
refers to economic deregulation in the neo-liberal economic sense of the
term but also in its broadest social meaning, which is in many respects a
consequence of the endo-colonisation of society by the market. In other
words, Virilio suggests that society has become progressively deregulated
as a result of the advance of modernity, capitalism and globalisation and
that this has coincided with the inward turn of the state as colonial power.
The irony of the process of deregulation is, therefore, that far from leading
to a minimal state and more individual freedom, it actually produces a
maximum state, which intervenes in every area of the individual's life to
produce what Virilio (*PW*, 110) calls a 'state of inevitability'. Put another
way, there is no sense of possibility in the endo-colonised society, since
everything is now under the sway of inhuman market forces and disciplinary state control.

    However, this form of state control is of a very particular kind. Virilio is

not a new right critic of the welfare state. On the contrary, he is support-
ive of the welfare state as representing a politics of lasting duration. For
Virilio, the welfare state is about creating a sustainable society. By contrast, his view of the deregulated society is that it is a society of the instant
and that it has no conception of time as extension, but, rather, regards time
as entirely intensive. There is then no idea of duration in the deregulated
society, but only ever a concern for the intensity of the instant, which
can be made ever more 'productive', 'pleasurable', violent, etc. Thus, it
turns out that it is not only the state that is endo-colonial, but also the
market, which seeks to mine the instant for ever more value. Against
the twin forces of endo-colonisation, which are the disciplinary state and
the market, Virilio tells us that the citizen has no chance of escape. There
is no social management of society. Citizens are not in control. Instead,
they must face up to the hyper-centralisation of social management, of the
market, and of the state and console themselves with the fantasy of self-
management that this situation produces.

The problem with the fantasy of self-management, which Virilio finds
in 'autonomous Marxism' (see, for example, Wright 2002), is that it is
completely in line with the dualistic tendency of the endo-colonial process
– the fragmentation of the social under pressure of deregulation and the
concentration of power in the abstract forms of market and state. What
this means is that it is clear that the turn to autonomy is by no means
revolutionary when we consider that this is exactly how endo-colonisation
works. It breaks the social apart and works on the individual, insinuating
itself into their life, transforming them into a person who acts, albeit in
line with market and state dictates. In this respect, Virilio's concept of
endo-colonisation cannot help but remind the reader of Michel Foucault's
(2010) theory of bio-power, which describes the way the state dominates
the individual, and Louis Althusser's (2005) theory of 'interpellation',
which similarly shows how the individual is constructed in ideology.
For Virilio, it is important that this endo-colonial process is understood,
because it represents a form of systematic state terror and the rise of a
kind of thanatalogical war machine committed to the destruction of true
independence.

See also: Globalisation; State; Territory; War

ESCAPE VELOCITY

Richard G. Smith

With the slow speeds of the transport age, relative speed is so low compared to the speed of light that the small difference between Albert Einstein's theory of relativity and Isaac Newton's classical theory is negligible. However, while at slow speeds the theories of Einstein and Newton are congruent, over very high speeds and large distances the two theories diverge as relativity links the effects of acceleration with those of gravity. But, despite the fact that it is only space travel (leaving the Earth and the solar system) that necessitates any meaningful abandonment of Newtonian understandings of space and time, Virilio is nevertheless insistent in *Open Sky* (1997 [1995]) that the topological shift in the nature of time that was heralded by Einstein's special and general theories of relativity is not solely a concern for physicists and astrophysicists.

Virilio's extraordinary claim is that Einstein's theory of the entire universe is relevant for understanding the world's interactive mass communications age. That information and communication technologies are a 'superconductive medium' that affords a speed of interaction that is not relative – that is, it has no frame of reference and so cannot be measured in relation to other objects – and consequently inaugurates 'the emergence of a *global* time that may well dispense with the concrete importance of the *local* time of geography that once made history' (*OS*, 122). In other words, *local* time (constant time) 'made history' through recourse to a geographical referent (fixed space); *global* or *world* time, in contrast, heralds the 'end of geography' because it is an 'instantaneous trajectory bearing no reference to the ground or to the surface' (*OS*, 134).

And it is through that dictum – 'the sudden *globalized expansion of the present*' (*OS*, 134), which today 'governs man's activities on a worldwide scale' (*OS*, 135) – that Virilio invents, and subsequently laments, the contemporary world as one that has lost its moorings, become bereft of the contingencies of place, and any system of reference to tell us what has happened to the geography of things, because it has achieved 'escape' or 'orbital' velocity or the minimum speed necessary to move away from the Earth's gravity field. The argument that the development of information and communication technologies has the consequence of erasing boundaries and shrinking distance is well known, oft-repeated and widely contested. Yet, it should be noted that Virilio goes even further than merely pronouncing the 'end of geography'. The replacement of the 'space-world' with the 'time-world' of the real instant also has the consequence, contends Virilio, that the very dimensions of material space – the point, the line, the surface or volume – also disappear in the 'superficial time' of telepresence. An outcome which is, we are told, nothing less than a catastrophe for the inhabitants of Mother Earth: 'The accident to end all accidents spreads in a flash and the centre of time – the endless present – leaves behind the centre of fixed space for good. There is no longer any "here", everything is "now"' (*OS*, 142).

EVENTS

John David Ebert

For Virilio, contemporary history is now composed of what he terms 'events', by which he does not mean large historical generalities, but rather small and local events of the micro type. This is what he terms the ascendancy of event-based history over global history. Macro events, for him, ended with the fall of the Soviet Union and Marxism, and what has taken their place is a collection of disconnected historical events such as terrorist attacks, accidents, the fall of the Berlin Wall, the attacks of September 11, and so on. History, for Virilio, has therefore lost its generality and instead has been replaced by what he terms 'fractal history', that is to say, a history composed of details rather than large-scale ideas. There are now no longer any overarching trends, according to him, but rather collections of disparate happenings.

For Virilio, two things have transpired to change the nature of events from their traditional historical basis in which they were anchored in the large-scale events of nation-state struggles, wars, revolutions, and so on. The first is that accidents, disasters and catastrophes have now largely taken over the role once occupied by the traditional historical event. Today's events, or at least the big ones which make the headlines, are mostly speed accidents resulting from the ever-accelerating nature of the world of our contemporary reality. Certain events, like September 11, are not so much historical events in essence as they are simulated accidents which, because of their simulation, have the effect of derealising the event and reducing it to the aleatory nature of an accident that is void of historical significance.

The second aspect that has changed the nature of historical events is that such events have now run up against the wall of real-time media technologies which tend to have the effect of derealising and desubstantialising them so that they no longer take place in any traditional sense of real events happening in real space. Instead, they have now shifted into the instantaneity of real time, in which the horizon of the event is delimited by the frame of the screen upon which the event takes place. Traditional events that took place in real space and present time tended to be configured by actual horizons, whereas the horizons of today's events disappear inside video monitor screens. Real time now means the collapse of time and the rendering simultaneous of all events.

In *The Administration of Fear* (Virilio and Richard 2012), Virilio points out that one of the results of the simultaneity of such events is that real-time media tend to spread fear as a ubiquitous environment precisely through the dissemination of its messages. Such media play a prominent role in establishing fear as a global environment because they allow for the synchronisation of emotion on a global scale. Because of electromagnetic speed the same feeling of terror can be felt all over the world at the same time. It is therefore not a local, but a global information bomb that explodes each second with every news report of new disasters. With live events, we thus arrive at the acceleration not of history, but of reality. Real-time technologies are not only opposed to the past, to delayed time, they are also opposed to the present, in the sense of the here and now of the concrete encounter.

Events, for Virilio, needless to say, do not mean historical episodes located in real space, but rather incidents that are flattened out by acceleration through audiovisual media, which tend to delocalise them and remove them from real space, thus placing them into the instantaneity of real time, where they move so fast that the mind cannot keep up with them and so fails to determine their significance adequately. In *Desert Screen: War at the Speed of Light* (2002a [1991]), for instance, Virilio points out that it was real-time technologies which gave us the Gulf War (1990–1), the first total electronic war, a war in two dimensions, plus a third dimension, that of real time, into which the historical events disappeared, since the war had become synonymous with its televisual projection. This was a war in which local space disappeared into a global and instantaneous military-managed operation.

The effect of these real-time media upon accidents, moreover, is that, due to their acceleration of reality, accidents take over the role of traditional historical events by virtue of their position, by their acceleration into real time alone. But the acceleration of time is also the acceleration of the event. The event now comes *from* the accident. Nowadays, according to Virilio, we no longer have to wait for historical events for, unlike the wars of the past, events now arrive without our even having to wait for them. The acceleration of reality by means of real-time media, in accelerating all events, thus becomes the question of 'history'.

See also: Accident; Media; Real Time; Space-Time; Speed

EYE LUST

George Katsonis

A term coined by Virilio to describe and encompass the various manipulations of visual reflexes and sensations brought on by perception-targeting technologies, and their disciplinary effects on mental imagery, emotional states and moral standards. The term was elaborated in a homonymous essay in *Open Sky* (1997 [1995]) where Virilio restages his earlier notions of 'kinematic energy' and 'synthetic vision' in relation to new developments and tendencies in the military–industrial complex, involving new realities in war, media, surgery and neuroscience. Virilio problematises the common optical element in these developments in a cultural and pathological context; whereas in *The Vision Machine* (1994b [1988]) his main focus was the nature and logic (logistics) of the virtual image, in *Open Sky* Virilio is largely interested in the perversity of vision machines, which is consummated in a delirious 'optoelectronic fetishism'.

Eye lust, which comes with a new set of optical anxieties, cravings, morals and politics, features prominently in a variety of milieus: from the logistics and conduct of war to its real-time mediatisation; from the surveillance and monitoring of the public to the domestic pleasure for surveillance and monitoring on television and the Internet; from multipurpose sensors and scanners to high-definition screens and the spherical three-dimensional cinema; from micro cameras to vision-correcting surgery and prosthetics; and, finally, in the developing quest in neuroscience for mental imagery processing and artificial intelligence, where Virilio foresees the veritable end of the automation of perception, and a catatonic future for mankind.

In 'Eye Lust' (*OS*, 89–102), as the problem of vision machines is approached culturally and pathologically, it naturally raises ethical questions proper not only to technoscientific research and development but also, and rather urgently, to the public that tele-participates in standardised vision. For Virilio, while vigilance is a much needed virtue, the ethical space for resistance to eye lust relates adamantly to less audiovisual consumerism and pollution, to an ecological movement that would be able to utter a 'right to blindness' and discuss thereafter limits to optoelectronic intensity (as in either bulk or immediacy).

At this stage, Virilio's thought arguably converges with Michel Foucault's (1991; 2010) disciplinary and biopolitical practices and Gilles Deleuze's (1995 [1990]) societies of control, since the question of power (war) resonates with that of subjectivity (perception). And, furthermore, there is a certain affinity with the interest, at the very least, of Deleuze and

Guattari (2004 [1980]) in desiring-machines and an ethics and aesthetics of intensity. But, whereas Deleuze and Guattari outline an ontology of the virtual and a baroque nomadic vision of humanity, one that is essentially linked to the passional cruelty of intensive time (becomings) and the 'foldings' of light, whether direct or indirect, for Virilio, after the experience of Italian Futurism, one must possess a fundamental vigilance towards the acceleration of culture and the optical nihilism it celebrates.

F

FAST FEMINISM

Shannon Bell

Fast Feminism (Bell 2010) is a work of speed philosophy, pornography and politics. It is situated simultaneously as a complement to speed theory and as the accident of speed theory.

Fast Feminism applies seven tendencies of Virilio's work: (1) critique the world quickly; (2) deploy speed to interrupt intellectual scholarship; (3) position the body as the basis of intellectual work; (4) write theory as art; (5) do theory from non-obvious points of departure; (6) speed and slowness work together as stability and motion, stasis, velocity, interruption and linkage; (7) use Virilio's (Virilio and Lotringer 2008: 52) 'staircase' method from *Pure War* for doing philosophy: once an idea is introduced and deployed, jump to linkages with another idea and always, always, do violence to the original context.

For Virilio, the accident, although an unintended and disturbing consequence, is inherent in, and created by, the very technology or knowledge system it undermines. *Fast Feminism* is the bastard offspring of Virilio's *The Original Accident* (2007a [2005]: 4), of the 'happy accident, the stroke of luck' and of speed theory. As Virilio is careful to point out in *The Accident of Art* (Virilio and Lotringer 2005: 63): 'the accident is positive [. . .] because it reveals something important that we would not otherwise be able to perceive', in this case, the importance of Virilio's method for contemporary feminism or feminism now.

How is *Fast Feminism* both the likely and unlikely accident of speed theory? An accident of any system, whether that system is ecological, technological or philosophical, is Virilio's *Unknown Quantity* (2003b [2002]) inherent in the original substance. Fast Feminism is intrinsic in Virilio's

speed theory in three instances: first, the ferocious speed style that profoundly critiques the world quickly and breaks intellectual scholarship;
second, the recurrent messianic instant that Virilio never fully hides: 'if
you save one man, you save the world [. . .] The world and man are identical' (Virilio and Wilson 1997: 46); and, third, in Virilio's positioning of the
body as the basis of his work: 'I am a materialist of the body, which means
that the body is the basis of all my work' (Virilio and Wilson 1997: 47):
'when I talk about speed, I am talking about bodies' (Virilio and Lotringer
2002: 56). Of course, the body has always been central in feminist philosophy and practice; the coupling with speed, however, is fast feminism.

Virilio's points of departure for speed theory are military history, architecture and aesthetics; *Fast Feminism*'s points of departure are the female
phallus, performative action and perverse aesthetics; they could, however,
easily be otherwise.

Fast feminism uses Virilio's method of analysis contrary to aspects of
the system of knowledge of its originator, making it the perfect intellectual
mishap. What fast feminism counters most obviously is Virilio's conception of the accident of art. At the core of the accident of art, for Virilio
(2011: 235), is the morphing and blending of genres into 'MAGMA', into
image, sound and text coupled with a blurring of the distinction between
reality (life) and the presentation of live art: body art, performance, installation work.

Fast Feminism is 'performance writing', wherein writing is doing; it is
embedded in praxis. Writing is, as Virilio (1999 [1996]: 51) contends, our
only hope: 'Salvation will come from writing and language. If we re-create
speech, we will be able to resist.' *Fast Feminism* presents a new technology of writing, writing as morphing, which remixes and blends materials
from different contexts. It does violence to the original contexts so that the
distinction among the three points of departure, philosophy, pornography
and politics, collapse.

Fast Feminism holds that many feminisms (second wave, liberal, socialist, radical) are forms of nostalgic theory, theory burdened by teleology
and ontology which can't theoretically capture the attention of the bored I
[eye]: 'the eye which flits from situation to situation, from scene to scene,
from image to image [. . .] with a restlessness and high-pitched consump-
tive appetite that can never really ever be satisfied' (Kroker 2002: 7).

Virilio's *Art as Far as the Eye Can See* (2007b [2005]: 90) deploys a
particular aesthetic affect to impact 'the globalization of affects' resultant
of the bored eye, to jar what he (*AFE*, 90) calls 'the communism of public
emotion'. This aesthetic affect is his method of working in 'staircases', as
he relates in *Pure War* (Virilio and Lotringer 2008):

I work in staircases [. . .] I begin a sentence, I work out an idea and when I consider it suggestive enough, I jump a step to another idea without bothering with the development [. . .] I try to reach the tendency. Tendency is the change of level. (*PW*, 44)

Virilio (*PW*, 52–3) deploys suggestion, breaks, stoppage and rapidity. He states: 'I don't believe in explanations, I believe in suggestion, in the obvious quality of the implicit' (*PW*, 52). Virilio notes 'the importance of interruption [. . .] The fact of stopping and saying "let's go somewhere else" is very important' (*PW*, 53).

Fast feminism is a feminism of affect, of intensity and influence. As a feminism of affect, there is no way of predicting what women influenced by *Fast Feminism* will do.

Virilio's *The Art of the Motor* (1995 [1993]: 147) cites Antonin Artaud: 'What defines the obscene life we are living is that all our perceptions [. . .] have been distilled for us.' According to *Fast Feminism*, one of the ways of stopping the obscenity of 'distilled perceptions' is to write philosophy obscenely and live obscenity philosophically (Bell 2010: 174).

While fast feminism is the accident of speed and of past feminisms, like any invention it can inadvertently give rise to its own accident, its own 'unknown quantity' on which it both thrives and disintegrates: 'If inventing the substance means indirectly inventing the accident, the more powerful and high performance the invention, the more dramatic the accident' (*OA*, 31). The potential accident in fast philosophy or speed theory may be that the intensity of life and the intensity of thought cease to be dynamic. The accident, then, of *Fast Feminism* might be an identitarian logic that congeals the process of doing live theory into '*this is* fast feminism'.

See also: Accident; Body; Feminism; Speed

FEAR

Ronald E. Purser

As an impressionable youth, Virilio witnessed the blitzkriegs and aftermath of the Second World War. It is not surprising, then, that fear is figural in almost all of his writings. Indeed, several titles have the word fear in it (*The Administration of Fear* [Virilio and Richard 2012], *Art and Fear* [2003a; 2000]), while others transmit the effects of fear (*City of Panic* [2005b; 2004], *The Original Accident* [2007a; 2005], *The University of Disaster* (2010a [2007]). Throughout Virilio's numerous books, it is this insidious normalisation of fear in the dromosphere that is his great concern. The rise of instantaneous new information and communications technologies from the Internet to the mobile phone has globalised fear; it can no longer be quarantined or contained to local times and spaces. This amounts to a contagion, a normalised-abnormal fear that is primitive, unconscious and regressive.

The Administration of Fear exposes how the accident of the instantaneous has accelerated the propagation of fear, making it equivalent to a sort of white noise that is accepted as a natural part of our environment:

It occupies and preoccupies us. Fear was once a phenomenon related to local-ised, identifiable events that were limited to a certain timeframe: wars, famines, epidemics. Today, the world itself is limited, saturated, reduced, restricting us to stressful claustrophobia: contagious stock crises, faceless terrorism, lightning pandemics, 'professional' suicides [. . .] Fear is a world, *panic* as a 'whole'. (*TAF*, 14–15)

Instantaneous interaction, what Virilio refers to as 'Weapons of Mass Communications', facilitates the 'synchronization of emotions', leading to a 'communism of affects' and collective panic. Talk radio with its syndi-cated shock jocks, a now popular genre, is aimed at mass activation of the amygdala – the ancient brain structure that is responsible for emotional states of fear and anxiety. This acceleration of fear feeds the neurological vulnerability of the amygdala response system, which relies primarily on millisecond signals – quick and dirty information from the thalamus – a system operating below the threshold of consciousness.

In *City of Panic*, fear is also a constant theme. Virilio traces the apoca-lyptic scenarios generated by globalisation of the instantaneous – global warming, the ecological crisis, the genetic biotechnology time bomb, high particle physics experiments and self-assembling nano-machines polluting the environment – not to mention war, hyper-terrorism and even the prospect of destruction of the earth by asteroids. He portends that warfare has become a war on civilians, which, aided by instantaneous telecommunications, as well as drones, will be a globalised civil war not just between the 99 per cent and the 1 per cent but eventually between the natural humans and the genetically enhanced. Global accidents, such as the insolvency of nations and the world financial crisis, are wars without borders whose casualties are the millions made homeless, uprooted by foreclosures, unemployment and loss of welfare state safety nets. Fear is therefore the bastion of what Virilio (*TAF*, 27) terms 'arrhythmic' socie-ties, which 'only know one rhythm: constant acceleration. Until the crash and systemic failure'.

FEMINISM

Ingrid Hoofd

Questions of feminism and the feminine receive little attention in Virilio's work. Nor have his writings been debated or adopted much in feminist theory. Nonetheless, conceptions of feminism, the feminine and the female do play a significant role in Virilio's theses on the development and consequences of modern technology. Moreover, his (Virilio and Lotringer 2008: 124) contemporary work does show a subtle parallel to French feminist thought such as that of Luce Irigaray, which probes questions of radical sexual difference. The presence of feminist arguments in Virilio's writings are due to the fact that his major critique is that of the militarisation of society and, by implication, of contemporary masculinity's global hegemony. Yet it must be said that Virilio's work in the sphere of feminism equates a kind of superior primordial femininity with the mysterious power of 'Mother Earth'. His 'feminist' position is, then, vulnerable to critique as a nostalgic romanticisation of women as the flip-side of their oppression (Conley 2000; Hoofd 2004; Beckman 2010). Furthermore, while Virilio's phenomenological position concerning the much-needed critique of militarisation and masculine rationality is to be welcomed, his stance on women's relationship to the Earth and to technology remains suspiciously coded as feminine. But the value of reading Virilio in relation to contemporary issues of feminism is that he draws out fundamental issues concerning technology, emancipation and sexual politics, all of which open up the possibility of feminism radicalising its project once more.

Virilio's *The Aesthetics of Disappearance* (2009a [1980]), for example, contains his strongest arguments concerning women and technology. Here, Virilio points to the ongoing reduction of the traditional function of the female to that of technologies of acceleration. He suggests that technology has appropriated the customary role of woman as primary 'seducer' and likens the Christian narrative of the Fall, namely, the expulsion of humanity from the Garden of Eden, to the technological expulsion of women from the territory and traditions of the Earth itself. For Virilio, the female was originally not so much an object or a subject but a 'vector' that made male 'movement' – as the 'passenger' of the female – possible. This meant that the 'Fall' engendered by subsequent technologies and techniques of speed did not constitute a form of technological transcendence but a form of technological enslavement and misery for women and men alike. Such technological dependence is further illustrated by Virilio's interpretation of the human body, which, by way of its loss of physicality, its senses, vision and, in the case of women, its 'femininity', disappears into technology under the reign of speed and virtual reality. In short, both female and male human bodies are becoming, in effect, the same body, or, alternatively, a 'unisex' body, which renders their prior male and female radical alterity reciprocally invisible as the technologically induced abolition of sexual differences continues.

Consequently, for Virilio, classical women's liberation narratives of 'emancipation', 'cyber-feminism' and liberal equality feminism not only fail to create a political space for the emergence and preservation of female sexual difference but are also implicated in the (wholly negative because technologically induced) 'liberation of the seduction of technique' (*AD*, 91). For instance, in *Speed and Politics* (2006 [1977]), he argues that the effect of cyber- and liberal equality feminism is to endorse and even, occasionally, to celebrate their transformation into a war machine; in *Negative Horizon* (2005a [1984]), likewise, he contends that, along with men, women are increasingly 'enlisted' in ever more complex technological mechanisms of dissimulation and disappearance; and, finally, in *Pure War* (Virilio and Lotringer 2008), Virilio argues that the vector-function, which was once the exclusive domain of the female, has been usurped by technology, leaving liberal equality feminism in particular without any possibility of resistance to technological speed. One can therefore understand why, when asked in an interview (Virilio and Armitage 2001a: 44) about Donna Haraway's (1985) cyber-feminist manifesto whether he would rather be a cyborg or a goddess, Virilio answered: 'neither'. For Virilio, therefore, the vicious objectification of living human beings through cybernetic technologies is not a form of liberation but a form of captivity. As he contends in *Open Sky* (1997 [1995]), so-called technological liberation or empowerment simply reduces women (and men) to objecthood. Additionally, given the technologically generated collapse of distance and duration (as well as of subjectivity, selfhood, the future, of man and of woman), not only human ethical relationships but also human sexual relationships subside into automated, online, or cybersexual relationships between mere shadows where technological acceleration transforms sex into misery and fear. For feminists, then, Virilio's critique of technological speed crucially draws fresh attention to the increasingly muddled political relationship between actuality and virtuality, action and inaction, while simultaneously problematising the possibility of feminist resistance.

See also: Fast Feminism; Resistance; Speed; Technology

FORECLOSURE

Mark Featherstone

Virilio explains the concept of foreclosure in his *Crepuscular Dawn* (Virilio and Lotringer 2002), where he explores the experience and processes of globalisation in relation to feelings of claustrophobia and incarceration. For Virilio, foreclosure refers to the problem of spatial enclosure, which occurs when the modern tendency to expansion reaches its limit with globalisation and folds back into itself as the condition of endo-colonisation, a term that Virilio uses to signify the intensive colonisation of the human body, territory and time. The effect of globalisation as the limitation of terrestrial space and the intensive colonisation of the temporal dimension by a form of society committed to expansion and 'progress' is, for Virilio, exemplified by the experience of claustrophobia in relation to space, so that we feel that there is nowhere to go, and time, whereby we feel that there is no time and that every moment counts or must be filled with activity. Under conditions of foreclosure, then, there is no outside, no external space and no free time.

Virilio notes that the idea of foreclosure has psychoanalytic roots in the works of Sigmund Freud and Jacques Lacan (2007). Although the concept never appears in Freud, Lacan translated Freud's term *Verwerfung*, which means rejection and disavowal, as foreclosure. Reading Freud's (2000) *Three Essays on the Theory of Sexuality*, where rejection is used to understand paranoia and psychosis, Lacan uses the term foreclosure to explain the collapse of the subject's symbolic universe. He argues that foreclosure entails the rejection or repudiation of the master signifier of the father who produces order in the psychological life of the subject. When this normal form of order disintegrates, the subject descends into psychosis, which represents a form of psychological chaos, and paranoia, whereby order is restored in a fantastical form characterised by megalomania and the persecution complex.

For Virilio, foreclosure means both a material condition, where global space becomes limited and time starts to fill up, *and* the human experience of these conditions, which is characterised by a sense of claustrophobia or paranoia where the subject is the centre of a total conspiracy that knows no end. Whereas in Lacan's work what is rejected and abolished is the symbolic anchor of the paternal signifier that authorises every other signifier, in Virilio's writings what is foreclosed is the possibility of an outside, of an external referent able to organise or orientate the subject within the interiority of global time-space. Thus, in Virilio's terminology, foreclosure is the 'bracketing out', to use a classical phenomenological concept, of a particular dimension of reality – the external referent, which is necessary not only to organise the interior of global time-space but also to prevent it from feeling completely overwhelmed by the experience and processes of globalisation.

FUTURISM

John Beck

Among the many artistic movements that emerged in response to the technological modernity of the early twentieth century, none shouted as loudly as the Italian Futurists about the thrilling violence of the machine. Filippo Tommaso Marinetti's Futurist Manifesto, first published in *La gazzetta dell'Emilia* on 5 February 1909 and reproduced in the French newspaper *Le Figaro* two weeks later, offers a nervy insomniac vision of steel-riveted sex and death that continues to speak to the ambivalent seductions of technological power. Committed to smashing through all social and artistic conventions with the apocalyptic force of a 'rogue locomotive', Marinetti (2005: 5) calls for the sensual embrace of danger, speed and contingency in a coupling of flesh and machine that kills time and space and replaces all measure with the ecstasy of the instant. Through this 'manifesto of burning and overwhelming violence', Marinetti (2005: 5) promises to deliver a backward-looking culture 'from its fetid cancer of professors, archaeologists, tour guides and antiquarians'. Translated into art, the Futurist sensibility dissolved concrete forms into the flows and fragments of matter in motion, typified in works like Umberto Boccioni's sculpture *Unique Forms of Continuity in Space* (1913) where the dynamic human figure is stretched and streamlined, or in Giacomo Balla's paintings of the blurred passage of objects in action.

   The Futurist Manifesto embraced war as the means through which the creative destruction of the old order could be most effectively achieved and Marinetti was an early supporter of Mussolini's Fascist Party. While Marinetti could not align himself with Mussolini's preference for classical art, the fascist celebration of violent self-becoming through blood and sacrifice reiterated the patriotic machismo of Futurism and, like Ezra Pound and Wyndham Lewis's Vorticism, the movement has come to be seen as an avant-garde articulation of the emerging political far right. This troubling combination of advanced aesthetic theory and reactionary politics situates Futurism as paradigmatic of the profound contradictions of twentieth-century technological modernity: it is utopian and nihilistic, emancipatory and a force of domination, creatively post-humanistic and brutally murderous. Any celebration of technology after Futurism stands in its disturbing shadow; any consideration of technology and politics must address its implications.

Virilio's work on speed and war, aesthetics and politics, technology and space, is inconceivable without Futurism. A self-proclaimed child of the blitzkrieg of the Second World War, Virilio's obsessions are shaped by the forces first enunciated in Marinetti's Manifesto, as is his propensity for provocative declarations and short, sharp bulletins from the front line of the present. Like the Futurists, Virilio believes that technology has collapsed space into time; that technology is inseparable from war; and that human experience has folded into its technological mediations. Virilio himself has admitted that his approach is Futurist, but that he has 'a score to settle with Italian Futurism' regarding its celebration of technology (Virilio and Zurbrugg 2001: 158). What distinguishes him from the Italian Futurists, he explains, is that 'their work is positive, mine is negative' (Virilio and Zurbrugg 2001: 158): 'Those who are optimistic about technology are very closely allied to Fascism. He who is critical of technology is not Fascist' (Virilio and Zurbrugg 2001: 158). While the Futurists were broadly right about the twentieth century, then, as far as Virilio is concerned their failure to develop a critical position led them into an appalling alliance with totalitarian barbarism.

What is perhaps most striking about Virilio as an analyst of technology and power is that his assessment is uniformly and consistently negative. His Christian phenomenology acts as a barrier that shields him from the seductions of technology and enables him to assess the encroachments of a dominating regime of spectacular violence while maintaining a commitment to relatively old-fashioned notions about the integrity of the human body and its somatic, aesthetic and spiritual experiences. Virilio may be a diagnostic Futurist but he is an adversary of the kind of aesthetico-political Futurism that has become the normative ideology of techno–militarised capitalism. In opposition to the affirmative vanguardism of Marinetti and his proto-fascists, Virilio argues that real art does not merely deploy and reproduce new technologies but resists and deforms them; technology is embraced by art only in order to struggle against its violent logic. This is a version of the avant-garde's collapse of the distinction of art and life that does not lead to a capitulation to the dominant culture but nonetheless accepts the necessity of engaging with domination from inside. Marinetti's Futurism, Virilio (Virilio, Geisler and Doze 2009: 94) claims, 'was still the futurism of History'; it was still inside measurable space-time. Now, however, we live, according to Virilio, in the futurism Marinetti longed for, the 'futurism of the instant' that will, tomorrow, 'render the Earth uninhabitable' (Virilio, Geisler and Doze 2009: 94). In other words, the collapse of history into real time has left us on the threshold of extinction as we disappear into the ever-accelerating instant. Virilio's Christian faith, however, refuses to see this as an end to hope; instead, like astrophysicists who use acceleration to lead them beyond the universe to multiverses, he identifies 'an aesthetic of successive extinction and appearance' (Virilio, Geisler and Doze 2009: 94). With Virilio, though, the negatives are usually easier to grasp than the positives. In *The Futurism of the Instant* (2010b), for example, any sort of fixed location – home, city, nation – has been destroyed and entire populations are placed in perpetual motion, the deracinated refugees of contemporary capitalist logistics held together only by the 'globalization of shared sensations' made possible by information technology (*FI*, 62). But if time and space have finally, as Marinetti hoped, been annihilated, the successive appearance of some new dispensation that Virilio claims will come after extinction is not readily discernible. Virilio's Futurism is indeed a critical response to Marinetti's terrifying affirmation of technological violence, but the strength of Virilio's work lies more in dogged negation rather than in plausible alternatives, which remain nebulous and indistinct.

See also: Art; Speed; Technology; War

GLOBALISATION

Mark Featherstone

Virilio's idea of globalisation differs from standard definitions and interpretations of the term in several important respects, including his emphasis on how acceleration is central to the endo-colonisation of space-time and his 'dystopian' theory of the exhaustion of the spatial and temporal dimensions of the world.

Described and articulated by writers such as David Held (1999) the notion of globalisation refers to ongoing processes of national and individual interconnectedness, interdependence and the creation of a sense of a global place. On this view, globalisation has transformed the social, political, economic and cultural spheres of nation-states and led to a global system based on individualism and international free trade, Postmodernisation, consumerism and technologically mass mediated communications and forms of spatio-temporal consciousness.

Post-Second World War American society has been central to the development of globalisation because of the United States's (US) export of an increasingly neo-liberal belief in international free trade, in its own advanced technological development, huge economic growth, ideologically powerful film and television industries, and, of course, the fall of its main rival – Eastern European and Soviet Communism – during the 1990s. Indeed, the American thinker Frances Fukuyama (1993) proclaimed the end of history and enthusiastically greeted the emergence of a unipolar world where US social, political, economic and cultural ideas dominate the global landscape. Moreover, since the end of the Cold War (1947–91), America has sought to police the neo-liberal internationalised system of free trade through a complex arrangement of hard technological and soft developmental power, but this has proved problematic, and economic globalisation in particular has become less associated with growth than with ideological chaos, mediated instability and post-industrial and post-Soviet politics. Neo-Marxists Michael Hardt and Antonio Negri (2000) suggest that the new global system, or 'Empire', as they call it, is essentially unmanageable, and certainly beyond the control of any one nation-state such as the US. In their view, this is because contemporary globalisation is unipolar but bi-directional, entailing both a tendency towards the domination of the local by the global, and the fractalisation of the local under conditions of generalised fragmentation that is beyond all territorial control.

Virilio's account of globalisation, by contrast, emphasises humanity's growing commitment to acceleration through the use of high-speed mass media and related information and communications technologies that enable the knitting together of the world. For Virilio, globalisation cannot be separated from the appearance of science, technology and a particular worldview obsessed with exploration, discovery, invention and newness. Globalisation is thus reliant on a specific attitude that embraces and facilitates human acceleration through the invention of accelerated media, information and technology. This last is important because it allows Virilio to locate precisely when and where globalisation began. Hence, while it is possible to trace the origins of globalisation in the European imperialism of the nineteenth century, the Americanisation of the mid-twentieth century, and the West's neo-liberal project of the 1980s and beyond, Virilio argues that globalisation stems from a specifically modern technoscientific mania with speeding up, which has today been realised as the Postmodern condition of worldwide 'time-space compression' (Harvey 1989). In explaining the starting point of modernity, and, consequently, Postmodern globalisation, Virilio's *Speed and Politics* (2006 [1977]), delineates the history of ballistics, arguing that it was in the heat of increasingly high-tech warfare that the principles of acceleration and humanity's desire to break through all speed barriers transpired. Virilio's contention is thus that the construction of modernity involved the smashing of norms (through innovation, improvements, progress and so on), the invention of the 'new' and a worldview predicated on human acceleration.

Certainly, Virilio proposes that modernity's first truly globalising force was that of the Jacobins of the French Revolution (1789–99) who overturned the static medieval order in favour of a new modern stance premised on the interconnected ideas of human acceleration, change, progress, technological development and modernisation. He claims that the restless and revolutionary spirit triggered by the Jacobins has driven the growth of ever newer media, information and communications technologies able both to shrink time and space and to endo-colonise the Earth.

Virilio's ideas regarding modernity and globalisation can usefully be compared to Hannah Arendt's (1973) concept of totalitarianism, which refers to modern political movements such as Nazism and Soviet Communism that were, in Arendt's view, concerned with complete planetary domination. Virilio's interest in Arendt's model of totalitarianism is evident in his invention and use of the term 'globalitarianism' to describe a new kind of technoscientific totalitarianism for our global age (see, for example, Virilio and Armitage 2001a: 15–47). By globalitarianism Virilio means that globalisation, which for him began with European modernity and with the French Revolutionary 'dromomaniacs', has now effectively been completed in the sense that it has transformed the world into a claustrophobic prison or an infinite black hole. He argues, for example, that, today, humanity has nowhere else to go in terms of global space, with the result that time becomes its new frontier.

However, in *The Great Accelerator* (2012 [2010]), Virilio goes even further, claiming that humanity has already exhausted itself in the search for ever-faster technoscientific acceleration. His contemporary theory of globalisation therefore contrasts the idea of the post-industrial 'big bang', which began the process of economic globalisation in the 1980s, with the notion of the post-geographical 'big crunch', which is ushering in processes of spatial contraction, claustrophobia and temporal confusion. In other words, for Virilio, the big crunch signifies not only the end of globalisation but also the end of geography, space and history. In response to this situation, characterised by a lack of time and space, Virilio asserts that globalisation generates its own utopian fantasy; that of humanity's escape from the Earth to another planet. Accordingly, globalisation is, in Virilio's estimation, a largely dystopic condition.

See also: Modernity; Space-Time; Speed; Technology

GREAT ACCELERATOR

Mark Featherstone

The Great Accelerator (2012 [2010]) is Virilio's critical commentary on the Large Hadron Collider (the world's largest and highest-energy particle accelerator), the contemporary global economic crash and what he calls the insecurity of history. Noting that globalisation and high-speed communication have resulted in the inertia of real time or the abolition of geographical distance by the acceleration of communication, Virilio argues that the temporal separation between transmission and reception has collapsed into a singular, endless, moment.

Explaining that historical time has given way to the moment, to a perpetual 'presentness' without a past or a future, Virilio contends that the insecurity of history is a dystopic condition that deprives humanity of the possibility of progress. For him, there is no hope here because there is now no way for humanity to reflect upon the events of the past in order to make changes in the present for the sake of progress in the future.

Relating these ideas to today's global financial crisis, Virilio makes clear that the turbo-capitalist market functions like a great accelerator, but one that has abolished the distance between buyers and sellers, senders and receivers, and, consequently, brought about an overexposed moment of live exchange where competition is eliminated. The outcome of this condition, which is premised on humanity's ability to function under circumstances dictated by real-time exchange, is the rise of a programmatic form of insider trader, universal monopoly, the end of free trade and confidence, the dominance of disbelief, and what Virilio terms the atheism of the market wherein systemic crashes are commonplace.

However, the light speed of exchange is not simply an economic problem. Indeed, Virilio indicates that the 'fractalisation' of the tempo of the market and the condensation of exchange into a moment of inertia and regular crashes allow critics to ponder the wider astronomic implications of the insecurity of history and the inertia of real time. Considering the acceleration of reality and its collapse into a singular moment, he discusses new global forms of habitable, or perhaps inhabitable, circulation beyond the city where people must live constantly on the move. But it would be a mistake to imagine that these new global forms of habitation mean that humanity somehow has more space in which to live, because the inertia of real time implies that geography itself collapses before a unitary world where here and there are now the same place. For this reason, claustrophobia is the spatial psychopathology of Virilio's inert world, a psychopathology that gives rise to the ultimate form of outsourcing: humanity's search for exo-planetary escape.

Certainly, for Virilio, exo-planetary escape represents the utopian or perhaps dystopian dream of dromocratic culture. For, faced with the spatio-temporal limits of the globe, people constantly on the move not only have to confront the final barrier of time but also the final barriers of progress and human habitation.

Caught inside this dead moment with no hope of escape, for Virilio, the Large Hadron Collider thus represents the contemporary fate of humanity. Buried deep under the Earth, the great accelerator creates a circular, totally enclosed, space so as to reproduce the original moment of the Big Bang, and to discover the famous God particle or the Higgs boson. Nevertheless, in Virilio's opinion, the central impact of the discovery of the God particle, which seeks to clarify the difference between the existence of something and nothing, is that of the completion of the modern scientific assault on God, which, in turn, creates a black hole called atheism at the centre of dromocratic culture. Thus, from Virilio's perspective, the great accelerator and the God particle are significant not simply because of their scientific importance, but also because of what they symbolise about our ongoing attempt to abolish history, promote the cult of light speed and collapse duration in such a way that is characteristic of nothing less than the modern death drive, which Freud (2003) discovered in the 1920s, and which was realised in the invention of the original atom-smasher by Ernest Lawrence at Berkeley in the 1930s.

GREY ECOLOGY

Julian Reid

Grey ecology is best understood as Virilio's alternative to green ecology. Green ecology refers to the sciences and movements oriented around the problem of the pollution of natural environments on which living organisms rely for their wellbeing. Grey ecology is concerned with the pollution of the self-created environment of the specifically human organism, its cosmos and culture, without which humans are no longer human. While green ecologists are generally concerned with the question of how to save the planet, the question for grey ecologists is that of how to save the humanity of human beings.

Virilio's *Open Sky* (1997 [1995]: 60) criticises green ecologists for their failures to recognise the pollution not simply of the natural environment, but of human culture and the human cosmos, caused by forms of scientific and technological 'progress', especially the 'empire of realtime communications' he associates with the information–communication revolution and phenomenon of globalisation. Likewise, Virilio argues that the ecological crisis with regard to the security of the natural environment is itself only understandable on account of the more profound crisis in the human environment. The temporal contraction or foreclosure that determines the process of globalisation, achieved through the ongoing acceleration of reality established by new technologies of information and communication, has functioned, according to Virilio's *Grey Ecology* (2009b: 50), to pollute the sense of distance between the human and its world that humanity relies on for its creative strength. The lack of effort required in teletechnologies for hearing, seeing and acting at a distance destroys our sense of the vastness of the world, a precondition of our ability to have meaningful experience of the world, and without which our perception of the very nature of the world and what is entailed in being in the world becomes debased.

Instead of being situated in the world, moving from place to place, as well as being moved, animated, desiring and loving elements of the world around us, we are delivered over to a condition in which all we perceive is the end of the world. While this end is fundamentally temporal it is also phenomenological. 'Everything is *déjà vu* or at least *déjà explore*: been there, done that' (*OS*, 65). What is polluted, therefore, in the context of the ongoing ecological crisis, is not simply the natural environment, but the relation with the geophysical environment on which we rely in order to be able to create new ways of living (politics). We have exhausted not only the sense of distance of the world but also the time of the world, without which we lose all sense of the future. Without a sense of a future, which emits from the experience of distance, we will not be able to find a way out of the ecological predicament, or, literally, the 'end of the world', because we are faced with an era of apparently apocalyptic processes. This 'end of the world' condition that now haunts humanity emerges from its false understanding of what constitutes the conditions for the development of human strength and security. The predicament of human subjection to the ecological crisis results from the hubristic desire of the species to master its world; to conquer and exploit it, most significantly through technological and scientific endeavour.

Overcoming this predilection for mastery requires humanity to recognise its fundamental humility in relation to the world, and, just as significantly, the 'finitude', both of humanity and of the world it inhabits. To recognise the finitude of the world is not simply to acknowledge that the world will end, Virilio argues, but also to recognise that we will have to learn to live after 'the end of the world'. Accepting the finitude of itself and the world gives, paradoxically, both the human and its world a future. It allows us to survive 'the end of the world' by recoiling from that end. It is a different kind of security device from that which has previously driven the history of human progress. Finitude is the ineradicable condition of (human) being, which elicits its resistance to the spatial-temporal contraction that threatens it. Facing the truth of its finitude and fundamental humility in relation with its world means that humanity must cast off the false faith in technoscientific 'progress' that has driven its historical development, the subsequent colonisation of time and space, and the establishment of the end of the world. Facing finitude allows the human to confront the end of the world and discover another path beyond it.

This act of facing finitude can only occur, Virilio argues, in the form of revelation: 'Grey ecology is revelationary' (*GE*, 43). Its purpose is to open us up to a new way of thinking and living. A way of thinking that will allow us to 're-civilize science', by making it come to terms with its exterminating dimension (*GE*, 47). Most especially, it requires us to address the militarisation of science that accounts for the exterminating dimension. Grey ecology exists in this sense in a necessary conflict with military intelligence and the art of war that has conditioned the technoscientific development of humanity. How we are to achieve Virilio's project of grey ecology remains an open question because we have not yet understood either finiteness or how to respond to its revelation. But the links that Virilio makes between the grey and green ecological problematics that humanity is faced with and with the art of war are necessary starting points. For in establishing these links Virilio asks us to understand the extent to which the militarisation of science and technological progress have functioned as extensions of an art of war that operates not for but upon humanity. For in destroying its own relation with the world, humanity has effectively waged war on itself, and, in doing so, is in the process of destroying itself. The task now is for humanity to face that catastrophe, confront it in its reality, not simply in proclamation of horror at it, but in order to step back from it, evade and move beyond it, by recovering a distance from it. The pollution of distance is the problematic of grey ecology, and the development of distance its task.

See also: Propaganda of Progress; Revolutionary, Revelationary; Technology

GROUND ZERO

Nick Prior

Ground zero is military nomenclature for the geographical point immediately beneath the detonation of a bomb. It was coined during the period of the Manhattan Project (1939–46), to refer to the spot chosen for testing the atomic bomb, the so-called 'Trinity' site of New Mexico. More recently, it has come to refer to areas of severe destruction wrought by any disaster, becoming synonymous with the attacks on the World Trade Center in New York City on September 11, 2001.

In Virilio's *Ground Zero* (2002b [2002]), the term stands for the state of the globalised accident, extending the point of impact to encompass the borderless territory of more or less everywhere and right now. As the grounds of war have themselves shifted from the military battlegrounds of yore to a state of deterritorialised hyperwar, we are left with the disturbing prospect that all technologically mediated life is lived at ground zero. The events of September 11 are, therefore, a specific instance of a more general state of technological terror manifested in the inability of a powerful state to control its own technoscientific unconsciousness and blind faith in the very machines that assault it. September 11 is emblematic of a globalism that has no moral compass and no ability to leash the worst vagaries of the technological complex. An act of 'total war', for sure, September 11 was 'remarkably conceived and executed, with a minimum of resources' (*GZ*, 82) and from within the USA itself. In effect, for Virilio, technologies of speed are boomerangs that return to wreak havoc on the forces that gave rise to them.

Three strands, then. First, the unprecedented emergence of the suicidal state represented in the twin images of the suicide bombers and the commercial production of human embryos for research purposes. The state-sponsored nuclear age finds its corollary in state eugenics and the death not just of God, but of the procreator in the race for a spermless genesis. In the aftermath, there can be no moral high ground to be taken by an American super-state whose arrogant superiority is, according to Virilio, based on its absolute technical power and loss of self-preservation in the form of embryonic destruction.

Second, in the razing of the twin towers by transportation vehicles, rather than military weapons, lies the ceaseless intensification of technologies of acceleration. This chimes with the idea of the inevitable accident, the invention of the passenger aeroplane and skyscraper being at one and the same time the invention of these two entities at some point colliding. Once the spell of technoculture is cast, and since the Manhattan project itself, there can be no social or ideological taming of progress. We are already at Hiroshima.

Third, the scene of the World Trade Center represents a derealisation of the event amidst collapsing ontologies of the real and the fictional. While images of the World Trade Center replayed in looped forms, the attacks were themselves a carefully managed image strategy, an 'event-instant' whose antecedents were reality game shows and the real-time conflicts of the Gulf and Kosovo. TV audiences, notes Virilio, momentarily believed that they were watching a disaster movie. But this is not Guy Debord's (1984) *Society of the Spectacle* as much as a self-perpetuating global electronic field with spectators fed on a diet of accidents.

The frenzied extension of a supposedly progressive technoscience is no more than an infectious hysteria located around the control of matter, the desire to endlessly compress and control everything, including death. But excess in all things (speed, proximity, circulation) invariably generates its opposite. The journey is replaced by a perpetual arriving that is itself redolent of inertia because we don't actually go anywhere. Electronic media, cybernetics, advertising, contemporary art, genetic manipulation, all annihilate the sensorial and spiritual registers of the body. The terrorist attacks index a profound absence, not only of a defensible state, America literally penetrated by its own transportation machines, but of an ethics of time and space once the desire for absolute speed governs communication. This 'philanoia' or love of madness at the behest of progress has been the polluting motor of history since at least the time of the Renaissance.

Like the German avant-garde composer Karlheinz Stockhausen, who believed that 'what we have witnessed is the greatest work of art there has ever been', Virilio entertains the notion that September 11 belongs to the realm of art (*GZ*, 45). Not as a statement of the sublime but as the folding of the body of the artist into the machine complex that had the Futurists in raptures. If the modern work of art is a dramaturgical event delivered by technologies of speed, it is also part of an 'electro-optical economy' (*GZ*, 60) managed by cultural promoters and transnational impresarios that favour the art of the cybernetic (Orlan, Stelarc) and the accelerated temporality of installation and video art. But the events of September 11 also reflect an extra-aesthetic manipulation of a displaced and radicalised 'global subproletariat' by a wealthy elite of Arab society as seduced by technological circumscription as Western elites. Wealthy Muslim students, technicians and military leaders, hence, resemble members of the American suicidal sect 'Heaven's Gate'. Virilio recognises no inevitable fracture between West and East, but rather a unifying state of technological virulence.

Like Jean Baudrillard's (2003) characterisation of September 11 as the absolute event, the mother of all events, Virilio recognises the era-defining properties of the attacks on the World Trade Center. Preceded by the bombing of the Center in 1993, September 11 heralded a new phase of the terrorist act as strategic event. On that day 'the Manhattan skyline became the front of the new war' (*GZ*, 82). Unlike Baudrillard, however, for Virilio there is no progressive moment beyond good and evil represented by the attacks, no logic of destructive potential. Instead, the attacks merely signal a dystopic vision of the system itself. For just as the rise of a 'global covert state' (*GZ*, 82) packs a charge of unknown criminality, so too the visions of the high priests of technological progress are pregnant with their ultimate and ironic opposite.

See also: Events; Globalisation; Propaganda of Progress; Technology

HUSSERL, EDMUND

Mark Wright

Edmund Husserl (1859–1938) was one of the most important Czecho-Austro-German philosophers of the twentieth century. Considered the founding father of phenomenology, the study of the construction of subjective experience and consciousness, Husserl's philosophy has influenced and been modified in the work of distinguished thinkers such as Martin Heidegger, Jean-Paul Sartre and Maurice Merleau-Ponty. In a career in which he wrote voluminously for over half a century, the effect that Husserl's prolific contributions to philosophy have had upon technological, textual and cultural hermeneutics is extraordinary. He composed numerous significant essays and books that interrogate the traditional philosophical concerns: mathematics, science, ethics, logic, epistemology, cognitive science, ontology, space and time. There are also several key lectures and texts that were published posthumously, such as *The Paris Lectures* (1998) and *The Crisis of European Sciences and Transcendental Phenomenology* (1970), which was Husserl's final endeavour to clarify and establish his phenomenological philosophy. Arguably, though, the most influential works appeared during Husserl's lifetime, including *Logical Investigations* (2001), *Ideas* (1983) and *Cartesian Meditations* (1977). Transcendental phenomenology, the study of the essential structures of pure consciousness, is the one discovery that Husserl would have wanted to be most remembered for. This is for him the authentic path of philosophy where he envisioned a community of co-workers interchanging phenomenological perspectives.

One such co-worker and phenomenologist is, of course, Virilio, whose immersion in Husserl's ideas has become increasingly evident as a set of motifs that run through his *oeuvre*. Indeed, Virilio integrates a number of critical Husserlian issues concerning the effects of technology in present-day societies, in particular the exploration of the potential loss of human presence, activity and experience in a world that is becoming ever more technologically determined. In clarification of the philosophical under-standing of the relationship between humanity, technology and modernity as it is conceived in the work of Virilio and Husserl, it is essential to begin with the analysis of Virilio's *Polar Inertia* (2000a: [1990]). This text pro-vides a synoptic treatment of time, space, bodies and the ego in orientation to the world and experience, demonstrating that through the deployment of new technologies these concepts are to be redefined. Virilio claims that the real-time telereality of telecommunications has replaced the real space of immediate action and that it is now possible to be remotely present any-where as spatial distances are compressed. Bodies are suspended as human action is transformed through high-velocity communications and trans-appearance in the global environment (*PI*, 8). Now everything happens without a requirement for action as continuous movement is exchanged for a state of inertia. In 'The Originary Ark, the Earth, Does Not Move' Husserl claims that this replacement discovers its ground in 'stationary kinaesthetic activity', or, for Virilio, in the realm of the 'absolute zero' (*PI*, 71) of movement. With the ego positioned at the centre of this zero point, human experience is altered or decentred as a consequence of the loss of place for bodies, which Virilio distinguishes as 'increasing man's behav-ioural ego-centricity' (*PI*, 73). This decentring, implying a loss of place for the body, is an actual deconstruction of human experience. In short, if the human sphere of activity has no restrictions, there are severe difficul-ties in perceiving how and where actual physical human presence can be located.

Technology's assault on the world, human body, lived experience and activity is the recurring concern in Virilio's work. In his phenomenological critique of acceleration, *Speed and Politics* (2006 [1977]), Virilio endeav-ours to clarify some of the difficulties in measuring the impact of military, transportation and telecommunications technologies on the alteration of the body, space and time. He claims that our experiences and modes of perception, which inform our interpretation of the world, are transformed through technologies of speed that have had a disparaging impact on human life. Referring to the railway, airway and highway infrastructures Virilio writes: 'the more speed increases, the faster freedom decreases' (*SP*, 58). Human beings have thus become accessories to technological instrumentation as telecommunication technologies accelerate beyond the restrictions of space and time. People are transported outside the familiarity of everyday life, consequently redefining human experience and the question of being.

In *The Administration of Fear* (2012) Virilio's astute understanding of human experience proper is identified when he refers to himself as a phenomenologist and as a Husserlian: 'Husserlian because of the attention he gave to thinking about our habitat, the earth, as the space in and through which we experience our own body' (*TAF*, 25–6). Certainly, Virilio claims that it was Husserl who originally 'asserted the inertia of being in the world, which makes it a world and not a flux' (*TAF*, 26). However, Virilio fears that phenomenology has been caught unprepared by new technologies, which result in 'the inertia of the instant (simultaneity of communications)' and which come to dominate 'the inertia of place (sedentariness)' (*TAF*, 26). In other words, in speeded-up technological society everything occurs instantaneously with no requirement for the human body to move; inertia is the governing contemporary condition. For Virilio, the meaning of inertia can be discovered in the cosmos, where 'absolute speed amounts to little, but at that scale, it is earth which amounts to nothing' (Virilio and Armitage 2001a: 31). Virilio thus establishes a relationship between absolute speed and inertia that he argues leads to absolute stasis, which, for him, means that the world 'remains "at home", already there, given' (Virilio and Armitage 2001a: 31).

In a world where everything is already given, the idea of alterity and a shared community with human presence has been replaced by inertia and pure egoism, or, as Virilio claims in *Art as Far as the Eye Can See* (2007b [2005]), the 'hypercentration of contemporary individualism' (*AFE*, 99). Virilio's thoughts on human presence and the ego draw certain parallels with Husserl's phenomenological 'epoché'. For Husserl, in the epoché, or the bracketing of the natural ego, the 'transcendental ego' is reduced in order for pure being to be found. Virilio's adoption and adaptation of these ideas gives them an entirely new value. Here, the body lies inert, suspended, with the ego roaming free in a virtual environment. Virilio describes the point of inertia as being the 'carnal centre of presence' (*AFE*, 20), which, under the rapid vicissitudes of reality, has extended itself as far as telepresence in the real-time world. As an effect of the 'hypertrophy' of the ego, the real world has therefore become the 'gigantic phantom limb of humanity' (*AFE*, 21), with the human body languishing in outer exocentricity. Physical movement is at a standstill under the duress of speed determined technology, which increases the authority of the ego with the consequence that the human being becomes a stationary inactive being. This is of enormous concern as it is impossible any longer to pinpoint a physical dwelling place: for the 'sedentary person is also a person who, thanks not only to displacement by terrorism and so on but also by the teletechnologies of information, of mobile and portable technologies, has been set adrift from his or her previous moorings in the city' (Virilio and Armitage 2011: 37). As Virilio explains in *Open Sky* (1997 [1995]: 25), the world as it was formerly experienced has changed as a result of the introduction of the 'real instant of instantaneous telecommunications'.

Virilio is a phenomenologist and he illustrates his obligation to phenomenological perspectives throughout his work. His reading of Husserl, which places emphasis on the body and on the ego as the permanent crux of experience and perception, amounts to nothing less than a rethinking of the wrenching away of the body from subjectivity as contemporary experiences becomes increasingly abstract in the era of virtual reality. Innovative technologies are responsible for the replacement of 'the body proper in favour of the spectral body, and the world proper in favour of a virtual world' (Virilio and Petit 1999 [1996]: 48). However, Virilio cautiously stresses how subjective human experience has been challenged directly through the serious threat posed by modern technological experience, with the will to mastery appearing to have slipped from human control.

See also: Body; Phenomenology; Polar Inertia; Space-Time; Speed; Technology

HYPERMODERNISM

Rob Bullard

A term used by critics to distance Virilio from Postmodern theory by emphasising his stress on accelerated modernity, military aesthetics and contemporary technologies. Following the translation of Virilio's writings into English, social theorists, including David Harvey (1989: 159–66), challenged his thinking, describing Virilio as a Postmodern theorist. John Armitage's (2000) *Paul Virilio: From Modernism to Hypermodernism and Beyond* explains how Virilio's work differs from Postmodern theory. With no interest or belief in structural linguistics, psychoanalysis, Marxism or the decline of metanarratives, Virilio, according to this analysis, carves out a distinct theoretical position as a Christian and as a pacifist, as an anarchist, and as a phenomenologist. But it is Virilio's constant use of Modernist terms and artefacts, coupled with his frequent references to Modernist writers and artists that distinguishes Virilio from most of his peers, with the notable exception of Gilles Deleuze (Virilio and Armitage 2011: 29–30). For Virilio's thought focuses on the ever fluctuating speed of modernity, on technology, urban surveillance, militarism and on the accelerating landscape of the mass media. In addition, Virilio believes that one of the crucial resultant characteristics of excessive speed is alienation. Consequently, it is not difficult to ascertain why so many Modernists fascinate Virilio and why labelling him as a Postmodernist is seen by Armitage, among others, as wide of the mark. Virilio's, then, is a cautious commitment to the project of modernity: 'we are not out of modernity yet', he declared in interview, before going on to explain how he is also 'not completely antithetical to reason', and remains committed to the concepts of justice and hope; humanist leanings wholly at odds with Postmodernism in particular (Virilio and Armitage 2001a: 16). Rather than provide a blanket condemnation of modernity, Virilio views his theorising as a 'critical analysis of modernity, but through a perception of technology which is largely [. . .] catastrophic not catastrophist' (2001a: 16). This catastrophic perception of technology leads to his persistent obsession with the technological accident, an 'event' utilised by iconic Modernist writers and artists as diverse as Virginia Woolf and Robert Musil, Aldous Huxley, Scott Fitzgerald and Filippo Tommaso Emilio Marinetti. In typically paradoxical Modernist fashion, Virilio sees accidents as something positive, as a means of revealing or exposing the concealed flip-side of technology. Accidents, in Virilian terms, can thus be seen as one of the outcomes, or intensities, of an excessively accelerated hypermodern culture that has its testing ground in the military–industrial–scientific complex. So, as a theorist primarily concerned with the cultural logic of speed or, alternatively, the cultural logic of late militarism, hypermodernism seems an entirely appropriate term for Virilio's work. His claim that 'we are only now entering the era of the postmodern' (Virilio and Armitage 2011: 29) complicates matters, but should not deter readers from the realisation that it is persistently the themes of speed, technology and military aesthetics that dominate Virilio's (aptly) frenzied writings. Lastly, the term hypermodernism captures the essence of Virilio's theory – that this is a world fuelled and framed by ever-increasing acceleration – far more accurately than the jaded term Postmodernism.

I

INFORMATION BOMB

Paul Crosthwaite

Introduced into Virilio's conceptual repertoire in the 1990s, the term 'information bomb' denotes a form of 'integral', 'general', or 'global' accident generated by the speed and connectivity of contemporary information and communication technologies. Virilio uses the term to refer both to particular, individual, 'explosions', in which data radiates across the planet's networks at near-light speed, and to the ongoing, ever-intensifying, 'blast' of signs, images and code tearing through the environments of everyday life in an age of ubiquitous real-time interactivity.

The 'information bomb' is, of course, so named in reference to the atomic and, latterly, nuclear bomb – a rhetorical move that Virilio borrows from Albert Einstein, the German theoretical physicist who developed the theory of general relativity and who, in the wake of the US attacks on Hiroshima and Nagasaki during the Second World War, spoke of 'the second bomb': 'the electronic bomb after the atomic one' (Virilio 1995: par. 13). The information bomb, Virilio explains, is '[a] bomb whereby real-time interaction would be to information what radioactivity is to energy. The disintegration then will not merely affect the particles of matter, but also the very people of which our societies consist' (Virilio 1995: par. 13). The information bomb, he remarks elsewhere, 'is similar to the atomic bomb but only to the extent that it is a device based on energy [. . .] Whereas the atom bomb was triggered by the energy of the atom, the information bomb is triggered by the energy of information and communication technologies' (Virilio and Armitage 2001b: 168).

In Virilio's elaboration of the concept, the information bomb takes various forms and has various consequences – some quite immediate and concrete and others more abstract and philosophical. Insofar as it entails the growing computerisation and automation of industrial production, the information bomb is implicated in the immiseration of swathes of 'the poor and the weak' (Virilio and Kittler 2001: 99), who, dispossessed of traditional outlets for their labour, and lacking the skills and resources to participate in the new 'information economy', find themselves effectively excluded from the mainstream of society. This 'structural unemployment', Virilio conjectures, is 'an effect, or a type of fall-out following the explosion of the information bomb' (Virilio and Kittler 2001: 99). Virilio finds further 'signs [. . .] of social disintegration' in the 'loss of social bonds [. . .] linked to the demise of the proximate human being' (Virilio and Kittler 2001: 99, 103). Privileging remote, mediated relationships over intimate, face-to-face ones – a preference evident in trends ranging from the phenomenon of couples 'living apart together' to the rise of 'cybersex' – individuals, according to Virilio, are becoming increasingly atomised, alienated and disconnected, even as the networks in which they are embedded become ever more densely interwoven (Virilio and Kittler 2001: 103). These 'metaphors of decay' are, again, 'effect[s]' of the information bomb' (Virilio and Kittler 2001: 103). Meanwhile, spewing forth a stream of undifferentiated semiotic material, in which historical events co-exist in a perpetual, holographic present, the information bomb threatens to have 'destructive effects on society's capacity to remember its past, a past that has a structure of its own and shapes the present'. 'We are merely the product of what was,' Virilio insists, '[a]nd whoever forgets the past is condemned to live it anew, as the saying goes. And yet this is exactly what is happening with new information and communications technologies' (Virilio and Kittler 2001: 105).

If, according to Virilio, we have yet to witness the full-scale, cataclysmic detonation of the information bomb – whose consequences would be incalculable and unimaginable – we nonetheless already find ourselves exposed to a host of lesser explosions. Among these various ominous events, it is the phenomenon of the stock market meltdown that Virilio has most often identified as the exemplary harbinger of the information bomb (Crosthwaite 2011: 177–99). Writing after the Black Monday crash of October 1987, for example, he (Virilio 1995: par. 15) remarks that 'the stock-market collapse' is a 'prefiguration' of 'a generalised kind of accident, a never-seen-before accident' arising from 'the globalization of telecommunications'. '[W]atch out,' he cautions, 'as you hear talk about the "financial bubble" in the economy: a very significant metaphor is used here, and it conjures up visions of some kind of cloud, reminding us of other clouds just as frightening as those of Chernobyl [. . .] ' (Virilio 1995: par. 15). Similarly, in *The Information Bomb* (2000d [1998]), Virilio, referring to 1997's financial turmoil in South East Asia, observes that '[i]f the cybernetics of the financial market had actually been globalized, the crash of autumn 1997 would have been instantaneously planetary and economic catastrophe would have been total' (*IB*, 108). By 2008, amidst the tumultuous financial upheavals of the global 'credit crunch', Virilio appeared willing to countenance the idea that interactivity was finally proving itself to be the genuine informational equivalent of nuclear radioactivity, remarking in a widely circulated interview with *Le Monde* that,

In 1979, at the time of the mishap at the Three Mile Island nuclear plant in the US, I did mention the occurrence of an 'original accident' [. . .] I said that our technical prowess was pregnant of catastrophic promises. In the past, accidents were local affairs. With Chernobyl, we have entered the era of global accidents, whose consequences are in the realm of the long term. The current crash represents the perfect 'integral accident'. (Virilio 2008: par. 3–4)

Just as the notion of the information bomb harks back to nuclear and atomic energy and – more specifically – weaponry, so Virilio argues that the new digital technologies 'will very soon require the establishment of a new type of *deterrence*' (Virilio *IB*, 108), akin to the nuclear stand-off that prevailed throughout the Cold War. If 'the emergence of the atomic bomb made very quickly the elaboration of a policy of military dissuasion imperative in order to avoid a nuclear catastrophe', then 'the information bomb will [. . .] need a [. . .] societal form of dissuasion to counter the damage caused by the explosion of unlimited information' (Virilio 1995: par. 14). As Virilio argues, however, the recent global financial crisis makes it abundantly clear that the task of implementing 'a policy based on the political economy of speed, the speed that technological progress engenders', remains to be accomplished. Such a project can only begin, Virilio suggests, in a frank acknowledgement of 'the "accidental" character of History' (Virilio 2008: par. 5).

See also: Accident; Catastrophe; Political Economy of Speed; Technology

KITTLER, FRIEDRICH, A.

Stephen Sale

Like Virilio, the late Friedrich A. Kittler (1943–2011) came from a generation that was too young to fight in the Second World War but which was old enough to experience the bombardment of the civilian centres of Europe first-hand. Kittler, who was born in Rochlitz, Saxony, remembered seeing Dresden ablaze and talked extensively about growing up in the former East Germany (Kittler and Armitage 2006). His mother used to take him on trips to Peenemünde, a Baltic seaport which was the centre for Nazi research into V2 rocket technology. Virilio, born in 1932, was a small child during the Second World War and fled Paris for Nantes with his family. The port was heavily bombed by the Allies in 1943. For both thinkers, a fascination with war, and the changes wrought by the Second World War in particular, guide their enquiries into the question of technology, leading both to productively examine the relationship between military technology and culture in a number of seminal texts.

Kittler's work on military technology is mainly associated with his so-called media-theoretical mid-period, which spanned the 1980s up to 2000. (His earlier writings had been focused on applying the insights of French poststructuralism to the hidebound discipline of German literary studies; his later work on 'cultural technologies' took him back to ancient Greece with an avowed rejection of war in favour of an exploration of 'love in Europe'.) During this time, Kittler emerged as the leading proponent of a new German 'media science' (*Medienwissenschaft*) that aimed to inject a new rigour into the humanities with a tech-savvy engagement with culture on the broadest terms. (Kittler was surely the only literary professor to teach his students the programming language C, arguing that scholars need to be able to understand the dominant contemporary cultural codes.) With his polemical claim that 'media determine our situation' (Kittler 1999: xxxix), Kittler aimed to expose the technological naivety of conventional literary theory, cultural studies, film studies, art history and sociology, whose ambitions were undermined by their inability to take into account their media-technological conditions of possibility. Instead, they had become befuddled by the 'eyewash' of medial surface effects.

In a number of his texts during this period, Kittler leans heavily on Virilio's work, in particular *War and Cinema: The Logistics of Perception* (1989 [1984]), which is used as a model argument in the 'Film' section of Kittler's *Gramophone, Film, Typewriter* (1999) and in the later *Optical Media* (2010), which is based on a lecture series from 1999. Kittler acknowledges his debt to Virilio, particularly on the military origins of optical technology, and has been keen to amplify Virilio's research and to 'demonstrate the plausibility of his often radical theories' (Kittler 2010: 42). Following Virilio, Kittler argues for the strict solidarity of war and film technology. The chain of assemblages that led to cinema includes Colt's multi-chambered revolver, Étienne-Jules Marey's chronophotographic gun, aerial reconnaissance in the First World War and the forging of the first mass audience in the trenches. Kittler also tells us that Thomas Edison, who was a telegrapher during the American Civil War, invented the phonograph 'in an attempt to improve the processing speed of the Morse telegraph beyond human limitations' (1999: 190), and that it was the gun manufacturer Remington & Son that began commercial production of the typewriter. On a broader canvas, *Optical Media* draws inspiration from

Virilio to produce a vivid historical account of the organisation of optical perception from the *camera obscura* to late twentieth-century computer graphics.

Together, Kittler and Virilio foreground the role of war in techno-logical development and reveal the martial origins of contemporary media technologies. For these thinkers, it is war, not the economic relations of Marxist orthodoxy that is the engine of historical change. They both subscribe to an inversion of Carl von Clausewitz's dictum that 'war is the continuation of politics by other means' (1968: 119), arguing that the political sphere becomes subordinated to the military. In their accounts, technology proceeds either by strategic escalation (Kittler) or through a logic of ever-increasing acceleration (Virilio). As Kittler tells us, the trans-mission technologies that emerged towards the end of the First World War were perfected by the time of the Second World War: 'VHF tank communications and radar images, those military developments parallel to television, meant total mobilisation, motorization and blitzkrieg from the Vistula in 1939 to Corregido in 1945' (1999: 243). Following the war, the 'total mobilization' that Ernst Jünger (1993; Armitage 2003) had called for in the 1920s was implemented in peacetime. Once media technologies lose their strategic advantage, they are then released to the public under strictly regulated conditions.

The mass media of the second half of the twentieth century, such as television, computer games and rock music, all served to implement military command structures throughout society and to produce mili-tarised 'machine subjects'. Accompanying the societal encroachment of martial technologies is the devolution of sensory perception from indi-viduals to machinic functions. Virilio also charts this displacement but where he offers a humanist lament for a world before the advent of the military–industrial complex after 1945, Kittler suggests that we cast off our sentimental anthropocentrism and start revising our ontologies. For Kittler, the isolation and reproduction of functions in technical devices offers us an opportunity to better understand some of the functions that we once believed were unique to human beings. Virilio's materialist phe-nomenology is interested in the effect of different intensities of light on the human sensorium; Kittler is equally interested in the effect of light on silver nitrate.

In a television interview recorded in 1995, the two theorists of 'total war' were brought together to discuss *The Information Bomb* (Virilio 2000d [1998]). Virilio suggested that the emergence of global communica-tion networks represents 'the limit point of acceleration' that would usher in a new 'archaism' as traditional social bonds are destroyed and violence is unleashed (Virilio and Kittler 2001). Kittler's measured response was to call for a revised philosophical and political framework that is able to address the changing technological paradigms. Critical to this is mastery of the languages and hardware of the computer systems themselves. While Virilio's pessimism remains faithful to phenomenology and existentialism, Kittler follows the later Martin Heidegger (1978) in looking for the saving power precisely where the danger is greatest: in computer technology.

See also: Media; Optics; Technology; War

L

LANDSCAPE OF EVENTS

Nicholas Michelson

Referring to Virilio's philosophy of history, as defined by his analysis of the present collapse of the spatial into the temporal; also the title of a book: *A Landscape of Events* (2000c [1996]). A landscape of events is the God's-eye view of history; all time being compressed into pure simultaneity and arranged as topography. Time is thereby no longer characterised, primarily, by sequentiality, but by the specific elements of its geography; events as landslides, hills, valleys and primal forests.

What is crucial about such a representation of time is that this landscape has no centre, no 'fixed meaning' or 'privileged vantage point' whence the whole can be understood, as in Karl Marx's historical materialism (*LE*, xi). Rather, this landscape of time must be explored; its constitutive events cannot be assessed only according to their visible scale or magnitude, since it is often the overlooked or ignored topographical features that most define the landscape of events.

If such a landscape was once disclosed only to celestial vision, its scrutiny has been democratised by the contemporary condition of general history, by the great panorama of time that today enacts only existential precariousness and terror, the definitive markers of 'dromocratic' societies. In embracing the rush of progress, we have achieved the totalitarianism of the momentary – a radical celebration of the instant – above all else which, rather than giving access to the present, has simply unfolded the evental vista before our horrified and bewildered eyes.

Time thus appears to us today, quite reasonably, as a far more important commodity than space. Modern technology, associated with the laws

of relativity, has rendered physical distance servant to temporal extension: all distance has been compressed as our capacity to traverse it has
expanded, guided by an unquenchable thirst for instantaneous arrival.
That spatio-temporal compression of the phenomenal world has, in turn,
fractured history, by destroying truly separate histories. Globalisation
is the end of finite or local times; time itself has now been finalised and
integrated into a single landscape.

This radical abandonment of extension for instantaneity obviates experience of the genuinely present moment. All events are simply situated
topographically. This is most obviously exemplified in the 24-hour news-
cycle, which has given birth to the sound-bites and obfuscation that stand
in for politics today, while ensuring that the noise of the evental plethora
displaces any resurgent aspiration to a measured collective response to
'current affairs'.

Virilio remarks that cybernetics (a creature of military science) plays
a crucial role in establishing and responding to this new conception of
time, framed as a definitely uncertain time calling for the securitisation
of the past. Indeed, the definitive mood that attends our perception of
the evental landscape is, according to Virilio, fear of the past. Past events
come to haunt the experience of temporality with their newly recognised
intimacy, which is always just over the horizon. Superseding the anxiety
about the future, which was mankind's traditional phenomenological
abode, the panic that besets us today is one born of our ability to trace the
infection of current events by their geographical neighbours. Rather than
being a repository of meaning and source of precedent, the past is now
seen as getting in the way of the present; its terrorisations hover threat-
eningly at our shoulders, calling up a surrender of agency to automated
response mechanisms that can cope with the perceptual onslaught. At the
limit we find a 'declaration-of-war-machine' (LE, 86).

We have, Virilio argues, accelerated so fast that we have hit the limit,
the speed of light, the wall in time itself, where reality happens all at once.
Is it any wonder that on this side of the wall events are getting compressed
on top of each other? This temporal compression is squeezing agency out
of history, leaving us only with a sense of panic at the unfolding of events
before our eyes. Virilio conjures up the German-Jewish literary critic, philosopher and social critic Walter Benjamin, and his evocative reading of
Paul Klee's painting, *Angelus Novus*: the angel of history is blown, facing
backwards, by the winds of time, so that he sees time itself as a 'single
catastrophe which keeps piling wreckage upon wreckage and hurls it at his
feet' (LE, xiii). For Virilio, this is the precise condition we find ourselves
in, and to which the concept of a landscape of events refers. Time now
resembles a car crash, in which the wreckage of each new event crashing

into the one in front leads us to resent the very passage of history. We are understandably repulsed by the horrific pile-up, but unable to look away from the panorama laid out around us.

Virilio's *A Landscape of Events,* which is made up of short essays written between 1984 and 1996, is 'halfway between an essay and a narrative' since it charts 'atypical' events over the course of ten to twelve years such as terrorist acts, wars, riots and kidnappings (*LE*, xii). The period is precisely that in which Virilio argues that the discontinuity with chronological history that defines our age became unmistakably clear as a kind of temporal crash. The Swiss architect Bernard Tschumi suggested in the foreword to the English translation of *A Landscape of Events* that it is a book about 'time, rather than space' (*LE*, viii). In an important sense it is about the crash of one into the other, leading to the collective experience of the implosion of space-time during the period addressed.

The text should, therefore, be understood as closely related to what Virilio termed the 'Accident Museum', which is in fact the title of one of its essays. In charting the passage of a landscape of events, Virilio seeks to create 'a new kind of scenography in which only what explodes and decomposes is exposed' (*LE*, 59). The evental landscape maps the decomposition of chronological history itself, exhibiting the seemingly inexorable progression of a temporal implosion, and as such, gives testimony to the accident of accidents.

See also: Accident Museum; Events; Space-Time

LAW OF PROXIMITY

Rob Bullard

The philosophical term applied by Virilio to signal the spatio-temporal differences between the mechanical machines and infrastructure of modernity and the electromagnetic transmission technologies of Postmodernity wherein the human body is subject to remote control. Delineating the topography and genealogy of such technologies, Virilio's *Open Sky* (1997 [1995]) explains modernity's 'transport revolution' (railways, highway networks, etc.) as a revolution of control over the natural world by way of 'volume and geography' (*OS*, 50). This 'law of mechanical proximity,' argues Virilio, is currently being eclipsed by technologies of miniaturisation or the 'transmission revolution', which is dominated by new information and communications technologies; a 'law of electromagnetic proximity' that manifests itself as, for example, mobile phones and laptop computers. Technologies of miniaturisation are also the forerunners of the 'transplantation revolution' that is presently under way. Here, mastery over the physical environment extends to control over the micro-physical environment, which includes human physiology and the Earth's climatology as well as the interactive capabilities of transmission tools, 'digestible' simulators and remote control scanners. Virilio writes of the transplantation revolution as 'the ingurgitation of micromachines', as the 'technological fuelling of the living body', and views the results as an endo-colonisation, as an 'imminent invasion of our bodies, the control of an endogenous environment, that of our entrails and viscera' (OS, 50–3). He thus recognises that the law of electromagnetic proximity has overtaken the law of mechanical proximity insofar as technologies of miniaturisation are now being transferred 'into the very heart of the living being' (OS, 52). Resembling the German phenomenological philosopher of Being Martin Heidegger's essay on 'The Age of the World Picture' (2002), Virilio claims that the 'law of proximity' should be understood relative to what he calls the 'principle of least action' and the ongoing miniaturisation of the world (OS, 54). For Virilio, then, the looming miniaturisation of humankind means that human beings no longer inhabit the energy of machines but, rather, are themselves occupied and governed by the energy of instantane-ity (OS, 54). Hence he declares that, in contrast to the spatially biased law of mechanical proximity, the temporally biased law of electromagnetic proximity is based on the 'real time of immediacy', on the acceleration of the urban realm and of the human body, both of which are increasingly, and perhaps fatally, colonised by technologies of control.

LOGISTICS OF PERCEPTION

Olga Alekseyeva

Interrogation of the impact of acceleration on perception is part of Virilio's research on 'dromology' or the science of speed. His key assumption is that the speed at which something happens affects the perceptual nature of the phenomenon in question. For Virilio, acceleration is one of the impor-tant forms of power; to be able to act at speed is thus a form of domination. In his view, then, the logic of acceleration underwrites both the power and the technological structures of contemporary society and culture.

In *Speed and Politics: An Essay on Dromology* (2006 [1977]), for example, Virilio analyses questions of power and technology relative to the ques-tion concerning perception. Assessing the development of contemporary warfare, he argues that the increased acceleration and therefore power of people, technical object and technical vehicles during wartime no longer involves the direct collision of armed forces but, rather, the indirect or mediated collision of immaterial military forces where actually killing the enemy has yielded to the virtual annihilation of the enemy's field of perception. Accordingly, war becomes less about material gain and more about appropriating the immateriality of perceptual fields in which the speed and power of new information and communications technologies are the keys to victory. Here, war becomes accelerated and the power of militarily and technologically enhanced logistics of perception turn speed into domination and, if necessary, into a wholly destructive force.

In *War and Cinema: The Logistics of Perception* (1989 [1984]), Virilio uncovers the parallels between perceptual-cinematic techniques, military technologies and weapons systems from machine-guns to aerial surveillance. Emerging jointly since the 1870s, the fusion of cinematic and military technologies signals a radical change in how the world is seen: from here on in, the function of the eye is equated with the function of the weapon. Such similar developments not only reveal new technologies and new and constantly shifting fields of perception but also new dimensions of war, aviation and acceleration that have continued to manifest themselves from the First World War to the Gulf, Kosovo and Iraq wars of the twentieth and twenty-first centuries (see, for instance, Virilio 2000b [1999]; 2002a [1991]; 2005b [2004]).

Yet these similarities between the development of contemporary war and cinema extend beyond the strictly military realm into the ostensibly social realm in which, for example, cinema's framing of visual material exploits the technical multiplication of images in space and time. Consequently, cinema ushers into the social realm a heterogeneity of perceptual fields wherein the object on screen (e.g. an actress's body) disappears into a momentary agglomeration of sense-data. Premised on the takeover of the spectator's gaze, cinema is then a social exercise involving the accelerated distortion of human perception by military technologies, a logistics and an aesthetics of disappearance, and the putting of the human eye into a powerful straitjacket.

The parallels with those societies such as the United States and the former Soviet Union that were embroiled in the destructiveness of the Cold War (1947–91), the largest ever war of human perception to date, replete as it was with strategies of appearance and disappearance, are obvious, and might even be extended beyond the human eye to the Pentagon's most recent military-strategic construct: network-centric warfare.

$$\boxed{\text{M}}$$

MASS INDIVIDUALISM

Hugh Davies

Mass individualism describes the diminishing subjectivity and emotional synchronisation of individuals temporally and spatially compressed within today's globalised environment, individuals who have been transformed into paranoid and compliant consumers of the 'free market'. The conceptual foundations of mass individualism are formed by Virilio in numerous texts including *The Information Bomb* (2000d [1998]), *City of Panic* (2005b [2004]) and *The University of Disaster* (2010a [2007]) where he outlines how the time-space compression resulting from globalisation has led to claustrophobia and incarceration. While the globe was once vast and undiscovered, and societies were comprised of collective masses, nowadays, global information technology and transportation networks have encircled and captured the world, thereby reducing critical reflection upon it and the apparent dwindling of existential space. With world geography conquered and regulated, now begins the urbanisation, domination and, above all, synchronisation of the mass individual.

The results, according to *The Information Bomb*, are 'pseudo-individualism' and 'liberal hedonism'; both far removed from the Canadian media philosopher Marshall McLuhan's (2001 [1964]) idealised citizens of the 'global village'. *City of Panic*, meanwhile, focuses on the media driven conformity and loss of freedom that mass individualism ushers in. For, despite the appearance of individual liberties and endless 'options', the actual scope of 'free choice' only exists within the emotionally synchronised limits prescribed and regulated by the 'free market'. Consequently, mass individuals become detached from one another while simultaneously becoming ever more attached to the cybernetic and synchronised systems of regulation. In *The University of Disaster*, for example, Virilio claims that the 'free market', posing as the 'Blitzkrieg of progress' (*UD*, 150), has introduced a new era of 'globalitarianism'; an alarmingly superior form of totalitarian control that fuses social engineering with telesurveillance to produce a globalised authoritarianism that appeals to, rather than repulses, the masses. Within this setting of totalitarian control, mass individuals are constantly tuned into the socially engineered 'messages' emanating from contemporary regimes of telesurveillance. Kept in constant telepresent contact through their mobile phones, 'captive' mass individuals are robbed of their spare time in the name of their 'freedom of expression' or the 'immediacy' offered by their digital communication devices, which, in reality, suppress mass individuals' 'freedom of impression' and their capacity for considered reflection (*UD*, 50).

Virilio's mapping of mass individualism and globalitarianism also instantiates a rare anti-capitalist stance. While technology assumes its usual role as a mechanism of information and power, he has recently begun to argue that mass individuals are in fact controlled by corporate rather than political or military forces. Political and military analogies are useful, though, and in interviews (e.g. Virilio and Armitage 2001a) Virilio has compared mass individualism and globalitarianism to the mid-twentieth-century mass totalitarianisms of Nazi Germany and the former Soviet Union. Here, he reminds us that, while the totalitarian nation-states of Adolf Hitler and Joseph Stalin sought to regulate every aspect of the lives of their citizens, their authority was, initially at least, contained within their national borders. However, with the advent of globalisation, nation-states have become detached from their national territories, achieving a globalitarianism wherein the mass regulation and collectivisation of the citizenry is unnecessary because mass individuals can today be directly targeted by the appropriate 'authorities'.

MEDIA

Bob Hanke

The arc of media traverses Virilio's work, beginning with his *Speed and Politics: An Essay on Dromology* (2006 [1977]) where the United States is the first country in which the 'means of its mediatization' becomes an instrument of necessity. Grounded in phenomenology and military history, Virilio analyses the mutation of warfare, the acceleration of reality and the eclipse of geography. With motion and speed as central concepts for exploring modernity, he illuminates both the continuity and the transformation in the nineteenth-century transportation and the twentieth-century transmission revolutions. In this context, media – beginning with photography – are the keys to understanding time, space and movement concerning warfare, urbanism, democracy, globalisation and the environment. Building on German phenomenologist Martin Heidegger's *An Introduction to Metaphysics* (2000) and Canadian media theorist Harold Innis's 'A Plea for Time' (2008), Virilio foresees the uprooting of Being and the annihilation of human-centred space and time by technologies operating at light speed. The telecommunications revolution explodes *The Information Bomb* (Virilio 2000d [1998]) that affords hyper-individualised reception and interactivity in 'real time'. Overall, a three-dimensional definition of media as metaphor, vehicle and vector shapes his discourse.

First, media are metaphors: translators and transformers of Being, perception and experience. In *The Information Bomb*, Virilio (*IB*, 141) revises the Canadian media philosopher Marshall McLuhan's well-known formula that 'the medium is the message': 'it is not the *medium* which is the message, but merely *the velocity* of the medium'. His analysis of technological evolution and mediatisation refutes the myth of progress and concentrates upon the deleterious consequences of the shift from relative speeds of transport to the absolute speed of electromagnetic transmission.

Second, starting from the idea of the human body in motion and technology as prosthesis, Virilio conceptualises the body as a metabolic vehicle and media as audiovisual vehicles of motorisation, exteriorisation, colonisation and synchronisation. What is at stake in understanding the transport and transmission revolutions of the nineteenth and twentieth centuries, then, is the growing immobility and disorientation of the body regarding temporality and Being, the here and now, territory, fields of vision and questions of human habitation.

Third, Virilio appropriates the mathematical concept of the vector as a metaphor for transport and transmission. Following the German theoretical physicist Albert Einstein, Virilio defines movement as a vector of force and as a change of speed with both moving in the same direction. The vector is the trajectory along which bodies and goods, money, messages, information and images travel. In his representation of Western history, the dimensions of territorial space, chronological time and Renaissance 'perspectivalism' are all suppressed or superseded by the geometric space-time of vectors, chronoscopy and 'luminocentricism'.

Virilio's media philosophy thus foregrounds an increasing disjuncture between technological speed-up, the human experience of space and time, and the relativist prism of perception. With the advent of 'real-time' media interactivity, human beings lose the value of distance and duration, of the difference between near and far, of their sense of there and then, and of the idea of nature and the real. In his account of technologisation, one tendency stands out: that today a 'real-time' perspective is privileged over real space and place. Every diagram of the unity of space, time, perception and action is shattered by the double movement of explosion and implosion. Teletechnology, Virilio argues, disqualifies the sense of sight, renders the real as an optico-electronic illusion, supplants democracy with geopolitical chaos and deterritorialises the Earth as humanity's habitat. His writing makes a plea for a vitalist perception and temporal diversity.

Accordingly, media vectors 'metamorphosise' topological space and relations of power. In *The Lost Dimension* (1991 [1984]: 35), 'speed becomes the sole vector for electronic representation, not only inside the micro-processor but in the terminal screen-writing itself: the numeric image'. What is at issue is not the content or the meaning of the image but rather its quantitative abstraction and the 'sensibility' of vectors of representation which, 'in the electronic interface, affect the order of sensations, and, above all, the capacity to have or not have sensations' (*LD*, 52). The speed and trajectory of the instantaneous synthetic image without any vanishing point thus redefines the sensible space of classical geometry.

Virilio's analysis of media vectors and territories is subtended within his wider examination of military techniques and vectors of war. His *War and Cinema: The Logistics of Perception* (1989 [1984]), for example, examines the photographic, cinematic and electronic mediation of the battlefield. Virilio's thesis is that a 'watching machine' develops in conjunction with the war machine. Beginning with the use of film for aerial reconnaissance during the First World War, the cinematic *mise en scène* and later automation of warfare is as much a matter of serial images, sounds and rapid feedback of data, as it is of projectiles and missiles.

Virilio's sampling of communication technology spans the rotary press, telegraphy, photography, cinematography, radio, television, satellite, computers, the Internet, mobile phones and geomedia. With electronic media, the transmission of information and messages reaches the speed of light. He also emphasises the kinetic energy of the visible and the audible, which conditions the cinema, analogue television and computerisation. In science, photography and cinema, for instance, the visible and the invisible become the bases for the production of appearances as audiovisual technologies and electronic visualisation become ever more salient and widespread. In the succession of screens, buildings and national boundaries become porous, and a mediatised information milieu supplants traditional notions of territory as in the example of Google Earth. In the world of 'stereo-reality', then, presence is disqualified by teletechnology and telereality is deprived of tactility, physical contact, empathy and privacy. Lastly, planetary sites and their populations are subject to surveillance and traceability by orbiting satellites, global positioning systems and mobile phones.

Virilio's *The Art of the Motor* (1995 [1993]) offers two propositions about the industrial media complex. The first is that mediatisation replaces 'natural' conditions of communication, which gave us the ability to distinguish between our environment and our representations of it. Paradoxically, the media's power to orchestrate appearances and disappearances has grown to the detriment of its prerogative to dissimulate reality. Second, '*Speed* guarantees the secret and thus the *value* of all information' (*AM*, 53). The military and the media industry are then folded together because both are at war with time. For example, for the news media, it is duration that is the enemy because, says Virilio, news 'is dynamite, information explodes like a bomb, opinion polls or war propaganda are time bombs [. . .]' (*AM*, 24).

In Virilio's metaphysics, the reality of what exists was once directly perceived and unmediated, and its solidity and stability was grounded in the hardness of the Earth and in cyclical time. However, following the demonstration by German physicist Heinrich Hertz of James Clerk Maxwell's electromagnetic theory of light and the subsequent invention of the wireless telegraph, radio and television, a 'telereality' emerges and transforms the subjects and objects of representation. Over the twentieth century, Virilio argues, there has been a 'de-localisation' of space-time, a 'de-corporation' of the eye and a 'de-realisation' of reality. The globalising deterritorialisation of audiovisual media and telecommunications networks are characterised as a speeding-up process wherein contiguity is vanishing in favour of ubiquity, and duration is minimised in favour of instantaneity and simultaneity.

To summarise: for Virilio, media are vectors that displace people, objects, appearances, representations and ecology. The fabrication of speed – first by transport, later by transmission – has intensified. Automated media culture is the just-in-time delivery of electromagnetic waves that ends in a 'zero-stock' of artistic, political and juridical representation. The chief consequences of Virilio's *The Vision Machine* (1994b [1988]), for instance, are the standardisation of human perception, synchronisation of sensations and the narrowing of our field of vision. Optico-electronic mediatisation hides unmediated reality by proliferation, deception, reduction and contraction. In digital technoculture, connectivity and circulation further overrule the autochthony of the real. In Virilio's accelerated movie of hyperrealism and technoscience, we are all 'voyeur-voyagers' and 'terminal citizens' mobilised for an empire of speed and cybernetic control.

See also: Space-Time; Speed; Technology

MERLEAU-PONTY, MAURICE

Felicity Colman

The work of the French philosopher Maurice Merleau-Ponty (1908–61) provides a resonant core for all of Virilio's writings. Merleau-Ponty's research develops a specific philosophy of an active, corporeal-centric phenomenology, looking at the relationships between consciousness and the natural world, and, in doing so, his work challenges previously held categorical distinctions in philosophy. Merleau-Ponty's focus on an active, bodily phenomenology is continued in Virilio's writings – with distinction. Although his work is subject to the criticism that sensory analysis fails to grasp the (political) intentionality of perception, Merleau-Ponty challenges the idea of a passive synthesis of the experience and knowledge of the world that the reductive methods of Husserlian phenomenology championed. Nevertheless, while philosophers divide Merleau-Ponty's work into early and late positions, he worked on specifically Husserlian topics throughout his short life (he died aged 53), including the notion of the pre-philosophical, intentionality, the body, perception and consciousness. After the Second World War, during which time he served in the infantry and was a member of the French Resistance, Merleau-Ponty taught philosophy at the École Normale Supérieure and the Sorbonne. Until their political differences caused his break from existentialist philosophy (he is critical of Marxist social practices), Merleau-Ponty was co-founding editor with Jean-Paul Sartre of the journal *Les Temps modernes*, from 1945 to 1952. Merleau-Ponty's core published works include *The Structure of Behavior* (1984), *Phenomenology of Perception* (2002), *Humanism and Terror* (2000), *Adventures of the Dialectic* (1973) and the posthumously published *The Visible and the Invisible* (1969).

Virilio became interested in Merleau-Ponty's work after studying phenomenology under him at the Sorbonne. References to Merleau-Ponty's texts are to be found throughout Virilio's writings – with and without direct citation – but the inflection and nod toward his former teacher are readily identifiable through the language and phrasing of the core issues of Merleau-Ponty's work on phenomenology; perception and visibility, cognition (mind) and corporeality (body), information, language and thought, temporality and presence. There is a metaphysical movement that is engaged through such twinned ideas, a metaphysics that Virilio develops in his theory of dromology, that describes the relations between the social and the technological in a similar way to that in which Merleau-Ponty addresses consciousness and the natural world.

Merleau-Ponty's phenomenological position argues for the examination of the points of movement where co-constitutive relationships are formed, between consciousness and elements of the world. For example, Merleau-Ponty's *Adventures of the Dialectic* points to how a skilled worker cannot be a revolutionary within the institution that requires and thus validates their skill (1973 [1955], 106–7). Merleau-Ponty identifies this lack of ability to move out of this mind-set as institutionalised stasis, arguing: 'The will believes only in itself, it is its own source' (1973 [1955]: 106). Here, Merleau-Ponty raises two of the core issues for philosophy, namely the problem of the analysis of things (given in the proposition *what is x?*), and the description of the apprehension of *consciousness* (given by propositions concerning *x*). The history of the philosophy of phenomenology is located in multiple cultures, and wherever there is a study of the components of consciousness, these questions are repeatedly asked. In Western philosophy, phenomenological problems determine many different thinkers' approaches to consciousness, and the phenomenological beliefs of the first half of the twentieth century stand in marked contrast to the poststructuralist positions of the end of that century. Philosophy at the beginning of the twentieth century is marked by new investigations into modes of analyticity, and evidentiary epistemology, found in the work of Austrian philosopher and mathematician Edmund Husserl, from whom Merleau-Ponty develops much of his thinking. Husserl wanted to develop a more 'scientific' method for the reasoning of experience. He demonstrates how philosophy is in error through its practice of a subjective consciousness, which can be 'overcome' through a phenomenology attendant to the relativity of knowledge, derived by a continuous teleological method of reasoning. How to describe consciousness, and thus the consciousness of *x* (inclusive of all the things in the world and life itself) becomes an infinite philosophical problem of the propositions of thought derived from (yet often at odds with) lived experience. In a move now described as transcendentalism, Husserl describes how phenomenology is critical of philosophical positions that fail to recognise or properly account for this problem of the intentional state of something with its external referent. Working with and ultimately against such conservative ideas, Merleau-Ponty developed a philosophy of an active phenomenology. To solve the phenomenological problem of co-constitutive relationships, Merleau-Ponty locates subjectivity arising from corporeal response to its surroundings in the chiasmatic. This chiasm, or middle, is where constitutive elements move between mind and body, enabling thought (1969 [1964]: 259).

The subjectivity that Virilio addresses is also subject to the contradictory positioning of the body by the chiasms of possibility. However, in Virilio, political positions are determined by directed activities within dromoscopy, and are not controlled by human consciousness, but by the activities of institutions that control militarism, government and the economy. Thus also influential for Virilio's philosophy is how Merleau-Ponty's phenomenology describes perception as a physically determined grasp of sensory and sensed data of the physical and social of lived space. For example, Merleau-Ponty's concept of 'motor intentionality', or how the body responds and inhabits its environment through its sensory, potential energy, is a concept that Virilio addresses with many historically informed answers (e.g. Merleau-Ponty 2002 [1945]: 138–9 and Virilio's *The Art of the Motor* 1995 [1993]: 136). This body is the focus of Virilio's address of how information and perception determine and direct the body, as it is subject to the manipulations of zones of militarism and motorisation – but this subject is lacking the autonomy, or sense of belonging to a spatial and temporal zone that Merleau-Ponty's body holds as a 'flesh of the world' (1969 [1964]: 123). Through Merleau-Ponty, an interest in German phenomenologist Martin Heidegger and Husserl's respective positions on phenomenology and ideas concerning presence and foundational meanings are found in Virilio's work (e.g. *AM*, 142).

On the second page of *War and Cinema: The Logistics of Perception* (1989 [1984]), Virilio cites Merleau-Ponty: 'The problem of knowing who is the subject of the state and war will be of exactly the same kind as the problem of knowing who is the subject of perception.' This quote is taken from Merleau-Ponty (1969 [1964]: 196). Yet Virilio has only given the first part of the sentence. However, the final phrase by Merleau-Ponty is perhaps indicative of Virilio's contribution to the role that phenomenology holds in philosophy, as it reads: 'one will not clear up the philosophy of history except by working out the problem of perception' (1969 [1964]: 196). And it is precisely this 'working out' of Merleau-Ponty's phenomenology that is, arguably, one of Virilio's key contributions to the contemporary philosophy of the history and ongoing development of human perception.

See also: Body; Husserl, Edmund; Perception, Perspective; Phenomenology

MILITARY–INDUSTRIAL COMPLEX

Brianne Gallagher

The concept of the military–industrial complex signifies the policy and financial relations between lawmakers, national militaries, the defence and other industries. Such relations comprise political contributions, the authorisation of defence spending and the industrial lobbying of legislative bureaucracies and the armed forces. The idea refers to the industrial-political 'system' behind the United States military and was coined by President Dwight D. Eisenhower in his farewell address on 17 January 1961.

For Virilio, however, the notion of the military–industrial complex indicates the development of the state war enterprise and the historical effects of Western revolutions in military–industrial power. In *Speed and Politics: An Essay on Dromology* (2006 [1977]), for instance, he demonstrates how the military–industrial complex actually emerged in the nineteenth century, when bourgeois-capitalist power became increasingly militarised through the expertise of military engineers and the establishment of a permanent military class. For the accumulation of bourgeois-capitalist wealth in nineteenth-century Europe in particular demanded the creation of an enduring 'state of siege' that was secured through the production of fortified cities and the configuration of the countryside into a network of transportation routes for the movement and facilitation of the military. Hence the rise of the bourgeoisie as a political-economic class during this period was accompanied by a revolution in military thought that scientifically mapped the sociopolitical landscape of the countryside and urban centres as strategic nodes of a broader militarised system of state power and its exploitation of mass movement. Significantly, the masses of the new military proletariat were mobilised through the production of industrial artillery and by the expansion of machine warfare into the movements of everyday life.

Moreover, from the nineteenth century onwards, such military-capitalist apparatuses of territorial conquest were accompanied by the military class's effort to control the seas to aid the movement of Western armies and bodies between its urban centres and its colonies. The expansion of Western military power was henceforth conditioned by mastery of the spatial cartography of the land and the seas as well as by control of the revolutions in speed and technical innovations in transportation. For example, Great Britain became the 'first great industrial nation' not only because of its technical advancements in transportation but also owing to its increased capacity to manufacture engines (*SP*, 69). For Virilio, therefore, democracy is best understood as a 'dromocracy'; as a revolution of speed and a strategic endeavour by the state to maintain technological superiority.

Likewise, in *Popular Defense & Ecological Struggles* (1990 [1978]), Virilio illustrates how twentieth- and now twenty-first-century West European expansionism, military revolutions and industrialisation have led to the 'domination of space by speed', to the rise of a military–industrial proletariat, and to the state's search for 'pure power' or the means of absolute defence and absolute attack (*PD*, 31). The military–industrial complex is consequently the historical result of these Western revolutions in pure power, of the military class's total colonisation of space by time, and of the movement of bodies within and without militarised and industrialised organisations such as the state. Somewhat distinct from Eisenhower's comprehension, then, Virilio's understanding of the military–industrial complex emphasises its dismantling of the unity of space and time, its inauguration and perpetuation of a militarised 'war of time' and its increasingly industrial management of the everyday movements of civilian populations (*PD*, 50).

MILITARY SPACE

Brianne Gallagher

A military field of action wherein according to Virilio's *Bunker Archeology* (1994a [1975]: 17–26) the armed forces reconfigure social space as a space of territorial, aerial and seaborne control through the deployment of a 'hierarchy of speeds', various projectiles and vehicles. Military space is then conditioned by historical shifts in the locus of power from the low speeds and infrastructural milieu of the pre-industrial era to the high-speed projectiles and vehicles of the industrial era. Significantly, projectiles and vehicles in the industrial age function not merely as objects in or of military space but, rather, as particles in or of a militarised field of 'energy' that destroys the space of the world (*BA*, 18).

Historically, the fortifications and the miniaturisation of weapons technologies during the industrial epoch led to a reduction of obstacles and distances within military space. Meanwhile, aeronautics and the deterritorialisation of the atmosphere through the production of the speeding fighter jet laden with bombs reduced the specificity and primacy of land forces. Moreover, the conquest of space through satellite and digital communication technologies has created a sense of an artificial space that has transformed how the military occupies time and space. For example, soldiers today rarely engage in face-to-face combat as a means of conquering the enemy but, instead, engage in combat at a distance as a way of defeating both the infinitely small spaces of nuclear physics and the never-ending large spaces of the cosmos (*BA*, 18). Hence, the increased speed of weapons technologies throughout the industrial period has led to a radical transformation of military space and the means of violence.

Yet these historical revolutions in industrialisation, military architecture, technoscience and communication networks in the industrial era not only reconfigured the spatial dimensions of modern warfare but also the temporal dimensions of contemporary conflict. For while the decreased time of modern warfare demands the continuous innovation and production of new weapons technologies during 'peacetime', it also insists on the temporal presence of more 'primitive' combat strategies and tactics. For instance, according to Virilio (*BA*, 22), the 'Oriental military-rural apparatus' tends to increase the time of war, as evidenced by the military structures and methods of combat used by the Vietcong during the Vietnam War (1959–75). Thus, while the 'time of war tends to disappear' with the 'Occident military apparatus', it is prolonged by the 'Oriental military-rural-apparatus' because the latter seeks to extend the time of war into the everyday life of the masses (*BA*, 22). Consequently, military space is dually constituted by the spatial and temporal co-presence of these sometimes competing military apparatuses, effectively blurring the supposed boundaries between the state of war and the state of peace.

MODERNITY, MODERNISM

Mark Featherstone

Although there are competing interpretations of the concept of modernity, arguably the dominant understanding is that of Karl Marx (Antonio 2002) so eloquently rearticulated by Marshall Berman (2010) in his *All That is Solid Melts Into Air: The Experience of Modernity*. For Marx and for Berman, modernity entails the dissolution of pre-modern social structures and cultural systems and the emergence of new social arrangements and cultural organisations based on the modernisation of science and technology, on rationality, progress and, primarily, on capitalism or that economic system founded on private ownership of the means of production and the making of goods or services for profit.

Yet the development of modernity also had cultural systemic effects, which are usually discussed under the rubric of modernism, which was itself a series of movements and set of cultural tendencies in the arts arising from extensive changes to Western society in the nineteenth and twentieth centuries. Surrealism, for example, was a cultural movement that began in the 1920s, and is best known for its visual artworks and writings featuring elements of surprise and unexpected juxtapositions underpinned by a Marxian inflected revolutionary philosophy.

Virilio's perspective on modernity, most clearly expressed in his *Speed and Politics: An Essay on Dromology* (2006 [1977]), is that, unlike the stasis of pre-modernity, modernity is concerned with the exercise of a new freedom to move, of a socially motivated projection of the self in and through time understood as a desire for a kind of kinetic development. The Jacobins of the French Revolution (1789–99), for instance, at least according to Virilio, became the first 'dromomaniacs' or a movement obsessed with kinetic expansion. However, for Virilio, the paradox of the Jacobins is that they were at once utopians searching for the stasis of the ultimate end and fully committed to endless kinetic progress.

Virilio's conception of modernity also extends to modernism and, especially, to Futurism, which was a socio-artistic movement that originated in Italy in the twentieth century. Glorifying innovative themes including speed and technology, youth, violence and objects such as the car, the aeroplane and the industrial city, Futurism for Virilio represents all that is amiss with modern society and culture. Consider, for example, the Futurist Umberto Boccioni's 1913 sculpture *Unique Forms of Continuity in Space* in which he excitedly depicts humanity transformed into a high-speed machine.

Finally, Virilio's ethical concern for modern society and culture can also be illustrated through his many references to another sort of futurism, to Nazism as the fascist ideology of the Nazi Party and Nazi Germany that included both biological racism and anti-Semitism (e.g. Virilio 1989 [1984]. Here, Virilio emphasises the socio-cultural and political dynamics of Nazism, a dynamics anchored, like that of Futurism, in the 'need' to transcend the 'weakness' of the human body through ever-increasing speed, technology, and through the turning of human corporeality into little more than a technical object that heralds not merely the end of modernity and modernism but also of humanity itself.

MOVEMENT, MOBILITY

Felicity Colman

The movement of bodies is central to Virilio's philosophy. Movement is not just a method or action for him, rather Virilio uses the terms and types of movement as an ontological force that determines the world: the world is movement. This ontology becomes visible through the variations of movement processes. According to Virilio, capitalism accelerates human culture. This acceleration is a process that he characterises as life in a 'dromoscopy', the central tenet of which is movement, and its related products and processes, including the notions of speed, transformation, resistance, time, space and mobility. The differentiation between various forms, concepts and consequences of movement are characterised by Virilio as a metaphysics of movement. In this metaphysics, theory and practice are not separate entities. Virilio developed his method through his architectural practice and experience of real situations. He describes the modalities for addressing the 'dromoscopic', such as the modes of speed, as regulated by its compression, or the technologies that enable or disable acceleration. It is a metaphysics that is itself characterised by movement, a coupling of positions and an incorporation of the process of movement to form subsidiary and dominant components. This is different from a binary or dialectical movement; Virilio describes the complexities of global and large-scale historical, social and political organisations of societies, and how they are able to determine human activities down to the microscopic level of deciding what art forms to create, and how to direct the thinking and activities of daily consumption toward the biological and technological interests of capitalist control. Virilio argues in *The Art of the Motor* (1995 [1993]: 23) that the communications and information industries that feed biological and military events are a result of the movement of the world: 'Since movement creates the event the real is *kinedramatic*.'

The problems that arise for life under perpetual movement – dromoscopic life – are framed as different types of political problems in each of Virilio's books. Each problem has a different focus; perhaps of a political situation, such as the Kosovo War (1998–9) detailed in his *Strategy of Deception* (2000b [1999]) or the events of September 11 discussed in *Crepuscular Dawn* (Virilio and Lotringer 2002). Virilio's focus is often on active mobilisation in a response to a condition, such as his thesis in *Art and Fear* (2003a [2000]) where Virilio describes how the global regulation of information and activities of militarism have enfeebled certain forms of science, and thus stifled creativity. Through every examination of a *kinedrama*, movement serves as a method for analysis of the situation and condition; a metaphysical description of how perceptual consciousness is directed, shifted and accelerated between positions of control and states of equilibrium (death) in and over society (see, for example, Virilio's arguments in his *The Vision Machine* [1994b] [1988]). Virilio's focus for each problem is guided by various aspects of his metaphysics, as a process of movement where the elements involved are productive of a constituent state or circumstance. Society, for example, is produced by the relationships between the multiple elements that come to compose our everyday reality, including events as they impose themselves upon our human bodies, resulting in what Virilio describes as '*the acceleration of human mutation*' (*CD*, 65). He describes how we do not have a singular body, but a constituted, 'territorial body' that is 'irrigated' by 'electricity and the energy revolution' (*CD*, 102–3). The movement of analogical moments of life, argues Virilio, is thus subject to a number of forces. An example of this is where he details the daily, economic and political reasons why the 'ethnic cleansing' of the Kosovar people was 'speeded up' (*SD*, 29).

Virilio's metaphysics of movement includes a range of comparative observations, themes, topics and events. These include (but are not limited to) the following: the mechanics of perceptual motion *and* intervention; experience of phenomena in mobility *and* perception of that experience; empirical memory *and* history's detailing; the concepts of dromocratic mobility; gendered mobility, repetition *and* potential radicalisation; aesthetic movements of art *and* life; radical possibilities *and* conservative reality.

The points at which speed may be discerned in society are also those where movement has been highlighted, or halted in some way. For instance, Virilio describes dwellings, cities and architectural forms as causing a 'slowing down' of history and bodies – through the enclosure, containment and restriction of movement (*CD*, 66–7). While some bodies are contained by the city, others are moved around for work, or others removed to peripheral positions (Virilio 2005a [1984]: 194–5). In describing the points of resistance to the speeds and movement of capitalism, Virilio offers a provocation to the process, suggesting methods for intervention in the flows of capital. For example, art forms of literature provide evidence, argues Virilio, of the 'power of *movement in action*', as a 'metaphysical poetics' (Virilio 1994b [1988]: 28). Virilio singles out the differences in biologically determined gendered mobility as moments where the dromoscopy fails or could be made to fail. He notes that activities of militarisation at different events lose their men due to enforced deprivations leading to loss of life (see, for example, *AM*, 82). Virilio offers a historical materialist perspective on the points at which capitalism allowed a speeding up of the female worker, while retaining her biological capacity to reproduce more workers and soldiers for the capitalist machine. His highlighting of woman as the first transport for man provides an example of where Virilio's argument concerning the technologisation of all humans describes how all things become dromoscopic devices at the service of capital (Conley 2000).

Virilio's work details countless examples of the histories of the movement and affective mutations of the human body in societies obsessed with their capitalist appearances and pursuits. Describing how perception arises and is given form, he explores different instances of bodies in motion, and the sensing of this motion (with Virilio, sense refers to both French language meanings of *sens*: the corporal senses and direction). The notions of movement and mobility provide both the metaphysical framework and critique of dromology. The spatial transformations of the world through dromocracy's velocity that refigures the human body and the possibility of a habitable society are singled out by Virilio as technological affects that control the bodies and the societies that humans continue to occupy.

See also: Body; Dromoscopy; Speed

N

NEGATIVE HORIZON

George Katsonis

A profoundly extensive concept in Virilio's phenomenological critique of speed, his idea of the negative horizon pertains to the perversion of vision within the accelerated perspective. Introduced in Virilio's *Negative Horizon: An Essay in Dromoscopy* (2005a [1984]), his notion animates simultaneously the forced negation and cinematic substitution through acceleration of the objective horizon of human sensible reality and a daring interrogation of the negative in its effective, affective and ontological topologies.

Virilio's revelation that speed is the new void culminates in the negative horizon of the desert, which facilitates the distorted quest for absolute acceleration and its surface visual effects: for not only does the desert serve the negative horizon of accelerated perspective as a reflective surface but the surface itself becomes a compulsive or sought-after void wherein all visual extension dissipates and a luminous mirage of horizontal speed erupts as a corporeal, vertiginous, illusion. 'At the height of desertification,' Virilio writes, 'the fascination with the negative horizon amounts to exhausting the last resource of space: the void' (*NH*, 146).

Questioning the harmful aspects of displaced perspective, Virilio concentrates on the results, influences and ontological topography of movement-power or the sometimes surprising relationships between speed and the void. Accordingly, his account of the negative horizon and of the accelerated dynamics of displaced perspective in the desert and elsewhere proceeds by a historical series (i.e. woman–horse–motor), a sort of zoophilous archaeology of movement-power, which Virilio utilises to illustrate the organisation of human cultures in an accelerated frame. For, ever since the invention of the horse and rider, the desire of humanity has been a desire for the displaced perspective of the desert, for the negative horizon of human subjectivity and for a form of movement-power that offers the effect if not the reality of accelerated escape, a form of perception that intensifies reflective surface forms to the detriment of the non-reflective ground, that repulses matter, mass and human-centred vision in the name of the surface and of the void, of virtual imagery, light speed and, ultimately, of total delusion.

Consequently, Virilio (*NH*, 105) denounces the desertification wrought by the negative horizon of the void and, especially, the damaging displaced viewpoint of the car windscreen where 'perspective becomes animated' and the 'vanishing point becomes a point of attack sending forth its lines of projection onto the voyeur-voyager'. Focusing on the outcomes, changes and ontological impact of such topologies of movement-power, Virilio highlights the relationship between the speeding technological vehicle that is the motor car and the emerging void at the heart of the metabolic vehicle that is the human body:

Let us disabuse ourselves of any illusions, we are here before the true 'seventh art', that of the dashboard. Opposite to the *stroboscopy* which allows us to observe objects animated by rapid movement, as if they were in slow motion, this *dromoscopy* displays inanimate objects as if they were animated by a violent movement. (*NH*, 105)

Moving through the accelerated dynamics and displaced perspective that are humanity's desertified fantasies and beyond the history of woman and of the horse, Virilio invokes the contemporary history of the movement-power of the motor as the negative horizon of the seventh art, which entails the organisation of mass human transport, mass cultural communication and the accelerated perspective of a dromoscopy driven by the ferocity of speed.

Yet Virilio does not believe that history is destiny and concentrates on the power of resistance as a way of diverting humanity from its present visual destination. No longer concerned with the horse and rider, he asks us to question our own desire for the displaced perspective of the desert, for the negative horizon of a form of movement-power that brings only surface effects, the nothingness of the void and the illusion of an accelerated escape from the confines of human perception.

OPTICS

Drew S. Burk

Virilio's work has always been interested in showing the relationship between vision and the war machine. Any novel invention with regard

to viewing whether it be in gaining an advantage over the enemy via the
creation of the telescope, to see the enemy coming from a distance, or the
discovery of depth perspective via artistic innovations such as those found
in the Italian quattrocento, are all first and foremost militarised.

Virilio's *War and Cinema: The Logistics of Perception* (1989 [1984]) and
The Vision Machine (1994b [1988]) use the examples of hot-air balloons
with cameras attached to obtain aerial photos of the enemy dating back to
the American Civil War and leading to the aviation photos and radar technologies of the Second World War where viewing is completely handed
over to technological vision machines. In these instances, the innovations
in viewing were based on novelties in perceiving images. Today, according
to Virilio, we are witnessing a movement from a militarisation of the image
to the militarisation of the optical field of vision. This is quite a leap within
not only how one views or perceives reality, but also in how one views the
construction of reality *tout court*. As increasingly predictive cybernetic
networks strive to 'pre-see', that is, to break through the walls between
the past, the present and the future, distance and duration are obliterated
and replaced by an instantaneous field of vision that predicates itself not
on objectivity or subjectivity but on what Virilio names tele-objectivity
and tele-subjectivity. This machinic vision of collectively viewing actuality from an illusory prefabricated distance based on viewing actuality via
a screen is no longer merely a question of a shift in the perspective of
images, but in the entire process of seeing itself. Namely, today, we must
begin to deal with the consequences of a shift in the construction of the
optical field. And here, we enter into a realm where one must constantly
take into consideration what Virilio often calls, following the term 'politically correct', 'tele-optically correct' and a 'newspeak of the eyes'. We are,
then, no longer involved with the militarisation of the image by means of
technologies like the camera, but with a militarisation of the optical field.
Virilio maintains that in order to have optics, one must have the speed
of light. And, nowadays, we risk losing the visual field created using the
light speed of the sun, of the physical world, for the light speed of illusory
optics, of real-time technologies. Furthermore, this sort of novel real-time
vision becomes a purely optical phenomenon, which leads the one viewing
to no longer believe his or her own eyes. Virilio (2002b [2002]) uses the
instance of the September 11 catastrophe as a good example of this new
type of optical field where the event itself can only truly be perceived or
comprehended by the use of the screen and a collective real-time viewing.

A purely optical phenomenon, the real-time machinery creates a sort of
lens, grinding the information algorithms of corrected vision, of a stereo-
reality whose dividing line between the virtual and the actual becomes
blurred within a field of machine vision, of a cybernetic vision which

demands novel lens grinders, to grind the lenses for viewing within an optical field of corrected vision. Today, the fight begins for the perpetual installation of optical phenomena, controlling no longer the images of the real, but one's audiovisual relationship with the real itself.

ORBITAL SPACE

Gerry Coulter

Virilio's thought concerning space begins in war. He has long operated with the assumption that modernity is not only a machinic regime of reorganisation but also a vast multidimensional compression machine. Virilio contends that all of Europe, for example, was compressed into one vast city. The actual compression occurred through increasingly vast and restrictive regimes of regulation, including the processing of human movement through space. This process moved toward its apex during the Second World War when the entire continent of Europe was transformed into a fortress. Virilio became aware of this vital aspect of modern space early in life when, as a boy, he first encountered the bunkers left behind by the Germans near his home in Nantes, France.

As modernity changed our relationship to territorial space according to Virilio, today, we witness the scene of a new relationship to space – orbital space. Orbital space circumvents territorial space for Virilio and he became aware of this development while watching his television and reading his newspaper. Among the events that tipped Virilio's understanding of space toward the orbital was the 1990s' war in Kosovo: 'what we witnessed in Kosovo was an extraordinary war, a war waged solely with bombs from the air' (Virilio and Armitage 2000: 4). This was, he contends, a reversal of the kind of war that brought us Fortress Europe – which was a fortress without a roof. Today, we have, according to Virilio, 'a fortress without walls – but with a roof' (Virilio and Armitage 2000: 4). Further, orbital space is not a European invention but an American development by the Pentagon in Washington DC.

Orbital space, as such, represents a deepening of automated war – and of America's effort to achieve total global information dominance. Orbital space creates Fortress World – a world inside of computer networks, but which, like old Fortress Europe, has real implications for how we interact with/in space. Orbital space is extra-territorial precisely because movement is controlled by computer networks that depend upon an extensive system of satellite links which orbit the earth. An important part of this includes the global financial system, which has also become orbital. The currency of an independent country can be devalued to the point of collapse in one afternoon. Just as people flee from their homes in territorial wars, thousands fled their homes after the housing bubble (part of the orbiting global financial system) burst.

For Virilio, the contemporary financial crisis can be understood not as the exploding of a military bomb but of the information bomb. As such, the effects of orbital space can be as devastating as those of war in territorial space. As in territorial space and war, whoever controls orbital space also 'possesses' it. Orbital space, then, is a theoretical device deployed by Virilio to understand America's recent effort to return to the position of global dominance it held when it was the sole atomic nation. For Virilio, resistance to orbital space and efforts to control it are hampered (if not defeated) by the lack of widespread technoscientific knowledge among the peoples of the world.

ORIGINAL ACCIDENT

Nick Prior

To interrogate the accident is to show, following Aristotle (2002), how the particular characteristics of an entity reveal its substance or essence. Virilio reverses this formulation because the invention of any substance is at one and the same time the invention of a distinct accident associated with its essence. Hence, just as the shipwreck is the by-product – the futurist invention – of the ship, so the air disaster is the hidden production of the airliner. The tragedy of modernity resides in its progressive inability to tame progress, resulting in the mass production of accidents.

In the absence of the science of the accident, Virilio proposes not merely a dromological programme, but a Museum of Accidents. This would be a place for the exhibition of technoscience's powerlessness to control itself and while never being built took inchoate form in Virilio's (2003b [2002]) exhibition of accidents at the Fondation Cartier pour l'art Contemporain in Paris in 2003. For Virilio, such acts of exhibitionary disclosure can transform the element of surprise of the accident into an automatic immanence and open up an intelligent awareness of the shadow of progress.

But what would the inventory of accidents include? Virilio is relatively indiscriminate: it would include ecological catastrophes and everyday incidents, happy accidents and terrorist attacks, those involving transport and those involving complex computer systems. Typological distinctions are present, however, in Virilio's characterisation of various categories of accident.

The integral accident (Chernobyl) opposes the local accident (*Titanic*) in its scale and impact. The integral accident is eschatological and global, extending into future geographies and timescapes while fuelling the apocalyptic scenarios of disaster movies and horror films. It necessitates a kind of consciousness and action befitting a new political movement, what Virilio terms in *The Original Accident* 'an eschatological party' (2007a [2005]: 40). The integral accident is the endless accident that integrates us and disintegrates us.

The original accident, on the other hand, is associated with the invention of a new technological artefact, process or motor, 'the equivalent of the first ship-wreck of the very first ship' (*OA*, 10). As the space shuttle *Challenger* explodes, so begins a new domain of failure attached to this mode of transport. As the nuclear containment vessel at Chernobyl ruptures, so a new style of accident in time is generated which pollutes the future, necessitating novel techniques of amelioration, in this case a huge concrete 'sarcophagus' to act as a barrier against time. In short, with every technological discovery comes an innovation in its breakdown, a new way of failing, contaminating and destroying. But each effort at improving the fallout of progress is countered by a newer threat generated by the same impulse. Just as the bunker is built in Chernobyl, so too are weapons designed by the US military to destroy these very bunkers.

Virilio calls for a temporal and conceptual reversal of the original accident by first inventing, or imagining, the accident to determine the substance to which it relates. To begin with the accident is not merely to reverse engineer the cause, but to potentially forestall future disasters and allow for a degree of forward planning for what would otherwise be inevitable.

OVEREXPOSED CITY

Scott McQuire

Virilio uses this term to describe the contemporary urban condition in which telematics increasingly defines power and access in urban space. The overexposed city is one in which ubiquitous electronic oversight triumphs over traditional forms of architectural space and urban enclosure.

Virilio introduced the concept in his landmark essay 'The Overexposed City' (1991 [1984]: 9–28). His general argument is that electronic networks progressively recalibrate the operation of traditional spatial boundaries at all levels, from the scale of the room to the division between country and city, right up to the delineation of the nation-state as a distinctive geographical territory. With the advent of electronic media, the city finds itself reframed by a new technological space-time in which the modes of spatial delimitation, security and access once granted by walls, doorways and gates, are displaced by media protocols.

Virilio posits three distinct trajectories contributing to this transformation of the city. The first is the transport revolution initiated by mechanical vehicles of rail and road. Its urban impact became manifest in various urban 'modernisation' projects designed to 'open up' the city and promote greater mobility, beginning with Paris in the 1850s. Automobility and the reconstruction of cities to accommodate the car confirm this mode of urban exposure dedicated to circulation. The second trajectory is the Modernist revolution in architecture, in which steel and concrete construction enabled the transformation of the archetypal city building from a solid, load-bearing structure to a soaring tower clad with glass curtain walls. For the Modernist avant-garde, glass architecture was synonymous with overcoming the constraints of the past; it constituted a welcome form of exposure thought to create a new 'openness' in social and political life.

The third trajectory, and the one that establishes overexposure as a definitive urban condition, is the communication revolution entrained by electronic media. The distinctiveness of Virilio's concept lies partly in its critique of the previous understandings of 'exposure' enabled by new forms of urban circulation and transparency. He argues that electronic media produce a tipping point in the urban milieu, in which the ubiquity of the screen interface erodes traditional distinctions between 'here' and 'there'. In this context, what Virilio regards as the properly human characteristics of place, based on the relative stability of physical dimensions, give way to a state of growing confusion.

While Virilio initially develops the problematic of overexposure in relation to electronic media, and especially television, the trajectory belongs as much, if not more, to digital networks. Thus, the mobile phone, and the enhanced capacity for spatialising information and providing 'real-time' feedback loops, is a critical element of urban overexposure in his more recent work.

Overexposure is closely related to other key themes in Virilio's work, notably the paradoxical 'inertia' of the city-dweller whose mobility is increasingly screen-based. It is also closely connected to Virilio's master trope of speed. The overexposed city is the urban space in which the management of speed and the administration and sequencing of time become the equivalent of older territorial strategies.

P

PERCEPTION

Jason Adams

Virilio's concept of perception begins with that developed by his teacher and mentor Maurice Merleau-Ponty, in his magnum opus, *Phenomenology of Perception* (2002 [1945]). In that work, perception is figured in contradistinction to the Platonic assumption that perception is only valid insofar as a distinction is maintained between mind and body, self and world, and the world and the realm of pure forms. Merleau-Ponty argues, in short, that all previous theories of perception have remained Platonist to the extent that they fail to consider the primacy of perception as lived experience, prior to second-order theorising about it. In other words, his approach to perception is a materialist rather than an idealist one, in that the perceptual field is always constituted by the interconnection of mind, body *and* world.

The experience of time that is one of Virilio's central concerns, then, and which he often conceptualises as speed, is filtered by the mind–body intertwining with the world, which constitutes a perceptual field in accordance with the qualities of a particular place and time. Thus, Virilio extends the primacy of perception found in Merleau-Ponty, just as Merleau-Ponty extends it from the phenomenological philosopher Edmund Husserl, considering the political significance of the technocultural alteration of the perceptual field. What he discovers, in summary, is that acceleration of communication and transportation speeds leads to a space–time compression that disrupts all previous instantiations of the mental environment, or what he (2009b) calls 'grey ecology'. Far from simply advocating a return to autonomous, embodied perception, however, Virilio takes the primacy of the perceptual field as a given throughout his analyses.

What he questions specifically is the often-unwarranted optimism about the cultural and political effects of contemporary vision technologies. Particularly in a period in which the technocultural habitus that co-constitutes mind–body experience is accelerating at an ever-greater pace, Virilio argues that the necessity of maintaining a critical perspective on the current and possible future effects of such developments is more crucial than ever. This can be seen in that one of his primary topics is the manner in which accelerated speeds are more often than not triggered by

the instantaneous financial transactions required by the globalised political economy as well as the ultra-rapid communication and transportation
relays necessitated by a planetary military apparatus.

One recent example of how the perceptual field has been altered in the
latter respect is the diffusion of Unmanned Aerial Vehicles (UAVs) within
global military zones, both externally and internally to the hegemonic
nation-states. What they produce in Virilio's account is a cinematisation
of the landscape, an overall militarisation of vision that changes the nature
of the cultural and political ecology just as it does the perceptual field with
which it forms a world. This is also the case, moreover, for those with as
well as for those without access to its renderings, although in an uneven
manner. Militarised vision in particular is predicated upon militarised
space-time in general. For Virilio, that means the acceleration of technological speed so as to collapse geographical difference, thereby subjecting
it to a more complete military dominance.

Virilio traces this specific training of perception to the American
Civil War (1861–5) in *War and Cinema: The Logistics of Perception* (1989
[1984]), in which aerial photography was first militarised, as the Union
mounted cameras and other optical devices on balloons. This early process
set in motion the development of more advanced reconnaissance planes
used in the First and Second World Wars, although, at the time, UAVs
were still only used to a limited extent. After the U-2 bomber was shot
down in 1960 by the USSR, the US Air Force expanded its programme
so that by the close of the Vietnam War (1959–75), over 3,000 pilotless
UAV missions had been dispatched, returning the data to IBM centres
in South East Asia. Rather than direct vision constituting the perceptual
field, Virilio (*WC*, 11) says, 'in the space of a hundred and fifty years, the
target area had become a cinema "location", the battlefield a film set out of
bounds to civilians'.

This, then, is why perception is of such political significance for Virilio.
As he sees it, the increasing acceleration of communication and transportation technologies privilege those positioned at the apex of national and
international hierarchies, providing their dominance over spatial as well
as temporal experience. Since the entire perceptual field is reordered by
technoculture, its very ubiquity is also what ensures its imperceptibility.
By drawing out the negative effects of acceleration on perception, Virilio
asserts that he opens up the possibility of contesting it, of reconstituting it otherwise. This, therefore, is why he holds that the greatest threat
to the dominant mode of perception today is the emergence of a new
Renaissance, the reintroduction of perspective into what has become
increasingly experienced as a form of objective perception that cannot be
questioned.

Virilio's emphasis on perspective derives, however, from the first Renaissance: the quattrocento of fifteenth-century Italy. His primary reference in this respect is Paolo Uccello, who, he argues, introduced perspective into Western visual culture by breaking with the objectivity of absolute space that prevailed up until that point and asserting the lived, experiential disjuncture of 'real space' (see, for example, Armitage and Bishop 2013). Just as idealist spatiality was contested half a millennium ago, Virilio argues that what is needed these days is a new materialist assertion of perspective with respect to contemporary temporal objectivism, derived from the perspective of 'real time'. Rather than simply refusing technology altogether, this would be achieved by contesting the ordering of the perceptual field in the interstices between time as it is imposed from above and time as it is experienced from below.

Thus, at this point, we can return to the practical question of the UAVs: in contrast to the 1960s and even in contrast to just a few years ago, nowadays consumer-grade drones can be acquired online for a low price, allowing the population at large to engage in their own surveillance and cinematisation of the landscape. But does this constitute the critical introduction of a real-time perspective into the temporal perceptual field in Virilio's sense? Not if doing so simply means using existing technology without thinking through the full implications of doing so, or how one might rework it in more self-determined ways. This is because, for Virilio, as for Merleau-Ponty before him, the reintroduction of perspective into perception requires working with the perceptual field as a whole: mind, body *and* world.

See also: Husserl, Edmund; Merleau-Ponty, Maurice; Space-Time; Speed; Technology

PHENOMENOLOGY

Ian James

The reference to phenomenological thought, and in particular that of Edmund Husserl (1859–1938) and of Maurice Merleau-Ponty (1908–61), permeates all of Virilio's thinking about bodily perception and experience. This reference is often explicit, however, as in texts such as *L'insécurité du territoire* (1993), *The Lost Dimension* (1991 [1984]) and *The Vision Machine* (1994b [1988]), and is nowhere more decisive than in *Polar Inertia* (2000a [1990]). Virilio's characterisation of polar inertia in this work is derived from his reading of Husserl's short 1930s' piece 'The Earth Does Not

Move', which is a satellite text of his *The Crisis in European Sciences and Transcendental Phenomenology* (1970). His engagement with phenomenology needs therefore to be understood in the context of Husserl's attempt in *The Crisis* to account for the rise of the technological worldview and of calculative thinking in Europe since the time of Galileo and, against the abstractions of technoscientific thinking, to rediscover the world of sense perception which constitutes our everyday activities and worldly engagements.

The phenomenological attempt to recover a 'first world' of primordial sense perception is articulated by Husserl around an analysis of what he terms 'kinaesthetic immobility'. According to this analysis, the human body at rest is understood as a fixed 'zero point' of our perceptual orientation towards a world. This zero point needs to be understood as absolute insofar as all worldly perception occurs with reference to the fixed orientation of the body at rest and insofar as all subsequent movement or displacement is experienced only with reference to that fixed orientation. In this context the earth beneath our feet must be understood not simply as one terrestrial body among so many other terrestrial bodies, but rather as the ground upon which our perception is oriented in the first instance. Similarly the sky above our heads would also be a primary horizon of perceptual orientation which, along with the ground upon which we stand, form the key axes according to which the primordially fixed stance of the body can experience movement through space, or any spatial apprehension of horizontal or vertical displacement. The phenomenological fundamentals of temporal presence, of worldly situatedness, of the body proper and of what Virilio himself calls 'the ego-centredness of being' (*PI*, 73) can all be seen to flow from the analysis of kinaesthetic immobility given by Husserl.

Similarly Virilio's own analysis of the transformation of spatial and temporal perception by modern technologies of transport, transmission and communication all flow from this Husserlian account. In particular, Virilio develops his understanding of polar inertia with reference to the development of rocket technology from the V2 experimentations carried out by the Third Reich in the late stages of the Second World War through to the space and Moon landing projects pursued by the US in the post-war period. The ability to transport bodies vertically through space, to place them on *another ground* (that of the Moon) and to take this other ground as a centre of perception effectively dissolves the axes of orientation which have up until the mid-twentieth century underpinned human apprehension of space, movement and time. Virilio understands the acquisition of a supplementary ground above our heads as paradigmatic for the way in which modern technology no longer allows us to take the first ground of the Earth and the originary arc of the sky as the primordial points of reference for bodily perception. According to his account, the loss of a ground of reference for the body leads directly to the loss of a traditional time of reference, that of temporal presence and the rootedness of time perception in an experience of duration centred upon real, lived presence.

The reference to rocket technology in *Polar Inertia* is exemplary of the way in which Virilio sees modern technologies of high-speed transport, instantaneous global transmission (by satellite, World Wide Web, etc.) and the real-time realities of digital and information technology, as effectively uprooting or deracinating perceptual experience and leading to a kind of immobilisation of the human body. His understanding of 'speed-space' is directly related in *Polar Inertia* to his engagement with Husserl's 'The Earth Does Not Move' essay. The loss of the first ground of the earth and originary arc of the sky means that our experience of places and movement between places, and the temporal rhythm or experience of space and time that accompanies this, is transformed into a speed-space defined by the temporal and spatial delays of technological transmission and transfer. The lengthy and infinitely variable spatial and temporal delays and deferrals imposed by earlier technologies (those of walking horse or sea travel for example) are replaced by the quasi-instantaneous delays and deferrals of high-speed transmission leading to a decline in the depth and richness of our real bodily spatial and temporal engagements.

It is in this context that Virilio comes to speak of an immobilisation of the body and a 'behavioural inertia'. If the body can be transported in a seated position at high speed across global distances, and if communication across those distances can occur instantaneously without bodily displacement, we are increasingly positioned within a sphere of activity freed from the limitations of our environment, but free also from using the bodily capacities that would allow us to overcome those limitations. In short, we approach the immobility of disability. Thus the polar inertia of which Virilio speaks, the loss of presence of which he warns, the virtualisation of space which he fears, and the bodily incapacitation which we may well already be in the process of collectively undergoing, are all understood from the phenomenological perspective first elaborated by Husserl and taken up later by the likes of Merleau-Ponty.

If, during the heyday of structuralism and poststructuralism, phenomenology was thought to have been consigned to a philosophical past, Virilio's assimilation of phenomenological thought demonstrates its ongoing pertinence and contemporaneity. For Virilio, it is the phenomenological perspective that may allow us to think ways of recovering a lost ground and thereby to step back from the void which modern technology opens beneath our feet.

See also: Body; Husserl, Edmund; Merleau-Ponty, Maurice; Perception, Perspective; Space-Time; Technology

PICNOLEPSY

Sean Cubitt

There is, according to Virilio, a medical condition called picnolepsy, a relative of epilepsy and narcolepsy. The word comes from the Greek root *leps-*, the future form of the verb 'to grasp or seize', and *picnos*, which means 'frequency'. Sufferers from the condition undergo brief episodes in which they are unconscious of their surroundings or actions. The term might apply more broadly to what drivers sometimes call 'automatic pilot': travelling a familiar route without noticing the time pass, surprised suddenly to find yourself at home without recalling how you got there. In *The Aesthetics of Disappearance* (2009a [1980]), picnolepsy is especially related to the automobile. We should credit Virilio with hearing the homophony of the 'auto', whose root meaning is 'self' ('automobile', mixing Greek and Latin, means 'self-moving'): the car only apparently obeys its driver; in fact, it is an automaton which its driver serves, not necessarily consciously.

There is another modern word that shares the grammatical misfortune of a mixture of Greek and Latin: television ('far-seeing', as in the German *Fernseh*). Television and film share with later digital imaging technologies a dependence on a kind of picnolepsy, one that brings us much closer to the etymology of *picnos*. Film is the easiest to understand. The 'phi effect' on which cinematic projection depends is the psychologists' term for the brain's ability to connect frames by interpolating imaginary movements between two disparate images. Shown two slides of a circle, one on the left and one on the right of a dark background, most observers will describe the circle as moving from one position to the other. Mistakenly called 'persistence of vision' in early literature, the phi effect, it could be argued, is like the experience of driving on automatic pilot: we invent a transition from place A to place B that we have not experienced. The frequency, however, of the momentary lapses between film frames lasts less than a twenty-fourth of a second.

That frequency is greatly increased in television, not only because it runs at twenty-five frames per second, but because broadcast TV, until very recently, used a combination of fields and frames to construct the flow of images. Each frame was analysed into two fields, corresponding to the odd and even lines of the cathode ray tube's scanning of the screen area. The 'odd' field (comprising lines 1, 3, 5, 7 and so on) filed first, before the scan recommenced on the 'even' field (2, 4, 6, 8, etc.). As the second scan began, the first was already beginning to fade; equally, as the 'odd' field of the next image began to scan, the remnant of the previous image was still fading from the bottom of the screen.

The interruption, in the case of film, is clearly marked on the filmstrip itself as a black area between frames, whose passage through the projector is made invisible by the repetitive closing of a shutter, which opens only to show the unmoving frame. Raymond Bellour (1990, 1999) refers to these phenomena as 'l'entre-images', the 'between-images' which, as absence, plays a structuring role in the production of cinematic illusion, whether of space or of narrative or its fundamental presumption, the continuity of time. As discrete entities, film frames partition time into discrete, static, moments. The operation of the shutter is a sleight of hand disguising this division into fragments, teaching those who become habituated to ignore these interruptions in temporal flow.

Electronic images try to overcome the problem of jerking between frames at first through the mechanism of fields in the process described above, known as interlacing. Since Virilio wrote *The Aesthetics of Disappearance* in 1980, there has been a proliferation of digital video including Internet (streaming, downloads, torrents, etc.), handheld devices (games consoles, tablets and smartphones), DVD and Blu-ray distribution media, and high-definition television (e.g. digital terrestrial and satellite broadcasting) among them. All these media share a set of standard protocols, known as codecs (compression–decompression), for handling the image streams. The dominant MPEG-4 codec not only scans the image (progressively, i.e. without fields) but divides it into separate areas known as blocks (4 × 4 pixels), macroblocks (4 × 4 blocks), groups of blocks or GoBs (4 × 4) macroblocks, in a hierarchy. These units (which can also be analysed in more irregular shapes called slices) are used in association with another technique called key-framing. Each sequence of images is analysed into short fragments by seeking out moments when a major change occurs (such as at an edit, but also if a camera pan moves from dark to light). During compression, the beginning and end of each segment is marked as a key-frame, and the key-frames's breakdown into the block hierarchy compared. Areas that seem not to change are stripped of their detail. A further technique simplifies transitions between key-frames (e.g. changes of lighting or the positions of objects) by interpolating a movement from position A to position B. Thus digital video replaces cinematic division with a new formalisation of the image stream. It takes as units not individual frames but segments of the flow. Within segments, it strips out the visual information in the middle of the sequence, replacing it with an invented (and simplified) transition between static states.

Virilio used the example of in-flight entertainment as a system for ensuring that airline passengers should not actually experience their journeys: picnolepsy as transport technology, imagining a further enhancement in which passengers would simply be drugged and awake at their destinations oblivious to their journeys. He could hardly have foretold that the technological aesthetic of the screens mounted in aircraft would reproduce and automate this narcosis, dividing first the time of experience into fragments, then analysing the fragment into scans, fields and blocks, and, finally, organising transitions between them not just as erasures (under the rotating blade of the cine-projector's shutter) but as rewritten memories in the form of key-frame technologies. Inattention to experience has never been solely a medical condition: every child has to be taught to watch where they're going, and whole societies have been required to learn how to concentrate (Crary 1999). Virilio's picnoleptic analysis suggests, however, that the mechanised and digitised erasure of experience that he calls the disappearance of reality is very specific to our epoch.

See also: Aesthetics of Disappearance; Real Time; Technology

PITILESS ART

Joy Garnett

In his lecture 'A Pitiless Art' in *Art and Fear* (2003a [2000]), Virilio begins by talking about the pitiful or pitiless nature of contemporary art, and then stops to wonder why no one ever asks: *'but contemporary with what?'* (*AF*, 27). That 'what', is, of course, our less-than-whole, post-war, human condition. In suggesting that the peace achieved in defeating the Nazi terror actually comprises and extends that terror in innumerable, insidious and indiscernible ways, Virilio posits an 'aesthetics of disappearance' whereby the body is subtly dehumanised, and all that is human is denigrated *without pity*, from within. In quoting the nineteenth-century French poet Charles Baudelaire, '*I am the wound and the knife*,' Virilio (*AF*, 29) asserts that contemporary art after the Second World War represents neither critique nor palliative to our state of continued cultural disarray, but rather constitutes a non-cognisant expression of our post-war, still-catastrophic, state of being. In other words, we are our time, each and every day.

Virilio inserts his discussion of 'A Pitiless Art' into the debate over contemporary art's relevance and its perceived 'awfulness'. This is not an assessment of contemporary art's terrorising aspects, nor a measurement of its piety or lack of it; rather, Virilio's approach to the art of our era is one that acknowledges its resounding lack of empathy or innate 'pity' regarding humanity, and posits the notion that contemporary art instead offers a figurative and metaphorical analogue to literal terror and terrorism.

Our pitiless contemporary art, then, according to Virilio, offers more evidence of the gaping wound left by our collective experience of the Second World War, an experience we have not fully acknowledged or accepted, nor have we engaged it philosophically as the authentic source and progenitor of our present condition. And because we cannot detach ourselves sufficiently from this state of obliviousness, we remain unable to stand outside or see beyond ourselves. Hence, our contemporary artists remain unable to see or acknowledge themselves as either wound or knife. Instead, contemporary post-war art flounders in oblivion, incapable of pity or empathy, and, by extension, incapable of self-love. Sustaining so heavy a burden of complicity – of culpability – for crimes against humanity, contemporary art has come to embody 'a pitiless art' in Virilio's eyes, one that leans on glib cynicism and a refined sense of irony in its attempt to escape the humiliation and culmination of misery in earnest self-destruction. However, as Virilio points out, citing the twentieth-century suicides of Paul Celan and Mark Rothko, often it is literal suicide and self-annihilation that go hand-in-hand with the figurative murder and self-mutilation that contemporary art has come to comprise. In other words, self-destructive metaphors and positions of intellectual nihilism are in fact contiguous with the literal suicide of both the individual and even the state (Auschwitz; Hiroshima).

Virilio (*AF*, 50) opines, quoting George Bernanos, that 'The world is sick, a lot sicker than people realize. That's what we must first acknowledge *so that we can take pity on it* [. . .] *The world needs pity.*'

In distinguishing an art that is full of pity, an art capable of illustrating atrocity (Grünewald's Isenheim Altarpiece; Picasso's *Guernica*), from an art that embodies it (Saatchi's Young British Artists), Virilio employs the terms 'demonstrative' versus 'monstrative', and names contemporary art as an art of 'presentation' as opposed to 'representation', noting that we have become slaves to real time, that is, we are wed to our new capability to express ourselves only in the moment of the absolute present. We are rendered incapable of the kind of sustained effort of reflection that leads to empathy and self-knowledge; hence we are deprived of the capacity to *represent* at all. Here, Virilio mourns the demise of the relative and analogical character of the pre-digital condition, charging the nihilism of contemporary technology with the loss of the poetics of the ephemeral. We can no longer represent because we are caught, seemingly eternally, repetitively, in the absolute present, expressing ourselves and our pitiable condition, now and always, only as it happens, and, above all, *without pity.*

PLACE

Drew S. Burk

Place is a very important concept in Virilio's project. In *City of Panic* (2005b [2004]), for example, he draws attention to the fact that this once crucial element of existence is in danger of disappearing. For Virilio, the disappearance of place can be traced to several technological advancements that, while being championed as progress, may in fact lead to a devaluation of place for the convenience of instantaneity, virtualisation and the unbridled pathology of the consumption of globalisation. In *City of Panic*, Virilio states that if the rest of the world lived at the same level of consumption as the United States, it would need three or four more Earths to maintain a liveable sustainable life-system. The level of consumption and the necessity of three or four more Earths demonstrate the extent to which both the idea and the reality of place is in crisis. At a technological level, embracing unconditionally new information and communications technologies that virtualise place such as Google Earth, and allowing for a virtual view of what one could normally consider place, carries with it the loss of place, the countering position of no longer moving or travelling but remaining at home within virtual places or spaces that take a precedence and fascination over real places and spaces.

As the acceleration of the global takes priority over our previous notions of time, place and space, there is also a new reaction of the body within a real-time sphere no longer limited by geophysical locations and temporalities. Inhabiting accelerated worldwide networks, we must also relate to the novel effects this 'twilight of place' (*CP*, 113–44) has upon the time and space of the body as we become what Virilio calls 'immobile travelers' (*CP*, 119). For him, this abandonment of our old notions of place for the non-place of real time leads to the temporal compression of geophysical distances, to atmospheric pressure, telescopic collision and to unknown tele-objective horizons that are presently supplanting previous human topographical limits. The alarming rate at which humanity has been called to embrace and to enter into a virtual/actual realm of living that no longer has its concerns focused on real places and spaces, indeed, assuring their continued success concerning the twilight of real places and spaces, leads Virilio to seek out the symptoms of this unheard-of shift into an accelerated global digital sphere. Examples of placeless space tourism and the continuing flourishing of gated communities show that there is already a desire to make one final desperate grasp towards something to inhabit within a world that is trying to do away with geophysical places and spaces. Yet, as our continuing reliance on a virtual sphere of communication, acceleration and 'tele-life' grows inexorably, the world of real places and spaces become that of a grand desertification:

From now on, *the desert of the screen* is expanding at the speed of the light waves that propagate the ghosts of a desire that has not only become platonic but telescopic [. . .]

After the invention of the telescope and of television, this transgenic species is even set to innovate *tele-life* in which amorous frenzy will come down to a few grimaces and a handful of smileys [. . .] (*CP*, 138)

POLAR INERTIA

Gregor Schuner

Virilio has discussed inertia in relation to movement and acceleration ever since *Speed and Politics* (2006 [1977]). Even though not central at that stage, and not yet developed into the idea of 'polar inertia', the concept of inertia appears and reappears in most of his books published prior to *Polar Inertia* (2000a [1990]). As a term that literally means to not be in motion, Virilio uses inertia to complicate the association between speed, movement, time and duration. His concept of polar inertia is arguably a concept that conflates a variety of arguments and is used ambiguously in his later work to refer to a collective sum of these arguments or some specific aspects of them.

Given the meaning of the polar moment of inertia in physics, that is, the force required to change the axis of movement of a spinning object, the metaphor seems fitting to discuss the way in which technology driven by speed is increasingly diminishing physical movement – just like with a spinning disk, Virilio argues that the higher the speed of technology the more difficult movement becomes in contemporary society. Real space gives way to real time. All becomes both quicker and smaller.

This movement in contemporary society is most extensively developed in *Polar Inertia*, where the concept of the same name is related to two phenomena: live video transmissions and related technologies on the one hand; theoretical physics (relativity and quantum mechanics) on the other. The latter seems to be employed more as a metaphor – something to illustrate what the increased speed of communication is like.

It is helpful to take a closer look at *Polar Inertia* to understand better what Virilio means by the claim that speeding up leads to slowing down.

The first concern is with the modern technology of videoscopy; Virilio's term for live video transmission, both related to, and distinct from, telescopy and microscopy. The image filmed in one place and then seen in another place instantaneously through transmission via optical fibres or radio waves results in the 'constitution of an instantaneous, interactive "space-time" that has nothing in common with the topographical space of geographical or even geometrical space' (*PI*, 2). What becomes important is not 'being there' but 'being now', or, put differently, 'being now' delivers all that is desired. A particularly effective example used by Virilio is the suppression of live video coverage of the Chinese protests in 1989 in Beijing's Tiananmen Square, which he describes as a 'temporal siege' (*PI*, 13). Space did not matter, but the live transmission of the protests was crucial.

Contemporary technology is (at times inconsistently) thus differentiated from other past technologies that resulted in the compression of physical space, since videoscopy transcends or bridges space, rather than permits a faster traversing of it. In other words, there is now 'the general arrival of images and sounds in the static vehicles of the audiovisual' (*PI*, 20), which no longer relies on anything ever departing.

As with most of his work, Virilio uses an extensive range of examples to illustrate this 'inertial confinement of space' (*PI*, 31): hotels with audiovisual 'screens' instead of windows, flight simulators and video-conferencing, to name a few.

Polar Inertia can make the claim that speed leads to inertia by showing how technology begins to accelerate movement by turning around a new axis: the world moves around the tele-viewer and not around itself. People no longer traverse space, but exist merely in time.

This egocentrism impacts on environmental control and a phenomenological egocentrism. Using Edmund Husserl's example of the world passing by a walking person (*PI*, 71), rather than a walking person moving through a space, Virilio returns to 'real time' as the cause for the loss of 'real space'. Environments, in much the same way, are increasingly shaped around the person that occupies them. The person becomes stationary in a world that arrives to him or her. The 'loss of exo-centricity is increasing man's behavioural ego-centricity' (*PI*, 73) to the point of inertia. This still requires us to both understand how this relates to time and why this is something that Virilio regards as other than progress – namely 'involution' (*PI*, 70).

The time of the live broadcast becomes real time. The transmission arrives the moment it is filmed (using active kinematic optics that are the hybrid of glass and electric optics) and traverses space at the speed of light. It is transmitted in the instant, when there is no longer a past or a future, but just the 'intensive time' of the instant, which is given depth. Just as there is speed without movement, Virilio also introduces the idea of time without duration (*PI*, 41), which is another aspect of inertia, of stopping: 'The yardstick of duration is no longer really "duration" but, paradoxically, the infinite and constant deepening of "the instant"' (*PI*, 42).

Returning to space, this depth of time replaces spatial depth as space is egocentrically delivered by suspending succession and replacing it with simultaneity – all is now. This is polar inertia.

Virilio fears certain consequences of this polar inertia. The problems raised in *Polar Inertia* are added to the repertoire of concerns, reappearing in several of his other works: the image of inertia as a state of siege reoccurs in *Desert Screen* (2002a [1991]: 12); too much speed leading to cessation of movement recurs in *The Original Accident* (2007a [2005]: 100); the egocentricity of a movement around an axis recurs in *The Futurism of the Instant: Stop-Eject* (2010b [2009]: 49).

Key to most of these concerns is the way in which telecommunication technologies overpower the human body and human politics to render them immobile. Virilio compares this slowing down through speeding up to 'old age' and 'fragility'. The blind, the paralysed, the couched and the comatose person are all visions of the self in the state of polar inertia (*PI*, 65–70). If the virtual world becomes the presentation of reality, then the living present is becoming the tele-living present. Virilio poses the question of presence: Where am I, if I am everywhere as a telepresence? If all is 'tele', where is the 'here'? The 'I' disappears through appearing everywhere at once. The political movement becomes the political broadcast while the moving actor becomes the virtual telepresence. All movement ceases as polar inertia sets in.

See also: Movement; Space-Time; Speed; Technology

POLITICAL ECONOMY OF SPEED

Robert Hassan

The concept and application of a political economy perspective runs through much of Virilio's work and constitutes a key mode through which to understand his whole *oeuvre*. Drawing upon classical conceptions of political economy that take as their organising principle the interactions of power and economics in modern society, Virilio builds upon this to construct a political economy of speed. He terms this analytical frame 'dromology', and deploys it to draw out and make salient the nature and effect of technologically driven speed in society. Virilio's political economy, though, is not subservient to the logic of value that drives the classical models, but instead is autonomously alive inside the logic of technology, the machines of war and, latterly, machines of information processing.

Virilio's interest in the political economy of speed emerged out of his earliest concerns with architecture, urbanism, war and military technology. His dromology was primarily concerned with the interconnections between speed, technology (increasingly information technology) and warfare. In terms of warfare, as Benjamin Bratton (Virilio 2006 [1977]: 7) puts it in his Introduction to *Speed and Politics*, conflict itself is not Virilio's main concern, but rather it is the logistics, the movement of war and 'everything that makes it possible'.

Speed and Politics marks the beginning of a distinctive political economy path that emphasises the function and the consequences of speed in politics, culture and society. Physical movement of people and things or logistical strategies is where power lies, and the development and deployment of timely technological 'solutions' makes the difference between winning and losing, being efficient or being slow, being alive or being dead. Revolution and domination, for Virilio, are implicated deeply in the possible trajectories of his speed economy. The producers of speed, those who develop and deploy the most technologically sophisticated machines, are those who will eclipse the producers of things (as a Marxian political economy would view as central) and it is they who become the 'deciders', the 'techno-logistical oppressors' or liberators (*SP*, 164).

There is one way that Virilio's political economy of speed parallels the classical political economy that emanates from the Marxian tradition and has its emphasis upon the contradictions that are inherent in the processes constructed to reflect and express human struggle. Political economy critique of capitalism would emphasise the bust that will inevitably follow the boom. Virilio sees similar fundamental oppositions in his political economy of speed. And so acceleration in automobiles or the increase in aircraft passengers tend toward gridlock (*La Vitesse*, 1991); in the increasing speed in the flow of digital information, the mind can become overstimulated but also runs the risk of incapacitation (*Polar Inertia* 2000a [1990]); in this networked stream, and contra Marshal McLuhan, it is not the medium that is either the message or the massage any more, but the velocity of the medium itself that is key (*The Information Bomb* 2000d [1998]); and in the accelerated flow of time, the real-time perspective afforded through cyberspace, the linearity of chronological and unfolding time is replaced by a chronoscopic time of instantaneity and a temporal alienation (*Open Sky* 1997 [1995]).

The 'politics' of Virilio's political economy of speed is a political process that is shaped decisively by acceleration and deceleration, by movement and inertia, a process he terms 'dromocracy'. The communicative politics of modernity based on presence and geography are replaced by communication through information technologies. Every society is based upon the relations of speed, and therefore every society is to a greater or lesser extent dromocratic. Virilio argues, however, that the owners and controllers of the technologies of speed in information production and dissemination are today concentrated to such an extent that our cyberspace dromocracy is in fact a dictatorship of speed.

The contradictions inherent in both classical political economy and Virilio's dromology can obviously be themselves the basis for conflict and warfare. Dromology therefore is a mode of analysis for the understanding of war as not necessarily ideological, and as not necessarily economic, but first and foremost about logistics and movement and the technologies that make these increasingly efficient and fast mediums. The interest in technologies for war, movement and logistics was expressed in his *Bunker Archeology* (1994a [1975]). Here Virilio posited that the military space of war was always susceptible to the countermeasures of speed. And so the Nazi-constructed Atlantic Wall, which was supposed to defend Europe from an Anglo-American attack, was, in Virilio's political economy of speed, an inert and ultimately useless mass of concrete in high modern functional form.

A more Postmodern form of war is described through Virilio's dromology in *Negative Horizon* (2005a [1984]) where he argues that the war of time reignites the war for territorial space. Space-shrinking electronic technologies are now able to project power and forces – as well as ideology – which, as he argues in *Desert Screen* (2002a [1991]), are presages of even more apocalyptic future warfare. Politics and ideology conflate through teletechnologies to diminish the function of media through the military's proprietary ownership of representations of warfare.

Virilio has often been accused of being a hyperbolic thinker whose McLuhanesque aphoristic style affords little real analytic purchase on problems of war and politics and culture. His work has been disparaged as a kind of social science fiction (see, for example, Thrift 2011). However, it is readily arguable that dromology is the cornerstone of almost all Virilio's *oeuvre*, and dromology is itself a form of political economy. What is therefore interesting to consider in the work of Virilio is whether his particular political economy (of speed) is a legitimate analytical frame. This raises the unavoidable question of whether the dimensions of time and space (relatively underdeveloped as they are) are themselves legitimate intellectual tools with which to frame social science issues and problems. In this context, Virilio's political economy of speed is very much a work in progress; a developing modality that nonetheless connects in often-fruitful ways with the equally emerging and changing dynamics of politics, economy, technology and society.

See also: Dromology; Politics; Speed; Technology; War

POLITICS

Phil Graham

For Virilio, the dromocratic political question is first one of military logistics which develops as a necessary science alongside the emergence of the city in history. The urban locus of political control is first based on vectoral concerns: the movements of goods, information and human bodies (2006 [1977]: 32). The city therefore emerges in history as a vectoral protectorate, a point in space for the development of political power that draws strength from the militarised control and protection of movement through space. The urban imperative is a guarantee of reliable movement of every kind, thus casting the urban as medium, information processor and logistics centre for resources of every kind. The contradiction in these functions goes to the very character of dromocratic political development. Its practical advantage has been to make political use of the tensions between sedentary settlement and actual and potential accelerations in any or all of the city's vectoral components: an increase in the speed at which ideas and information can be communicated; general increases in the rate of transportation and exchange; the sudden ability of large groups of people (labour) to move or be moved about faster and more freely. All of these are threats to dromocratic control, which can only deal with such threats by exceeding them in sheer intensity (a function of organisation), and by denying or systematically limiting access to the means of acceleration among the general population: '*highway surveillance*' as primary political method (*SP*, 39).

Dromocracy is a systematic 'protection racket' that barters with the human spirit for the means of survival in return for its accession to exogenous purposes – a literal colonisation of human will: since power can never be free of labour, labour must be made pliable (*SP*, 97). Central to the ongoing achievement of this core political concern is terror: the immediate or imagined threats that provide states with the cultural rationale for permanent 'high-alert' security measures. In *Speed and Politics: An Essay in Dromology*, the contemporary terror is nuclear war. Virilio accurately predicts that:

We will see the creation of a common feeling of insecurity that will lead to a new kind of consumption, the consumption of protection; this latter will progressively come to the fore and become *the target of the whole merchandising system* [. . .] The indivisible promotion of the need for security already composes a new composite portrait of the citizen – no longer the one who enriches the nation by consuming, but the one who invests first and foremost in security, manages his own protection as best he can, and finally pays more to consume less. (*SP*, 139)

The root of all human terror is a perceived and imminent threat to survival. The closer we are collectively brought to the perceived precipice of annihilation, the more willingly will individuals accede to exogenous ends.

With the collapse of the Cold War (1947–91), the new source of mass insecurity first fell to abstract financial concerns: personal, civic, national and global financial insecurity was promoted at every level of public discourse as a matter of the utmost concern. A decade later, the definitive answer to the 'Manichean' security riddle posed by the post-Cold War vacuum and the collapse of global finance was delivered in spectacular fashion with the bombing of the World Trade Center and the Pentagon in September 2001 (Kellner 2004). As if to demonstrate Virilio's dromocratic formulation, the coup was delivered first in the apparent form of an accident. The first air assault was not read as anything else until the second and third attacks had occurred:

Indeed, not to use weapons, military tools, any more but simple air transport vehicles to destroy buildings, and being prepared to die in the process, is to set up a fatal confusion between the terrorist attack and the accident and to use the 'quality' of the deliberate accident to the detriment of the quality of the aeroplane, as well as the 'quantity' of innocent lives sacrificed, thereby exceeding the bounds once set by ethics, religious or philosophical. (Virilio 2007a [2005]: 7)

The laws of physics speak decisively on matters of mass and acceleration. To increase the likelihood that previously unseen subatomic particles will collide, matter is accelerated to near-light speed in a synchrotron. At maximum acceleration, particle speeds are such that energy is transformed into mass and an 'accidental' collision of previously invisible parts becomes more and more inevitable. This much is self-evidently true: the greater the mass and speed, the more likely the accident, the more spectacular its impact. To put this in the context of dromocracy: 'the smaller the world becomes as a result of the relativistic effect of telecommunications, the more violently situations are concertinaed' (Virilio 2000d [1998]: 67). The more suddenly a phenomenon emerges at accelerated speeds from its background, the more disruptive and dangerous are its effects to dromocratic stability. Dromocracy thereby inevitably produces its own 'political economy of disaster' (*OA*, 46). This is as much a function of light-speed, globally connected communication technologies – what Virilio calls *The Information Bomb* (2000d [1998]) – as it is of globally active, nuclearised militaries: 'The information bomb gives rise to the integral and globally constituted accident. The globally constituted accident can be compared to what people who work at the stock exchange call "systemic risk"' (Virilio and Armitage 2001b: 172).

Post-September 11 dromocracy has cast off any pretence to democracy; it is, for the entire world to see, a globally active militaristic system fully geared to the anticipation of all possible accidents – disruptions, attacks and breakdowns of every kind. Today, the dromocratic political bargain operates on a guaranteed attempt to protect citizens against all accidents waiting to happen, whether expected or unexpected, and as such remains directed at the basest level of human existence: survival in the security state.

Virilio sees the information bomb giving rise to transpolitics: the post-democratic deterritorialisation of individuals on a global scale and a concomitant 'tyranny of real time' (1999 [1996]: 87) in which reactionary impulses and global communications lead to 'the globalization of public opinion' (*PVW*, 37). The city becomes merely a 'borough among others of the invisible world *meta-city*' (*IB*, 11). The transpolitical is, for Virilio, a bleak prospect. It is a delocalised space of 'non-rights [. . .] the decline of the city as a territorial localization, and also as a place of an assumed right, affirmed by a policy' (Virilio and Dercon 2001: 80–1). In other words, light-speed connectedness means the destruction of space and the 'loss of place, alas, generally means the loss of rights' (Virilio and Dercon 2001: 81).

See also: City; Dromology; Information Bomb; Speed

POLITICS OF THE VERY WORST

Bob Hanke

Politics of the Very Worst (1999 [1996]) is the title of an interview with Virilio conducted by Philippe Petit. In this book, Virilio discusses how new technologies require us to pose a political question: what kind of specific accident do new technologies convey? He answers that the invention of technical objects is the invention of unpredictable, local and specific accidents. However, for Virilio, the invention of worldwide communication networks and the ever-increasing speed of information bring about new integral accidents that are likely to occur everywhere simultaneously. He presents the 1987 stock market crash exacerbated by New York City Stock Exchange program trading strategies as a precursor to future, automatic, accidents that will affect the whole world.

Yet, for Virilio, the question of speed is also a question of democratisation because political history is inseparable from economic history. Consequently, once a society reaches industrial speeds, geopolitics gives way to speed or chronopolitics where real time prevails over real space. Virilio also asks whether it is possible for us to achieve a democracy of real time because, for him, technologies such as television and telesurveillance represent a tyranny of real time that is analogous to classical tyranny. Media time, for example, destroys the time for citizens to reflect and to make considered decisions. During the 1990s, for instance, liberal democracy was thought by many, including Virilio, to be increasingly precarious even as the Internet revolution gave impetus to hopes of democratic renewal. Nevertheless, in Virilio's estimation, visions of electronic democracy on a computer screen suffer from the illusion of speed as salvation in an age in which the *demos* of relative speeds has been overruled by the *dromos* of instantaneous communication.

Beyond the clear political concerns expressed in this interview, it is worth noting that Virilio experienced the 'politics of the very worst' in the form of the Second World War at a very young age (he was born in 1932). Following Claus von Clausewitz's (1968) *On War*, for whom famously 'war is the continuation of policy by other means', Virilio shows how the Second World War and the dropping of atomic bombs mutated into the arms race and into deterrence; into, in other words, disinformation, deception and the logic of mutually assured destruction (MAD) as represented in Stanley Kubrick's well-known film, *Dr Strangelove or: How I Learned to Stop Worrying and Love the Bomb* (1964).

In Virilio's thought, therefore, the acceleration of transport and transmission affects the very nature of politics because these vectors are at the heart of the city (the political form of history) and the state apparatus. In *Negative Horizon* (2005a [1984]), for instance, Virilio defines chronopolitics as a war of time that is beyond that of territorial space and regards temporal administration and management as keys to the understanding of our post-national, transpolitical, state of emergency. For, due to the revolutions in transport and transmission, the spaces of the nation, of the law and of regulation are increasingly liquidated. Chronopolitics emerges with the steam engine, railways and aircraft, and later intensifies with advances in telecommunications and telematics. Thus the progress of democracy at relative speeds is stalled when citizens become engrossed in instantaneous control and regulated systems of interactivity within cybernetic societies.

Two ideas are prominent in Virilio's political ruminations: totalitarianism and terrorism.

Indeed, in Virilio's perspective on the history of what the German philosopher Ernst Jünger (1895–1998) called 'total mobilization' (see, for example, Armitage 2003) in the 1930s, the Allied defeat of Nazism in 1945 was followed by the 'balance of terror' between nations, which threatened each other with nuclear weapons. Totalitarianism, suggested Hannah Arendt (1973), refers to political states that operate through the suppression of information and through censorship. But, in *Strategy of Deception* (2000b [1999]), Virilio posits a 'globalitarian' state of disinformation flows and local/global feedback where subjects are flooded with information and contradictory data that prevent them from functioning democratically owing to an oversupply of information that amounts to a new kind of censorship.

Similarly, Virilio has long observed terrorism with great acuity. In *A Landscape of Events* (2000c [1996]), for example, he discusses the end of nuclear deterrence and the beginning of the post-Cold War era of terrorism. In *Ground Zero* (2002b [2002]), written in the wake of the September 11, 2001 terror attacks on New York City and Washington DC, Virilio portrays the rise of a global 'covert state', an 'unknown quantity' of privatised illegality. Lastly, in *The University of Disaster* (2010a [2007]), he notes a 'finalistic terrorism' in which terror simultaneously occurs live on the ground and as a recording, thanks to the replay and constant 'looping' of terrorist attacks (see, for instance, Armitage 2012: 95–110). After the September 11, 2001 terror assaults, Virilio says in the 'Third War: Cities, Conflict, and Contemporary Art' interview (Virilio and Armitage 2011: 32), that we have entered a 'logic of pure or individualized terrorism' or the last stage of war. Here he defines the 'Third War' as a 'war against civilians that does not include regular armies but only privatised armies, war lords, gangs in the suburbs, and terrorists' (2011: 33). In contrast to military dissuasion, Virilio warns that globalitarian civilian dissuasion threatens everyone's right to be human. Moreover, he thinks that war and politics have become part of the integral accident of ecological, economic and political collapse. At the beginning of the third millennium, then, Virilio registers the 'politics of the very worst' as the metamorphosis of the armed forces into police forces, as the administration of fear, and as the dissolution of liberal democracy into 'temporary authoritarian zones' (Armitage 2010: 18–19).

See also: Accident; Politics; Real Time; Speed

POSTMODERNITY, POSTMODERNISM

John Armitage

Postmodernity and postmodernism are concepts that Virilio rarely uses, either individually in interviews or critically in his major texts from *Bunker Archeology* (1994a [1975]) to *The Administration of Fear* (Virilio and Richard 2012). Fredric Jameson's (1991) landmark text, *Postmodernism, Or, the Cultural Logic of Late Capitalism*, for example, does not feature at all in Virilio's main works. Being a 'war baby', Virilio has little use for these terms' flexible imprecision, allusions, ascriptions and alleged critical significance for academic debate across the arts and technoculture. He attempts no definition of either postmodernity or postmodernism, preferring instead to focus on the symptoms of the accident, on the atmosphere or state of catastrophe, both terms that routinely escape the purview of many postmodern theorists. This does not mean that Virilio is indifferent to the contemporary issues that fall under the headings of postmodernity, postmodernism and postmodern theory.

Thus, while postmodernity is frequently used to signify a historical and cultural era, first and foremost in the leading information and consumer societies of the West, with the exact dating of this era still a subject for debate between, for instance, Jameson (postmodernity began in the 1950s and 1960s) and David Harvey (1989) (postmodernity began with the financial crash of the 1970s), Virilio points to 1947 as the beginning of the history of contemporary acceleration (Virilio and Armitage 2001a: 16). Unlike a number of postmodern theorists, furthermore, Virilio does not consider this transition as involving a radical break with previous stages of modernity. Consequently, while Virilio does have a certain affinity with those who understand postmodernity as an escalation and as a speeding up of existing developments, such as Arthur Kroker (2003), as far as Virilio is concerned: 'we are not out of modernity yet, by far. I think that modernity will only come to a halt within the ambit of what I call the "integral accident"' (Virilio and Armitage 2001a: 16). As such, Virilio has little need of an awareness of the intricacies of the prefix 'post'. It is also apparent that whereas Marxists like Jameson and Harvey discuss the multiple transformations that have transported Western capitalism into a new stage, whether similar to or radically different from the preceding regime, Virilio is less concerned with describing global capitalism and more concerned with explaining 'globalitarianism', the 'convergence of time towards a [. . .] world time [. . .] which comes to dominate local time' (Virilio and Armitage 2001a: 29).

Equally, although the term 'postmodernism' is used by others to indicate specific cultural texts and the responsiveness to or state of the age of postmodernity, Virilio appreciates postmodernism as an idea that might make sense in architecture because 'it is a clear-cut phenomenon: styles are mixed up, history is ignored, one goes for a "melting pot" of approaches' (Virilio and Armitage 2001a: 15). Hence, if the goal of postmodern theorists is to explain a contemporary aesthetic, so conspicuous in today's literary texts, movies, TV, music, architecture, urban atmosphere and fashion, then Virilio's goal has almost nothing to do with postmodern theory:

I simply cannot understand why people are talking about postmodernism. Poststructuralism? Yes, OK. Postmodernism? It doesn't make any sense to me [. . .] Moreover, as a teacher in a college of architecture, I believe postmodernism was a catastrophe in the history of modern architecture. Therefore there is no linkage between me and postmodernism. (Virilio and Armitage 2001a: 15)

Distinct from Jameson, therefore, Virilio has little intellectual interest either in identifying or in discussing eye-catching postmodern parades of decorous self-consciousness, textual or stylistic poaching across disciplinary fields, or even the disintegration of the differences between 'high' and 'low' and Western and other cultures. Virilio is, however, intellectually interested in the breakdown of the distinction between the past and the present, in the way that, today, 'the past and the future loom up together in all their obvious simultaneity' (Virilio 2000c [1996]: x). What is more, for Virilio, the outcome of all this is not a call for the investigation of irony and eclecticism, pastiche and parody, let alone enjoyment or pleasure-seeking. Rather, for him, the outcome of the crumbling of the differences between the past and the present is our arrival at a 'place where nothing follows on from anything else anymore and yet where nothing ever ends, the lack of duration of the perpetual present circumscribing the cycle of history and its repetitions' (Virilio *LE*, x). Far removed from those purported media-savvy TV audiences, readers and artists of the postmodern epoch, then, Virilio is anything but frivolous, light-hearted or allusive. His writings are most definitely not self-referential intertextual metafictions. As he puts it:

Basques often say that they enjoy themselves seriously and I must be part Basque. It is hard for me to talk about happiness and collective pleasure. I am an only child, and my experience was less pleasure than pain and solitude [. . .] I do not believe in hedonism [. . .] True joy does not need to be promoted, it is striking. (*TAF*, 59)

Yet, for all that, one thing that Virilio does have in common with the texts and varied cultural forms of postmodernism is a concern for the fate of the here and now in our ostensibly perpetual present wrought by new information and communications technologies. He explains the experience of living in the here and now of telepresence and virtual reality: 'Being is being present here and now [. . .] telepresence delocalizes the position or orientation of the body. The whole problem of virtual reality is that it essentially denies the *hic et nunc* [here and now], it denies the 'here' in favour of the 'now' (1999 [1996]: 44).

At its most expansive, consequently, Virilio's standpoint on the aesthetics and 'lifestyle' (not an actual life but a *style* of life) linked with postmodernity and postmodernism is a manifestation of his doubt about it, except on the question of the preceding divisions between the past and present being broken down and the outward disappearance of the here into the now of our technologically induced eternal present. Certainly, for Virilio, as for postmodern thinkers, contemporary issues relating to the arts and media, to technoculture, to the role of the intellectual, politics and the troubles of everyday life are vital issues (Virilio 2000b [1999]); 2000d [1998]; 2002b [2002]; 2003a [2000]; 2003b [2002]; 2005b [2004]; and 2007a [2005]). Indeed, these issues provoke numerous comparable questions concerning the loss of uniqueness and a real historical awareness, of genuine individuality and principles in art and ethics (see, for example, Virilio 2007b [2005]). But Virilio's reaction to these issues is not to view them as a kind of liberation from conventional suppositions and snobbish hierarchies. Instead, his reaction is, primarily, to censure postmodernism's reprocessed meaninglessness and showiness. He argues, for instance, that 'the postmodern period has seen a gradual drift away from an art once substantial, marked by architecture, music, sculpture, and painting, and towards a purely accidental art that the crisis in international architecture flagged at practically the same time as the crisis in symphonic music' (*AFE*, 2).

Virilio's contemporary theories, then, touch on the broad scope of postmodernity and poststructuralism, but his contribution to these discussions are notable not only for their absence of reference to the writings of Jacques Derrida and Roland Barthes, Jacques Lacan, and Louis Althusser, but also for their opposition to the 'explanations' and construction of 'clear systems' of the kind produced by Michel Foucault (see Virilio and Lotringer 2008: 52). What, in that case, differentiates Virilio's theories from postmodern theories and arguments? Let us take Jean-François Lyotard and Jean Baudrillard as two important postmodern philosophers and contrast their work with that of Virilio. For Lyotard's *The Postmodern Condition: A Report on Knowledge* (1984), the 'grand narratives' of human progress and emancipation, founded on the philosophy of the Enlightenment, have lost our trust because they turned into authoritarian governments such as those of Nazi Germany or the former Soviet Union and also because of the West's conceit that it alone could provide a truly global knowledge of the world. Nonetheless, for Virilio, and while he concurs with Lyotard regarding 'the end of the grand ideological narratives', he does not agree that the grand ideological narrative of justice has faded away: 'to me', he declares, 'even if I accept the demise of the grand historical and ideological narratives in favor of the small narratives, the narrative of justice is beyond deconstruction' (Virilio and Armitage 2001a: 30). For Baudrillard, the logic of a media-inundated consumer society has given rise to simulation, to 'the generation by models of a real without origin or reality: a hyperreal' (Baudrillard 1983: 2). But, once more, for Virilio:

as far as Baudrillard is concerned, there is for sure something about his work that I do not like at all, and that is his concept of simulation. I do not believe in simulation. To me, what takes place is substitution [. . .] The reason why is that I believe that different categories of reality have unfolded since the beginning of time [. . .] This means that reality is never given, but is the outcome of a culture [. . .] (Virilio and Armitage 2001a: 34–5; see also Virilio 2009b: 42)

In other words, Virilio disputes both Lyotard's and Baudrillard's arguments relating to, respectively, the waning of all the grand ideological narratives and the concept of simulation. The joint result of Virilio's contentions is to expound a dual response, of justice (because justice remains an essential notion) and of substitution (because diverse types of reality develop over time and are, consequently, never given).

Postmodernism and postmodernity are thus terms that Virilio feels distinctly ambivalent and uneasy about. Accordingly, his work is best understood as relating, initially, to the contemporary 'excesses' of a previous modernism and modernity or what I have called elsewhere 'hypermodernism' and 'hypermodernity' (Armitage 2000). However, there is, in addition, the problem of the relation between what hypermodernism and hypermodernity stand for in the fields of culture and society. Virilio's major contribution is to reflect on hypermodernism as the cultural logic of contemporary warfare. The chief issue his writings present is whether war in this wide-ranging, globalitarian stage of the supposed 'War on Terror' can make an allowance for a critical theory of art, technology and culture that is resistant to its 'accidents', catastrophes, unexpected transformations and disturbances. His explanations are crucially concerned with the domains of the morality of orbital warfare, the history and contemporary politics of acceleration, the defence and redefinition of a critical point of view on the problems of modernity, on the reality or otherwise of human perception, justice and the democratisation of technology, terms emanating from the catastrophic dimensions of modernity, which postmodern arguments largely ignore, such as the prospect of an integral accident (Virilio and Armitage 2001a: 16).

Even so, there are intimations that Virilio's attitude to postmodernism is becoming more favourable. In a recent interview, for example, he remarks that we are 'only *now* entering the era of postmodernism' (Virilio and Armitage 2011: 29). Questioning his own former sceptical viewpoint on postmodernism and his own past preference for the term 'hypermodernism', he argues that, now, 'we have truly entered into the postmodern age. And we have left the era of the hypermodern for that of the postmodern first and foremost due to acceleration, due to the fact that, currently, it is *the instant that dominates*' (2011: 29).

The concluding implication of Virilio's position is that he has little interest in providing detailed, authoritative accounts of either postmodernity or postmodernism, still less a dictionary definition of his own major concepts. And, notwithstanding his more positive recent attitude towards postmodernism noted above, hypermodernism and hypermodernity, in lieu of and therefore more than any other terms of contemporary theory, inclusive of postmodernity and postmodernism, at least clarify that Virilio is principally concerned with the extreme facets and meanings of modernism and modernity (e.g. excessive speed): hypermodernism and hypermodernity, then, sooner than postmodernism and postmodernity.

See also: Accident; Baudrillard, Jean; Hypermodernism; Modernity, Modernism; Speed

PROPAGANDA OF PROGRESS

John Armitage

The idea of the propaganda of progress or the propaganda about the Internet and related new information and communications technologies such as mobile phones was primarily developed by Virilio in his book-length interview with Philippe Petit, *Politics of the Very Worst* (1999 [1996]: 45–7), and in his study of human 'advance', technical progress and destruction, *Ground Zero* (2002b [2002]). The concept is derived from the theory and practice of modern notions of progress where, in various episodes of 'development', we have sought to enjoy a wholly technical environment and in the process plan the arrival of televisions and computers, high-speed monorails, moon rockets, weapons of mass destruction, robotics and domestic automation. The propaganda of progress therefore adapted to the profit motive and can be seen as 'the irruption of a host of machine-toys for adults who could, with their aid, *do what they had been forbidden to do as children*' (*GZ*, 2–3). This 'technical change' similarly forced upon us the idea that, from here on in, everything 'would be done in the name of this *prohibition to prohibit* which, for each human being, brought onto the stage the child they had once been' (*GZ*, 2). Virilio (*GZ*, 3) argues that this 'progressive' mode was adopted as a form of 'gigantism' by a 'dangerous gang of dwarves' and employs what he identifies as the key features of 'a scientifically naïve conception of the world in which positivism would become a veiled nihilism, and growth a negative growth – the satisfaction of a stubbornly repeated infantile refusal' (*GZ*, 2).

The propaganda promoting technology has become an especially important theme in Virilio's technocultural studies in the last decade, as his writings have become increasingly widely circulated. Given that the vigorous technoculture associated with the propaganda of progress has escalated in the West, Virilio applies his idea aesthetically or by extension to other theories and practices in discussions of contemporary art, ecology and fear (see Virilio 2003b [2002]; 2007a [2005]; 2009b; and Virilio and Richard 2012). While seeking to develop his concept for current technocultural analysis, Virilio is predominantly scornful of those who, in marketing 'progress', refuse to acknowledge that it has now turned into a marker of catastrophe: 'To the qualitative achievements of discoveries that have benefitted humanity has stealthily come to be conjoined the quantitative, baleful, achievement of Progress's many depradations' (*UQ*, Frontispiece). The propaganda concerning technology is, for example, adept at censoring the fact of technological accidents. Consequently, Virilio's concept is proving a relevant, technoculturally referenced and creative theme in his theoretical analyses and curatorial activities. The film *CROSSROADS* (1976–7), for instance, directed by the American artist Bruce Conner, and featured in Virilio's *Unknown Quantity* (*UQ*, 184–5) exhibition, bases its own aesthetic critique of the propaganda concerning military technology on the atom bomb's obliteration of Bikini Atoll and its rhapsodic dimensions, but does so in a self-reflexive film essay upon contemporary nuclear horror. As William C. Wees (2010: 5) observes, the text performs or exemplifies a critique of the spirit of the propaganda of progress by transforming the documentary archival footage from the American National Archives into a 'sustained, thirty-six minute evocation of the nuclear sublime'.

Virilio's (2009b) discussions, in a study of the application of his thought to grey ecology and temporal contraction, art and perception, explains the continuing appeal of invoking the concept of the propaganda of progress, above all for those seeking to discover a rebellious, if occasionally challenging, critique of technoculture. He (*GE*, 30) both focuses his theory of 'the failure of the success of progress' and substantiates its radicalism, because, in exposing the propaganda of progress, declares Virilio, the 'failure of progress is the failure of progress' success up against the finitude of the world'. His book-length interview with Bertrand Richard (Virilio and Richard 2012: 16) further proposes how his theory that 'technological progress' is accompanied by 'real propaganda' can be put to work in the discipline of technocultural studies, 'notably in the way the media covers the new creations' presented by Apple, Google, Microsoft and so forth. Here, Virilio (*TAF*, 16) suggests how this 'combination of techno-scientific domination and propaganda', so often considered 'cool' and 'informative' and 'counter-culturally' at odds in its popular manifestations with official culture, can be seen as reproducing 'all the characteristics of [military] occupation, both physically and mentally'.

PURE WAR

Chris Hables Gray

In a series of 1982 interviews with Sylvère Lotringer, Virilio introduced the concept of pure war, which indicates the period of the Cold War (1947–91) when humanity lived under the shadow of the balance of nuclear terror between the United States and the Soviet Union. *Pure War* (Virilio and Lotringer 1983) mapped, in chilling and compelling detail, the militarisation of the late twentieth century by the reality of nuclear and other weapons of mass destruction, which were, in effect, waging a kind of invisible war against humanity. A second edition of *Pure War*, with a new postscript, 'Infowar', was published in 1997. And, in 2008, Virilio and Lotringer released *Pure War: Twenty-Five Years Later*, which included the original text, the 1997 postscript, a 2007 postscript, 'War on the Cities', and a new introduction by Virilio entitled 'Impure War'.

Thus we cannot understand the idea of pure war outside of the development and deployment by the United States of the atomic bomb, the weapon of the catastrophe. During the Cold War, for example, humanity lived with the possibility of a pure war which, nevertheless, failed to appear, except as a global fear of what nuclear war would entail: the total annihilation of humanity itself. However, such nuclear deterrence did generate a technoscientific upsurge. For technoscience applied to war not only produces new technologies such as the Internet but also produces a massive acceleration of war machines (and potentially combat as well), the perfection of weapons of communication that generate spectacle and panic, and the proliferation of weapons of mass destruction. Together, they allow a pure form of war to emerge, which, in potential terms, remakes the blockade of nuclear deterrence and the world technological order and in practical applications, especially in the deserts of Iraq, for instance, leads to sharp, speedy and yet somehow indecisive battles and 'victories' (see, for example, Virilio 2002a [1991]). At its heart, then, pure war isn't an actual war at all, but a 'logistical' war in which it is very often difficult to locate its destructive character. This is because pure war is in reality the continual, perhaps infinite, preparation for war that militarises and exhausts society, threatening to eventually eliminate it. Pure war therefore produces a transnational state whose only ideology is military order based on technoscience, not a politics grounded on the polis. It is a secular version of Holy War, and Virilio equates the total release of religiously justified conflicts with the apocalyptic potential of weapons of mass destruction. So he argues that there can be no 'just' pure war, in large part because nuclear war has no need of people, and that is why for him the notion of pure war is particularly appropriate.

Consequently, according to Virilio, the emergence of pure war generated a new form of resistance:

It was no longer about resisting an invader, German or other, but about resisting the military-scientific and industrial complex [. . .] that is, against the invention of ever-crazier sorts of weapons, like the neutron bomb, and 'Doomsday machines', something that we saw, for instance, in Stanley Kubrick's film *Dr Strangelove*. Thus resistance to pure war is of another nature than resistance to an oppressor, to an invader. It is resistance against science: that is extraordinary, unheard of! (Virilio and Armitage 2001a: 28)

Today, though, Virilio (Virilio and Lotringer 2008: 9) writes not about pure war but about 'impure war', given that the 'whole question of deterrence has changed in nature'. No longer aimed simply at the military sector, deterrence is now directed at the civilian population through state legislation, extra-judicial 'camps' such as Guantanamo Bay, and, of course, the supposed 'War on Terror'. Yet, for Virilio, the War on Terror is a war of disequilibrium, with the civilian deterrence of impure war aimed at resisting the disequilibrium wrought by the proliferation of asymmetric enemies in the shape of hyper-terrorists. Focusing on the contemporary threat that impure war represents to democracy everywhere, Virilio argues that the advent of civilian deterrence is not merely a warning sign for supporters of social equality but also a precursor to the coming insecurity and the resulting need to oppose the pervasive disequilibrium and chaos that hyper-terrorism brings to the city:

This is what we're up against with when we raise the question of Pure War. Pure War is still around, it's still possible to press the button and send out missiles – Korea can do it, Iran can do it, and so can others; but in reality the real displacement of strategy is in this fusion between hyper-terrorist civil war and international war, to the point that they're indistinguishable. (Virilio and Lotringer 2008: 13)

See also: *Desert Screen; Fear; Resistance; Speed; War*

REAL TIME

Ronald E. Purser

Virilio (1995 [1993]; 1997 [1995]; 2000d [1998]) has gone to great lengths to show that the essence of post-Second World War telematics involves the virtual elimination of both spatial and temporal distance between events' occurrences and their representations. The will-to-speed unleashes the absolute speed of real-time technologies, annihilating real space. For Virilio (*OS*, 3), this causes a massive distortion in our perceptual field. Speed is no longer limited by moving across geographic distances by means of physical transport – that is, movement through the real space of chronological time. Rather, speed is equated with data transmission moving at the absolute speed of light – giving rise to what is now understood as real time.

   Clearly, a key driver of real time is the shift to an instantaneous mode of production and consumption, or just-in-time systems. Flexible accumulation, or 'post-Fordism', was a response to the previous crisis of capital overaccumulation during the 1970s and 1980s. The shift from a flexible to an instantaneous mode of accumulation is what I have referred to as 'Gatesism' (Purser 2000). This configuration is coupled to the dynamic and logic of late capitalism, in which new information and communications technologies provide the means for accelerating turnover times of capital in production (Harvey 1989; Hassan 2003; Hassan and Purser 2007).

Emerging real-time technologies remove the friction of the real world, by promising ever more 'user-friendly' interfaces. For example, Regis McKenna's (1997: 3) book, *Real Time*, opens with the invitation: 'Imagine a world in which time seems to vanish and space seems completely malleable. Where the gap between need or desire and fulfillment collapses to zero. Where distance equals a microsecond in lapsed connection time.' The ideal for McKenna is to eliminate the temporal distance between desire and the commodified objects. Such time-negation has become a reality, for new information and communications technologies compress the distance between 'here and there', 'now and then'.

Geometry is negated with real-time technology, no matter what the distance. Hence, the need for cumbersome networks of distribution is abolished, and much physical movement can be eliminated. For example, commuting is replaced by telecommuting; attending meetings is no longer necessary with the availability of teleconferencing; going to school is seen as a laborious inconvenience in light of the choices that online distance learning now offers.

Time compression of this sort, which for McKenna is the cause of celebration, is for Virilio a matter of deep concern. 'With acceleration,' he writes, 'there is no more here and there, only the mental confusion of near and far, present and future, real and unreal – a mix of history, stories, and the hallucinatory utopia of communication technologies' (Virilio 1995 [1993]: 35). And, in *The Information Bomb*, Virilio (2000d [1998]: 117) traces this trend as leading to the 'ending of all localized *durée*' and the establishment of a universal world time based on the limit-speed of real-time telecommunications.

In *Open Sky*, Virilio (1997 [1995]: 60) characterises this as the 'empire of real-time telecommunications', noting how an indirectly transparent 'optoelectronic' layer has enveloped the globe. Limits traditionally associated with terrestrial and geographic space (real space) are swallowed up by real-time instantaneity (*OS*, 62–3; *IB*, 119). The 'trans-apparent horizon' of digital media supersedes physical and cultural horizons, where 'the far prevails over the near and figures without density prevail over things within reach' (*OS*, 26). Moreover, real-time technologies introduce a 'bug' or mental virus into perceptual fields as a new horizon (trans-apparent) generated purely by digital media and the electronic transmission of images (trans-appearances) that take hold over the normal boundary line of the physical horizon, and also play havoc on the deep horizon of our collective imagination and memory.

Virilio (*IB*, 118) claims that acceleration of real-time technologies narrows down our attention to the flickering present, or what Walter Benjamin (1994) simply calls, 'now-time'. This is similar to Virilio's (*OS*,

10) quotation of Paul Klee: 'To define the present in isolation is to kill it.' In other words, real time is chronoscopic in nature. A temporal orientation that is fixated on instantaneity places limits on our attention span. Knowledge is reduced to knowledge of the present, a bundle of information that can be instantaneously consumed. In so-called real time, there is no history or future – no time available for serious reflection or creative imagination. Virilio explains real-time technologies as functioning as monochronic filters that screen or cut out concern for the past and future. Noting this trend, Virilio (*OS*, 137) states:

the time of the present world flashes us a glimpse on our screens of another regime of temporality that reproduces neither the chronographic succession of the hands of our watches nor the chronological succession of history. Outrageously puffed up by all the commotion of our communication technologies, the perpetual present suddenly serves to illuminate duration.

In a chronological world, time as duration was coupled with space as extension. Calendars and clocks served as the dominant means for regulating and synchronising political, social and economic activities. The emergence of a chronoscopic world parallels the advance of electronic data transmission technologies, which send and receive signals at the speed of light. This amounts to a new time standard based on real-time capability for instantaneity, and an accelerated perspective focused on intensive duration of the 'the real' moment replacing extensive duration of history.

In his early work, *Speed and Politics: An Essay on Dromology* (2006 [1977]), Virilio anticipated the emergence of real time and the dramatic transformation it would have on politics and war. He (*SP*, 133) states: 'The instantaneousness of action at a distance corresponds to the defeat of the unprepared adversary, but also, and especially, to the defeat of the world as a field, as distance, as matter.'

Politics in a chronological world was enacted within the limit speeds of terrestrial movement across geography. Similarly, war (politics by other means) was primarily about movement and intrusion into foreign territory. State politics was concerned with maintaining a territorial economy and defending national boundaries. Empires with superior transport and war technologies could traverse space and gain control from a distance, colonising distant lands and countries. Politics based on a tyranny of distance required mastery of spatial movement. Politics based on a tyranny of real time requires mastery of absolute speed. For Virilio, absolute speed is the royal road to absolute power.

Real-time technologies obliterate the barriers of distance, which erase the clear demarcations between 'global' and 'local', leading to an increasing

168 RESISTANCE

homogenisation of cultures. The new political economy is based on a tyranny of real time, where the speed of commerce dictates local behaviour. War in the new global economy is based more on a policy of dissuasion and global control of information. As Virilio (2002a [1991]) pointed out, the Gulf War was the first 'live war', which occurred in a local space, but was global in time. Virilio foretold, with uncanny accuracy, privacy issues, electronic surveillance and other associated risks of cybernetic control as global information networks would become ubiquitous.

See also: Politics; Space-Time; Speed; Technology

RESISTANCE

Ingrid Hoofd

That increasingly disappearing capacity or potentiality for opposing, decelerating or thwarting late modernity's propensity for and logic of technological acceleration. Combining the insights of Newtonian physics and a phenomenology of the subject with the modern ideal of political subversion or confrontation, the question of resistance entails for Virilio primarily an analysis of how any force – legal, military, political or ethical – must emerge from actual tradition, territory and duration. In *The Vision Machine* (1994b [1988]) Virilio identifies the contemporary dwindling of the possibility for resistance as related to the impossibility of consolidating subjective and communal memory because the 'I see' is less and less mapped upon the 'I can' under conditions of acceleration. Resistance is therefore, as he states, for instance, throughout *Art as Far as the Eye Can See* (2007b [2005]), 'telluric', insofar as it must start from, and hence today must seek to make possible again, actual places and spaces of physical proximity required for political or ethical dialogue and confrontation. As he likewise contends in *Speed and Politics* (2006 [1977]), the acceleration of the social by way of transportation and information technologies results in the emergence of displaced 'speed-spaces' and the destruction of 'olden time', creating a situation in which 'dromocracy' (speed-politics) increasingly replaces democracy. Since dromocracy is a tactic of intensive penetration or 'endo-colonisation' by way of modern techniques of speed, it becomes pertinent for Virilio to strictly reject the progressive or liberal reading of technological empowerment, emancipation or liberation, as in any way truly resisting at all. Worse even, such a liberal understanding not only (literally) buys into the belief that emancipation is effectuated through what he calls in *The Vision Machine* the exalted 'interpretosis' surrounding media representation and content analysis, but also reproduces what he calls in *Pure War* (2008: 166) the 'echo of progress-illusion' and its mechanisms.

We are, therefore, according to *The Vision Machine*, in the age of the image's 'paradoxical logic' in which the era of total illumination is simultaneously the era of total surveillance and exclusion. The condition of acceleration splits humanity into 'hopeful' and 'despairing populations' while the unnatural law of technological survival reigns supreme under the illusion of social progress. Here, the actual natural law of today's world seems to be 'stasis is death', and Virilio implies, for instance in *Pure War*, that true resistance must re-create an awareness and contemplation of death as that which is intrinsically bound to any meaningful or ethical relationship to the other, and by extension to the political. As he reiterates in *Pure War*, the possibility of resistance can only consist of creating a politics of interruption regarding the incessant interruptions of total war, wherein the lethality and despair that are essential to modern technology's functioning (and which it manages to obscure for example as if these are mere accidents) are again revealed. It follows that a critique of technology – and by implication true resistance to dromocracy – as he explicitly asserts in *Negative Horizon* (2005a [1984]: 25) while echoing Heidegger's (1978) phenomenological position, 'is not simply anti-technology [. . .] it is necessary to obey' while 'also to resist'. In other words, remaining faithful to an ethics of proximity, duration and the 'telluric' necessitates becoming 'an atheist of technology' and of technological fundamentalism. The latter, after all, as he sums it up in *The Vision Machine*, threatens to become the only remaining truth through a 'preemptive abortion of the diversity of mental images' (*VM*, 12) and of human and biological diversity as such. One could therefore finally argue that the speed at which Virilio throws new books and neologisms at his audience aims not only to bring the reader back to the duration and materiality of a written *oeuvre* but also aims to generate a lingering sense of paradox, nostalgia and doom as the central characteristics of the technological condition into which we must first enquire if we want to resist at all.

REVOLUTIONARY, REVELATIONARY

George Katsonis

The juxtaposition between two types of political thought and movement based on the historical superseding of material space and geopolitics by technological progressivism and its temporal milieu of acceleration and contingency. The distinction is most explicitly made in Virilio's interview with John Armitage for the latter's edited volume *Virilio Now* (Virilio and Armitage 2011: 39) where Virilio proclaims:

I am not a *revolutionary* but a *revelationary*! This is very important! Ancient and modern societies were revolutionary and brought into being revolutionaries. But I am a revelationary. For *what is revealed forces itself above what is past and forces itself upon our situation as a revelation*, as in the case of the integral accident and finitude. Revelationary thought is a new type of thought.

However, this distinction also features noticeably among Virilio's most recent writings that focus on globalisation, insecurity and his theory of the accident.

Already in *Popular Defense and Ecological Struggles* (1990 [1978]), Virilio had heralded the twilight of revolutionary agents and avatars in the face of the terrorist movements of that time and advocated the urgent necessity for a pragmatic ecological struggle against speed-politics. Yet, by the time of *The Original Accident* (2007a [2005]), Virilio would double this call by presenting the need for a second, eschatological, or revelationary political movement able to predict in 'meteorological' fashion the imminent disasters of technological inflation. In addition, such a movement would deflect 'clapped-out' revolutionary discourse, sensational aesthetics and a certain 'academicism of horror', all contemporary phenomena that Virilio considers equally contributive to the acceleration of culture.

Augmenting the bold apocalyptic tone of his previous works, the notion of 'revelation' appears in Virilio's writings, first, in relation to a discourse on the accident in *Politics of the Very Worst* (1999 [1996]), where the accident in itself reveals the negativity of a given technology, and then in relation to globalisation in *The Information Bomb* (2000d [1998]), where the reality of spatial foreclosure reveals finiteness as the 'negative horizon' of speed. It is after the terror attacks on New York City and Washington DC on September 11, 2001, nevertheless, when the revolutionary/revelationary juxtaposition takes place; in *Crepuscular Dawn* (2002) where it suggests the double nature of technological progress, in *City of Panic* (2005b [2004]) where it is employed in terms of historical transition, in *The Original Accident* where it is used to situate the politics of post–September 11, 2001 globality within contingency and its spectre, and, finally, in *The University of Disaster* (2010a [2007]) where it denotes the vulgarity of the revelationary scientist (genius or madman?) who is compared by Virilio to the universal revelationary figure of a man reminded of his birth and humility.

In this sense, revelationary thought is a matter of both ecology and eschatology, interested equally in the nihilism of matter and the hidden negativity of technoscientific knowledge, as well as the perceptibility of speed, mediated reality and the apocalyptic accident.

$$S$$

SEDENTARINESS

Josiane Behmoiras

Virilio is preoccupied throughout his work with the situation of the human body within the environment and with the history of its physical and social sedentarisation: the sedentariness of the body upon the seat of a moving vehicle, the transition from warrior nomad to sedentary urban civilian, and the mutating patterns of sedentariness in times of accelerated modernity.

In *Polar Inertia* (2000a [1990]), Virilio contends that our 'civilised world' has been intent on extending urban sedentariness from the fixed habitat and the means of 'seated' transport to technological sedentary living aided by remote control and the telepresence of communications. Ultimately, Virilio points out, sedentariness will be extended towards the 'stationary vehicle' in which the personality of an individual will be 'fixed forever' and from which that individual will be able, without actual movement, to command the actions of other actor-bodies in remote locations (*PI*, 85). This is a condition where it is possible to 'transfer over distance sight, sound, smell, and tactile feeling' and in which the physical journey becomes obsolete, since 'one has already arrived' (Virilio and Armitage 2001a: 31).

The shifting of human civilisation from the original sedentariness of the agricultural–mercantile model of settlement onto the global techno-industrial model of transience and transhumance is also at the core of Virilio's *The Futurism of the Instant: Stop-Eject* (2010b [2009]). He argues that in times of ubiquity and instantaneity, the right to sedentariness in one's place of origin is compromised by telecommunications' prioritisation of real time over real space and the ensuing effects of globalisation, and by the multiple environmental, political and social consequences of advanced technologies. The post-industrial era heralds a fundamental unsettling of the orientation of human activity under ubiquitous terms such as 'deregulation' and 'relocation', annihilating sedentariness as 'localization within a historic space that is our cultural heritage' (*FI*, 11–12). Moreover, he contends that the portability of objects that were once 'happy to be "fixed" and precisely situated' has reversed the relationship between nomadism and fixed settlement, eliciting a favouring for mobility over localisation and sedentariness: paradoxically, the sedentary individual is now at home everywhere with the aid of electronic devices, while the nomad is at home nowhere, wrenched away from his or her native land, and forever driven into marginal inhabitancy (*FI*, 14).

Lastly, Virilio (1997 [1995]: 25–6) also warns us about the '*terminal* – and final – *sedentarization*', a sort of sedentariness of the moment, a 'civilization of forgetting' within the 'third and final horizon of indirect visibility', that 'square horizon of the screen' generated by *the speed of light* of telecommunications. This is a '*live* (live coverage) society' in which the past and future are removed from human history in favour of the endless present of 'real time' – a society with 'no extension and no duration' (*OS*, 25). The 'second [. . .] deep horizon of our memory' is thus reordered into a fixed inhabitancy of the moment, altering our orientation in the world – within the first horizon – and our perception of it, while the evolving forms of human sedentariness are reconstructed 'around the screen and the time slot' (*OS*, 26).

SPACE-TIME

David B. Clarke and Marcus A. Doel

One virtue of Virilio's thought is that space and time are always thought together. While the terminology of 'space-time' is used differently in different contexts, the most significant use Virilio makes of the term marks its contrast with 'speed-space'. Loosely speaking, 'space-time' articulates the sense of space and time that preceded the advent of telecommunications and information technologies, when, quite simply, crossing space took time. The limited (vehicular) technological capacity for traversing space rendered geographical space a resilient matter of extension. The 'old reality', in Virilio's (Virilio and Dercon 2001: 70–1) description, 'can be presented as a space-time reality', a reality marked by 'an extensive *space*, a space where the duration of time was valued'. The sense of time as duration accompanying extensive space is, in fact, crucial to Virilio's claim that we have since entered a new era. While many would contend that the 'old' reality is still with us – in many ways it undeniably is – it is equally undeniable that the 'new' reality of 'speed-space' has become a powerful force in changing the shape of the world. What is arguably of greatest value in the contrast Virilio sets up is the way in which it sensitises us to otherwise opaque qualities of technological developments that have, over an appreciably long time-period, transformed space and time in the ways to which Virilio's thought attunes us.

In the 'old' reality of space-time, 'Man lived in a time-system of his actual presence: when he wasn't there, he wasn't there', says Virilio (Virilio and Dercon 2001: 70), obliquely confirming the opposition between presence and absence this situation underpinned. By extension, one may add that when he wasn't there he was elsewhere: 'space is that which keeps everything from occupying the same place' (Virilio 1991 [1984]: 17). If extensive space was the definitive quality of the old reality, however, one may say that intensive time is the paradigmatic feature of the new, not least insofar as its capacity to abolish distance retrospectively reveals that distance was, all along, a function of the time, and cost, it took to overcome it. The transition between the two is aptly illustrated by Virilio (1994b [1988]: 4) in his discussion of technological prostheses like the telescope:

The telescope, that epitome of the visual prosthesis, projected an image of a world beyond our reach and thus another way of moving about in the world; the *logistics of perception* inaugurating an unknown conveyance of sight that produced a telescoping of near and far, a *phenomenon of acceleration* obliterating our experiences of distances and dimensions.

If visual prostheses initially transformed experiences of space – 'with telescopes, of the infinitely large, and with microscopes, of the infinitely small' (Virilio and Dercon 2001: 71) – increasingly, Virilio claims, they reconfigure time. 'We witnessed the shift from extensive to intensive time with cinema', he (Virilio and Dercon 2001: 76) proposes. Ever since, our technologies have further intensified time, ultimately to the point where they reach the limit-speed of '*the time frequency of light*' (Virilio *VM*, 71) – at which point 'distinctions of *here* and *there* no longer mean anything' (Virilio *LD*, 13).

SPEED

Jason Adams

The most important starting point from which to begin to encounter Virilio's concept of speed in his works such as *Speed and Politics: An Essay on Dromology* (2006 [1977]) lies in recognising that, while it always retains contextually specific qualities, for him, speed is not inherently negative.

While Virilio is often misunderstood on this point, his work as a whole constitutes an inventive, new materialist assertion that, today, speed tends to promote deleterious outcomes not because of its essence, but because perception has not apprehended the cultural effects of acceleration thus far and is therefore rendered powerless to shape it. What Virilio contributes, then, is a political economy of speed in which resistance to the present would not just be about slowing down, but also about becoming a producer of speed.

In his writings, Virilio identifies two primary forms of speed: relative speed and absolute speed. As he sees it, modernity has moved from the former, in which speed is relative to space and time, to the latter, in which space and time are relative to speed. Contemporary communication and transportation technologies, in other words, at the bidding of various bureaucracies and hierarchies, have accelerated everyday experience tremendously, with almost no opportunity for popular negotiation. Thus, perception has been subordinated to the pace, content and form imposed upon it. Virilio does, however, posit a variety of ways in which the politicisation of speed might occur: for instance, within art, science or politics.

One example that is both typical of a Virilian politicising aesthetic choice and a useful metaphor for grasping his project is that of time-exposure photography. Here, the camera's shutter is left open for an extended period, producing the blurred motion normally eschewed by photographers used to seeking a precise, still image. In conventional, fast-exposure imagery, by contrast, critical capacities are often overcome by an image of exactitude, one in which precise moments are simply captured and presented. In essence, one might say, what Virilio's writing provides is a series of time-exposure images rendered theoretically. Like many of these photographs, they are calibrated to render the relativity of speed perceptible in a time that presents it as absolute.

Two major scientific paradigms frame Virilio's concepts of relative and absolute speed. The first is that of Sir Isaac Newton, whose positivist conception of space also affirmed an absolute image of speed. If speed is defined in modern science as the magnitude of the velocity of an object discovered by dividing spatial distance by the temporal duration used to traverse it, Newton's assertion made no allowance for how the everyday experience of speed changes the experience of space as this velocity increases. It is, then, like conventional photography, also a paradigm in which an image of exactitude prevails, which has the effect of precluding questioning and interpretation.

Virilio often refers here to the example of a tree one passes by in a train. Is the true tree that of Newtonian space, the tree we imagine in a close-up, as a still image devoid of movement? Or is the true tree the one registered in the very different form of time-exposure photography, a motion-blur produced while the viewer speeds on by? Newtonian conceptions, of course, provide only for the decontextualised tree as the true tree. Whether filtered by the illusion of stillness or the apparentness of motion, the materiality of the situation is of no consequence to this idealist framework. Virilio, then, argues no more for this than he does for simply slowing down.

Rather, he is much closer to Albert Einstein, for whom speed is always relative. The tree is always the true tree, whether perceived in a time-exposure image or a still image, because it is situational. The point, for Virilio, is that when perception is conditioned by the speed of technology rather than by the speed of technology conditioned by perception, we lose our grasp on relativity, the co-existence of multiple realities. Absolute speed, in other words, takes over, fitting a positivist filter onto experience so that acceleration as it is deployed from above becomes the only mode of acceleration conceivable. Rather than Einsteinian time-exposure images, we might say, Newtonian concepts are time-concealment images.

Ultimately, the most crucial dimension of this thematic for Virilio is the relationship between speed and politics. What he means when he refers to a political economy of speed is that the multiple temporalities within which people co-exist are unevenly distributed. If our bodies move physically in space yet also move perceptually in time by way of technology, the manner in which this occurs, Virilio avers, should also be open to popular negotiation. Just as time-exposure images negotiate a freer relationship to visual culture, so too can an analogous politics do so in relation to the political economy of speed.

There is, of course, a reason that Virilio is often seen as pessimistic with respect to speed. It is that he generally begins with the negative dimension of acceleration, since this is what allows him to politicise speed as it is materialised in specific situations. Indeed, Virilio (e.g. in Virilio and Armitage 2009: 102) describes himself as a 'critic of the art of technology', just as one might describe oneself as an art critic of painting. It is not, then, that speed is inherently negative or positive, but, rather, that, because it retains the potential for a multiplicity of material expressions, we should emphasise a critical disposition to it. In doing so, Virilio holds, we become better positioned to enable new, more affirmative, technocultural developments to emerge.

See also: Perception, Perspective; Politics; Space-Time; Technology

SPEED-SPACE

David B. Clarke and Marcus A. Doel

'The new space is speed-space; it is no longer a time-space', claims Virilio (Virilio and Dercon 2001: 71). At its most basic, this suggests the end of an era dominated by vehicular transportation technologies – dedicated to overcoming the friction of distance – and the inauguration of an era defined by virtual information technologies – devoted to enabling instantaneous communication over space, to realising the fiction of distance. In Virilio's (1991 [1984]: 18) words, '*Speed distance* obliterates the notion of physical dimension. Speed suddenly becomes a primal dimension that defies all temporal and physical measurements.' At the limit – the speed of light – lies a world 'devoid of spatial dimensions, but inscribed in the singular temporality of an instantaneous diffusion' (*LD*, 13). To gain a fuller grasp of the intended sense of 'speed-space', it is important to consider the term in relation to Virilio's (1997 [1995]: 9) claim that 'we have not yet digested relativity, the very notion of space-time' (in Einstein's sense of a four-dimensional continuum, with all that this implies) and, crucially, in relation to the phenomenological register of Virilio's thought, particularly the sense in which 'speed metamorphoses appearances' (Virilio 2005a [1984]: 105). Only when these two aspects converge does the full force of Virilio's argument become apparent.

Distinguishing 'speed-space' from 'time-space' demonstrates the kind of insight Virilio consistently achieves by 'deterritorialising' concepts devised in other contexts; suggesting, in this instance, the importance of shifting social thought from a Newtonian to an Einsteinian conceptual framework. Rather than defining speed in relation to absolute and independent notions of space and time, Virilio borrows from the theory of relativity the sense in which space and time are, so to speak, in the eyes of the beholder: strictly speaking, relative to the state of motion of the observer, amounting to substitutable aspects of a four-dimensional continuum in which space is translatable into time, and vice versa, such that the speed of light remains constant for all observers. 'If the categories of space and time have become relative (critical), this is because the stamp of the absolute has shifted from matter to light and especially to light's finite speed', says Virilio (1994b [1988]: 71). 'From now on', he (*VM*, 71) argues, 'speed is less useful in terms of getting around easily than in terms of seeing and conceiving more or less clearly.' The upshot, as the sociologist Zygmunt Bauman (2002: 13) points out, is that 'speed is no longer a means but a milieu; one may say that speed is a sort of ethereal substance that saturates the world and into which more and more action is transferred, acquiring in the process new qualities that only such a substance makes possible – and inescapable'. The implications of this are legion: numerous aspects of Virilio's thought fall into place when considered in this frame of reference.

Insofar as speed conditions perception, the liminal speed of action-at-a-distance defining speed-space is marked not merely by the sudden appearance [*surgissement*] of things but, more pointedly, by their instantaneous disappearance. This is a source of consternation for Virilio, insofar as technologically mediated perception removes from vision its 'prophetic' quality: 'Today we are no longer truly *seers* [*voyants*] of our world but [. . .] merely *reviewers* [*revoyants*]' (Virilio 2005a [1984]: 37). Accordingly, one should properly speak of reception rather than perception: 'An indirect and mediatized reception succeeds the instant of the direct perception of objects, surfaces and volumes [. . .] in an interface which escapes daily duration and the calendar of the everyday' (Virilio 1991 [1984]: 84). Here, Virilio's phenomenological background becomes apparent, as the lived experience of the present moment is reduced to 'real time', which he (1997 [1995]: 10) accuses of 'killing "present" time by isolating it from its here and now, in favour of a commutative elsewhere that no longer has anything to do with our "concrete presence" in the world, but is the elsewhere of a "discreet telepresence" that remains a complete mystery'. The instantaneous disappearance associated with action-at-a-distance may equally be characterised, then, in terms of absence – 'the absence of the actor from the scene of the action, the actor's presence *sous rapture* – appearance and disappearance, so to speak, rolled into one' (Bauman 2002: 13). In this paradoxical state, 'The philosophical question is no longer who I really am but where I presently am' (Virilio 2000a [1990]: 85).

Just as one only really notices things once they begin to fall apart or fade from view, the most crucial aspect of Virilio's musings on the new form of 'speed-space' is the revelation that 'speed-space' was, in fact, there all along: all space is speed-space. In a manner directly comparable to the French philosopher Jean-François Lyotard (2011), Virilio decries the 'geometricising' of vision inherent to the quattrocento tradition of representation, which freezes the observer in order to constitute the world as a picture. For Virilio (1991 [1984]: 102), 'acceleration and deceleration, or the movement of movement, are the only true dimensions of space [. . .] This space is not defined as substantive or extensive; it is not primarily volume, mass, larger or smaller density, extension, nor longer, shorter, or bigger superficie'. This phenomenological insight becomes increasingly apparent in an era where:

Past, present and *future* – that old tripartite division of the time continuum [. . .] cedes primacy to the immediacy of a tele-presence [. . .] in which the fourth dimension (that of time) suddenly substitutes for the third: the material volume loses its geometrical value as an 'effective presence' and yields to an audiovisual volume whose self-evident 'tele-presence' easily wins out over the nature of the facts. (*NH*, 118)

This belated recognition is, for Virilio, a source of lament, as our technological prostheses take us ever further from an immediate, sensory experience of the world, inducing a motion that puts an end to movement by transforming the actor into a tele-actor. 'This tele-actor will no longer throw himself into any means of physical travel, but only into another body, an optical body; and he will go forward without moving, see with other eyes, touch with other hands from his own [. . .] a stranger to himself, a deserter from his own body, an exile for evermore' (*PI*, 85).

See also: Critical Space; Phenomenology; Speed; Technology

STATE

Eric Wilson

As with art, Virilio has no formal theory of the state, regarding it as the arena of the exercise of the hegemony of optics and visual culture. Speed-politics, which governs the state, revolutionises the relationship between the sovereign and the subject. As Virilio puts it in *Polar Inertia* (2000a [1990]: 56–7):

[The] subject or *subjugated* observer thus becomes inseparable from the observed object, because of the very immediacy of the interface, of the aptly named 'terminal', that perfects the extension and duration of a world reduced to man–machine commutation, where the 'spatial depth' of perspectival geometry suddenly gives way to the 'temporal depth' of a *real-time perspective* superseding the old real-space perspective of the Renaissance.

The modern state, like modern art, originates in the Italian Renaissance with the development of civic ritual as a form of virtual politics: 'Renaissance painting (linear perspective; depth) lays the foundation for the Enlightenment "anthropic principle", which regards the existence of any observer as inseparable from the existence of rationally observed phenomena' (*PI*, 51). The virtual re-presentation of the state as optical phenomena through civic pageantry underlies the successor political project of the Enlightenment, which is grounded upon a strict correlation between modernity with vision. The state can now be understood in terms of optical considerations of 'high resolution' or 'high definition' as factors governing the invisibility underlying power relations; a constant, and rapid, alteration between foreground and background, between the visible and the invisible (Virilio 2005a [1984]: 26–38). Conversely, the state, as the final arbiter of all definitional thresholds of political reality, may be reconceptualised in terms of the entirety of its existence as an optical effect; juro-political truth is mediated through surveillance and transparency. Virilio has made this point clearly through a striking example taken from the modes of political control developed during the French Enlightenment:

It is no longer the body of the army that passes back and forth in tight ranks beneath the regard of the intendant, now it is the inspector general that files past in review of the provinces, aligned as in a parade. Yet the repetition of these reviews that triggers *the unfolding of the regional film is only an artifice, only a cinematic special effect* which benefits the itinerant observer. Perceiving the sequence of geographic locations in this isolated fashion, the general loses sight of the local realities and immediately demands the reform of the common law in order to advance the administrative standard. (*NH*, 68)

The state is 'real' precisely to the degree that it is capable not only of perception but, also, to the same degree, and in the same manner, that it is capable of being perceived. The paradox, then, of Michel Foucault's (1991) 'surveillance society' is that its optical hegemony, achieved through the expansion of surveillance, always stands in inverse relationship to the visibility of the state. The state creates its own virtual existence through time by means of the continuous recirculation of the externalised signs of its visibility through space; the 'procession' of the intendant through the virtual geospatial territory of the state both sees and is seen.

This ritualistic act of mutual constitution, however, serves as the grounds of a dangerous metaphysical 'trap' for the state: in effect, the reality of the state is reduced to its virtual appearance. Here, of course, 'real' means 'lawful'. The prejudice of modern liberalism is that the mutual conditionality of the reality and the legality of the state is guaranteed by the state's co-determinate existence with the visible, or 'public', realm; 'The State apparatus is in fact simply an apparatus of displacement [*déplacement*], its stability appears to be assured by a series of temporary gyroscopic processes of delocalisation and relocalization' (*NH*, 56). The demarcation of the political body of the state rests largely upon its successful deployment of its arsenal of optical devices. Panoptical techniques and their variables, most crucially their velocity, or 'speed of apperception', serve as the parameters within which the state regulates the politics of appearance

(*PI*, 45). Political control of such a high-velocity virtual reality ultimately threatens the state with a form of ontological 'disappearance' into the aesthetic techniques of its construction of political reality.

In an anti-Hegelian pun, Virilio (1989 [1984]: 33) defines the post-Enlightenment state as 'pure' – that is, it attains its highest form of being through disappearing: 'The state's only original existence is as a visual hallucination akin to dreaming.' Politics 'disappears' into aesthetics precisely through its inability to successfully uphold the 'reality principle', which is premised upon conventional representational demarcations between the 'real', the 'visual' and the 'virtual' (Virilio 2009a [1980]). In one sense, the 'purity' of the state is the perfect realisation of its (self-) annihilating will towards universal transparency. This ontological and political 'loss of reality' is identified with the kinematic, which assumes two forms. 'Kinematic optics', or 'cinematic motion', effectively 'dissolves' substance through the acceleration of perception; time supplants space which 'deletes' Being (*PI*, 45). 'Kinematic acceleration' is thus realised through the 'dismemberment' of space/time into isolated 'frames' or editorial 'cuts'. In both instances of the kinematic, the virtual re-presentation of reality is now governed by alterations in the rate, or speed, of perception: 'It is reality [that] we have to measure in a cinematic way' (*WC*, 79–89). The final outcome is a total 'virtualising' of reality arising from 'the unprecedented limits imposed on subjective perception by the instrumental splitting of modes of perception and representation' (1994b [1988]: 49). In the second sense, the optical/ontological collapse of politics into speed underlies Virilio's identification of the 'pure state' with 'pure war' (Virilio and Lotringer 2008), a military metaphor that signifies the centrality of the panoptical to the contemporary mode of combat. 'The primacy of speed is simultaneously the primacy of the military' (Virilio and Lotringer 2008: 51); pure war is the master-sign of a (post-) modern world-system that is governed by speed-politics, signifying the total reversibility between the 'political', the 'military' and the 'economic'. Politics disappears into a tripartite 'logistics of perception' (*WC*): military, tele-cinematic and technoscientific. Pure war is a more ontologically sophisticated rendering of the 'Revolution in Military Affairs' (RMA), the Pentagon's theorisation of future wars and their technological organisation, which is more commonly known as 'shock and awe' or the US military doctrine founded on the use of irresistible power:

It is a war of images and sounds, rather than objects and things, in which winning is simply a matter of not losing sight of the opposition. The will to see all, know all, at every moment, everywhere, the will to universalized illumination: a scientific permutation on the eye of God which would forever rule out the surprise, the accident, the irruption of the unforeseen. (*VM*, 70)

By attaining purity, the state becomes 'suicidal'; the unlimited projection of pure war simultaneously into external space (exo-colonisation) and internal space (endo-colonisation) yields a military and political struggle devoid of temporal and spatial duration – the antithesis of Carl von Clausewitz's (1968) account of the 'correct' relationship between war and the state. Yet, for Virilio (*PI*, 78):

Everything that was acted out in dividing the territory is now acted out not only, as before, in organising the social body, but in controlling the animal body of the human being, less 'in the world' than *within himself*. Hence the fragility of human 'self-consciousness', which has been more invaded by technologies than invested with new responsibilities.

In other words, Virilio's pure state culminates in the decomposition of the political, social and bodily subject.

See also: Optics; Perception, Perspective; Politics; Speed; Virtual Reality

STATE OF EMERGENCY

Jason Adams

Virilio's concept of the state of emergency, most notably featured in his *Speed and Politics: An Essay on Dromology* (2006 [1977]: 149–67), focuses on the politics of time and technoculture. Virilio argues that the triumph of absolute speed over relative speed in the contemporary period has displaced earlier modes of dictatorship, which were based upon a temporary state of siege in separate, national spaces. Today, Virilio argues, a permanent state of emergency cuts through all such distinctions, insofar as it amounts to a permanent dictatorship of time.

One example Virilio uses to elucidate this is nuclear war. Whereas the state of emergency has traditionally been understood as a decree made by a single representative authorised to invoke extraordinary constitutional powers within national space, Virilio foregrounds the rise of autonomous technological decision, which functions temporally to govern the entirety of space as such. The development of automatic responders, for instance, authorised in advance to return nuclear warheads within moments after launching in other countries, renders the traditional concern with human decision less central as a unit of analysis.

Just as dauntingly, as the temporal state of emergency increasingly replaces the spatial state of siege, perspective is subtracted from the perceptual field such that autonomous technological decision appears as the only world possible. As a result, Virilio makes visible to us what often goes unnoticed: that, as Andrew Stratton has observed, decision has moved 'from the action stage to the conception stage', which, as we know, characterises automation (*SP*, 156). In this respect, institutionalist approaches to the state of emergency miss one of the central developments of contemporary forms of control, the manner in which technological design can itself become a domain of absolute power and authority.

The difference it makes can be seen in the Arab Spring, the revolutionary wave of protest marches that occurred in the Arab world and which began on 18 December 2010: those sympathetic to it often invoked the relationship between power and technology through a reductive understanding of what is involved in contemporary forms of the state of emergency. While the Egyptian uprising was overthrowing its president, Hosni Mubarak, in January 2011, for instance, it was widely noted that Internet and texting services were cut off, creating a communication vacuum in which only the state retained access to interactivity at accelerated speeds. But, as we have seen, for Virilio, it is not simply the power of the state to invoke a temporary state of emergency within a geographically limited space that counts, but, more importantly, the technological design that creates dictatorial power.

The truly radical development for him, then, would not only have been the democratisation of the state functions but, crucially, the transformation of technological development itself, so that, at a minimum, operability and accessibility would be ensured regardless of who is in power. In other words, in the Egyptian case, it was not the political constitution that granted Mubarak dictatorial power, but, more importantly, the constitution of technology. Just as we fail to perceive the 'emergency lighting system' of telecommunications that has replaced the circadian rhythm that once tied human sleep and wakefulness to the rising and setting sun, we also fail with respect to the permanent state of emergency.

STEREO-REALITY

J. Macgregor Wise

Stereo-reality is Virilio's idea that, rather than replacing reality, virtual reality sits alongside actual reality, so that our current reality consists of two overlapping 'channels', much like stereo vision or stereo sound:

A *stereo-reality* in which the 'high notes' and 'low notes' of the sound landscape of high fidelity acoustics will be replaced, on one hand, by the gravity, the weightiness of bodies and so of the real distances of a *whole* world and, on the other, by the absence of weight, of gravity, of the signals of a kind of visual and tactical high definition appropriate to the exotic arena of electromagnetic fields. (Virilio 1997 [1995]: 41)

Virilio (2000d [1998]: 13–15) writes in *The Information Bomb* that the 'temporal compression of instantaneous communication' creates a 'new vision of a world that is constantly "tele-present" twenty-four hours a day, seven days a week, thanks to the artifice of this "trans-horizon optics" which puts what was previously out of sight on display'. Rather than the horizon line of Renaissance perspective, he suggests in *Open Sky* (*OS*, 41), we now have the new 'square horizon' of the screen. But, unlike much writing on virtual reality, Virilio does not then go on to argue that this new horizon becomes our only horizon, but that one space sits alongside the other in a relation of interdependence. However, this is not a relationship of equals; for the virtual dominates and is imposed on the actual:

As with *stereoscopy* and *stereophony*, which distinguish left from right, bass from treble, to make it easier to perceive audiovisual relief, it is essential today to effect a split in primary reality by developing a *stereo-reality*, made up on the one hand of *the actual reality* of immediate appearances and, on the other, of the *virtual reality* of media trans-appearances. (*IB*, 15)

Stereo-reality is therefore not just passively perceptual (being able to see and hear what is proximate and what is distant at the same time) but active in that one can move, touch and manipulate real objects close by and also (through technologies of telepresence and telerobotics) at a distance, which means that it is an issue for a whole variety of academic disciplines from media and cultural studies to, for example, philosophy and architecture.

In sum, for Virilio, there are three consequences of stereo-reality. The first is our loss of bearings, an inability to orient ourselves in and to the world, and to others, particularly given that today we are increasingly delocalised or rootless. The second consequence is political. For our loss of orientation to the other denotes that we are often more influenced by virtual reality, by media reality, than by actual reality. Virilio writes that, today, '*far* wins out over the *near* [. . .] media representation winning out by a long way over the classic political representation of nations' (*OS*, 74). The loss of the near, of the local, also paves the way for the rise of what he calls the '*omnipolitan* periphery whose *center will be nowhere and circumference everywhere*' (*OS*, 74). And this leads to the third and final consequence, which, Virilio argues, not only signifies that the new reality effect of stereo-reality is the forerunner to real globalisation but also that it is a reality effect of what he terms 'globalitarianism' or worldwide cyber-netic totalitarianism in the form of constant surveillance and information warfare.

STOP-EJECT

Josiane Behmoiras

In this symbolic reference to the now archaic gesture of stopping the cas-sette and ejecting the tape, Virilio refers to the huge movement of global migration that is occurring in our current millennium, when, by 2050, a forecasted one billion people will be forced out of their homes for ecologi-cal, political and economic reasons. In *Native Land: Stop Eject* (Virilio and Depardon 2008: 16), for example, he argues that in accelerated modernity the city is changing from 'a place where we elect to live – to a place of ejection'. Virilio is thus concerned with the way in which this new tran-shumance reshapes human identity, from one that was based on belong-ing to a particular place to one that is founded on movement across the globe.

Similarly, in *Negative Horizon* (Virilio 2005a [1984]: 95), Virilio con-ceptualises the '*révolution de l'emport*' (the transport revolution), contend-ing that the 'urban nebulae' which surround our cities are sites of transit (e.g. railway stations, airports) that are presently being developed as 'sites of ejection', thereby replacing our former 'sites of election'. Equally, in *The Futurism of the Instant: Stop-Eject* (Virilio 2010b [2009]: 25–6), he proposes that, because of the introduction of portable teletechnologies, sedentary people are now at home everywhere while nomadic people are now nowhere at home, except, perhaps, in the ever burgeoning transitory settlements, border crossings and deportation camps that signal a forced depopulation exercise of global proportions (see, for instance, Armitage 2010). Indeed, Virilio suggests that, in our era of global technological instantaneity and ubiquity, the reality of globalisation is such that it rep-resents a fundamental disturbance in our notion of human activity within a settled community; economic practices, such as the 'just in time' mode of product delivery and the outsourcing of human labour, for example, displace populations from their native land, from the here and now of their place of origin. This disruption of human activity, he maintains, amounts to nothing less than a 'war of movement of civilians' in which the 'purchasing power' of the credit card supplants the 'staying power' of the identity card (*FI*, 29):

What is shaping up here, in this universe that's so much busier excluding than expanding, is no longer, no matter what they say, the return of the cosmopolis, or even of the claustropolis of gated communities or high-rise towers. What is shaping up, above all, is the marshalling yard, that 'terminus of last wishes' that Cendrars talked about in *Trans-Siberian Prose*. (*FI*, 29–30)

To understand that the Earth has become too small for both progress and short-term profit, Virilio suggests that we need to rethink the finiteness of real space and challenge the illusion of real time that reduces past, present and future into an omnipresent instant. He argues that the protracted miniaturisation of our earthly habitat and its proportions is, in truth, the desertification of the world. In the end, then, after the transience and hoped for utopia of 'suburbia' and the ensuing ejection of 'exhurbia', Virilio warns of the coming final dystopia: the extraterrestrial exodus of humanity from planet Earth.

STRATEGY OF THE BEYOND

John David Ebert

That principle whereby contemporary state formations appropriate the religious vocabulary of soteriology (the theological doctrine of deliverance as advocated by Jesus) in order to further their own political aims. In *Negative Horizon* (2005a [1984]: 179–200), Virilio holds up 'Democratic Kampuchea', the Khmer Rouge-controlled state that ruled Cambodia between 1975 and 1979, as a paradigmatic example of this phenomenon: he contrasts the Khmer Rouge assertion that revolution is a more pure form of purification than religion, with Buddhism, where the punishment is always deferred to the next lifetime and, as a result, one never knows when, or for precisely which sin, one is being punished. With revolution, on the other hand, the Khmer Rouge point out that the guilty individual is punished immediately and that revolution is therefore superior to traditional religious soteriology. However, it is a nihilistic strategy, since, along with this, traditional state infrastructures – such as the process of incarceration and the documentation of individuals with birth certificates and so on – disappear. As a result, Virilio says that the utopian socialism of the Khmer Rouge reveals itself as an atopian eschatological power determined to hasten the Last Judgement.

Virilio asserts that there is a conflict in these current state formations between priest and warrior, a conflict in which the transpolitical beyond is at stake. What instantaneity is for the warrior – in the case of the Khmer's immediacy of punishment, for instance – eternity is for the priest. No more duration, no more topography.

The context for the advent of this transpolitical beyond, however, is the post-Cold War (1947–91) disintegration of the nation-state, with its traditional geopolitical orientation of geographical extensivity – capable of generating World Wars – to be contrasted with the current chronopolitical orientation of state formations whose intensivity is causing them to implode, thus creating wars of endless duration – as in the case of Cambodia – wars which are often internally directed against the state's own citizens. These are wars of humanitarian crises, intensive guerrilla wars, or little wars with separatist demands which oppose traditional nation-state formations out of a stated demand for self-autonomy in the era of decolonisation. Virilio points out that with the breakdown of the nation-state and its traditional ideas of the constitutionally guaranteed rights of the individual, new forms of terrorism are arising, some of them state-sponsored and backed by unstable regimes that go 'beyond' all traditional forms of politics – hence their 'transpolitical' orientation. For such supernumerary populations deprived of civil rights, transpolitical tactics are becoming the new norm. The imploding contemporary state, with its transpolitical city, deprived of both territory and corporeality, is a regime founded more on the immediate survival of the body rather than, as in the past, the post-mortem survival of the soul.

Virilio points out that a military–scientific messianism has crept into the contemporary state formation, which no longer bothers to conscript the individual in the service of defending the state, but is rather more concerned with converting him to a faith in salvation by the virtues of absolute armament, and hence, the salvation of the body. Thus, this parody of the religious state actually inverts the traditional religious soteriology of the salvation of the soul with a salvation of the body in its place.

SUICIDAL STATE

Mark Featherstone

Virilio (1998, 'Suicidal State') discusses the idea of the suicidal state in his *L'insécurité du territoire* (1993), starting with the premise that modern society wages war on its own environment. In his view, following the Nazi declaration of Total War in 1943, Western society entered a period of 'Total Peace', which we may define as Total War fought by other means. In *Pure War* (Virilio and Lotringer 2008), Virilio explores a similar idea through the notion of 'pure war', which equally shows how the pursuit of total social security collapses back into a state of total insecurity. His key conception here is that, following the Second World War, the Allied powers – and he refers to post-war era Britain as the main example – sought to wage war on poverty and thereby create a society defined by freedom from want. However, in doing so, Britain and other Western countries produced a totally administered society, which essentially took away their citizens' freedom and left them entirely dependent on the state for their survival. Virilio notes that the state became a life support system, which could be turned off at any time, thus killing the citizen. As such, the state-sponsored attempt to create a society of security and safety inadvertently produced a society of insecurity because citizens became dependent on the state milieu for their survival.

Virilio also considers the American attitude to imperialism, noting that US presidents from Wilson to Nixon dismissed the idea of American colonialism, preferring instead to export the American way of life. Virilio's idea is that America does not colonise others but, rather, exports a cultural way of being, a milieu or environment, which functions as a frame of integration for ordering life. This frame of integration entails the market and related sociopolitical and economic principles such as democracy, individualism, consumerism and, perhaps most importantly, freedom. Yet Virilio's belief is that this sort of freedom is foreclosed by the statist milieu because it abolishes the natural environment, and thus our phenomenological relation to the world, in favour of a new constructed state reality, Total Peace, which he associates with pseudo-freedom. Freedom is, therefore, impossible in the state of Total Peace and social security because being and movement are controlled by police and military powers. Virilio's notion of the state of Total Peace is thus comparable to Michel Foucault's (2002) theory of the disciplinary state, which is organised around the principle of governmentality. But where Virilio's idea differs from Foucault's is in the way he explicitly maintains a Heideggerian (see, for example, Young 2001) view of the natural milieu. In other words, for Virilio and for Heidegger, the new life support system of the social state is ultimately 'suicidal' for the state and for its citizens.

Virilio excavates these suicidal dimensions of the social security state by tracing the idea of Total Peace, and the creation of the totally administered system, back to the Nazi Total War state, which dominated the freedom of its citizens to the extent that it would become a kind of second nature to them. Virilio points to 'Telegram 71', in which Hitler declared that if Germany should lose the war, the population should perish with it. Here, the existence of the state and the population it governs are seen as one artificial being that attempts to unify people, time and space within a new milieu. Since it functions as a life support machine, this new milieu is, then, not only omnipotent but also destroys the biosphere in the name of a totalitarian, phenomenological, apocalypse. Focused on the human death drive, the new milieu is thus humanity's attempt to escape from itself and its environment. Beyond the Nazi example, Virilio finds evidence for humanity's tendency to destroy itself through the creation of an artificial 'second nature' in, for instance, the American obsession with cinema, cars and war. Resembling the Nazi equation of state and population, Virilio sees this American industrialisation of the tendency to take flight from the world as evidence of the tragic human desire to achieve escape velocity through the creation of the suicidal state.

$$\boxed{\text{T}}$$

TECHNOLOGY

John Armitage

Although occasionally understood as identical with Virilio's contemporary theoretical approach, which he often characterises as the 'critique of the art of technology' (e.g. Virilio and Armitage 2009: 103), this term designates principally his theoretical writings on the relationship between aesthetics and technology. Virilio's critique of the art of technology was instituted as the critique of military technology at the 'Atlantic Wall' – Adolf Hitler's Second World War defensive system against an expected Allied attack that extended from France to Scandinavia – in 1958, developed in Paris in the 1960s and 1970s and matured from the 1980s onwards. Its most important influences are Edmund Husserl (1859–1938) and Henri Bergson (1859–1941), Martin Heidegger (1889–1976) and, more recently, Hans Jonas (1903–93). Virilio also contributes to numerous academic journals, periodicals and newspapers on problems relating to technology.

Virilio's interest in the association between aesthetics and technology is beholden throughout to his and Claude Parent's architectural theory (Virilio and Parent 1996 and 1997) but embraces a less 'oblique'-based model in Virilio's writings on *Bunker Archeology* (1994a [1975]) and the contemporary impact of military technology on the organisation of space. This differentiated it from the geopolitical intonation of certain of Virilio's (1993) works, conceived in what some might think to be too close an empathy with the Marxist philosophy of Herbert Marcuse (1991

[1964]). Virilio's first major work on the connection between aesthetics and technology is his *Speed and Politics: An Essay on Dromology* (2006 [1977]), a critique of the military and political impact of the nineteenth- and twentieth-century revolutions in transportation and transmission technologies, which are perceived by Virilio as complicit with 'the time of the finite world [. . .] coming to an end' and the 'beginnings of a para- doxical *miniaturization of action*, which others prefer to baptise *automation* (*SP*, 156). This book includes the much-reprinted essay, 'The State of Emergency', a remorseless condemnation of what Virilio understands as the 'violence of speed', which has 'become both the location and the law, the world's destiny and its destination' (*SP*, 167).

At its most demanding, Virilio's *The Aesthetics of Disappearance* (2009a [1980]) maintains a rigorous aesthetic examination of the inconsistencies of contemporary technologised vision, but while in this respect indebted to his architectural theory and to phenomenology, he looks to the socio- cultural consequences of modern cinema and visual slips (absences, departures, interruptions) for an oppositional receptivity to technology rather than to the customary phenomenological activities of human consciousness and temporality. The technologically mediated city, in particular, Virilio sees in his *The Lost Dimension* (1991 [1984]) as corrod- ing physical space and as threatening to soak up all but the most essential of metropolitan buildings. He makes his point of view known through a discussion of American cities and a focus upon the aesthetic and techno- logical aspects of 'the overexposed city' (*LD*, 9–20). Here, we no longer enter the city through a gate but through an 'electronic audience system' as 'interlocutors in permanent transit' where 'continuity is ruptured in time, in a time that advanced technologies and industrial redeployment incessantly arrange through a series of interruptions, such as plant clo- sures, unemployment, casual labor, and successive or simultaneous disap- pearing acts' (*LD*, 11). His later writings, *War and Cinema: The Logistics of Perception* (1989 [1984]) and *Negative Horizon* (2005a [1984]), where he sought to comprehend the use of cinematographic and interrelated technological techniques during the First and Second World Wars and the connections between technological speed, culture, politics and society, have become important texts for the critical study of technoculture in the twenty-first century. In *Negative Horizon*, for example, Virilio (*NH*, 199) not only perceives 'technological excesses' as replacing 'war objectives with ideologies' but also a 'scientific excess' that is currently installing a 'technological idolatry (the Gnostic belief in a transcendence of science) in place of political economy'. His *The Vision Machine* (1994b [1988]) likewise ascribes a critical role to challenging the propaganda of progress that surrounds the computerisation of post-industrial production and our perception of the world, although in terms other than those of his previous architectural and phenomenological theory (Armitage 2012).

Virilio's theoretical critique of the art of technology is exercising a broad influence upon contemporary technocultural theory, especially through his writings on *Polar Inertia* (2000a [1990]), which is a series of essays on the relationship between space, time and technology. Yet, in *Desert Screen* (2002a [1991]: 2–3), his reports on the Gulf War of 1990–1 for European newspapers, he rejects the association of 'the development of air-land military units using "forward projection" – such as the American Rapid Deployment Force (RDF)' – with military success of the kind claimed by other commentators (e.g. de la Billiere 2008), arguing that 'the essence of the strategy' was to be 'found elsewhere in the extraterrestrial components of the US Strategic Defense Initiative, the orbital deployment of independent satellite or reconnaissance forces, of advance alert or transmission, depending solely upon "the American spatial high command", a true *deus ex machina* of planetary peace or war', and many have found his censure of 'the outdated arguments of military leaders concerning [. . .] "rapid" action or reaction' intricate and productive. Nevertheless, Virilio's *The Art of the Motor* (1995 [1993]) is appalled by the seeming technologisation of the human body and by the expanding of the body's abilities through technology in the postmodern age, as evidenced by his searing critique of 'hyperactive man' (*AM*, 111; see also Armitage 2013). A supplementary development, linked with Virilio's *Open Sky* (1997 [1995]), wherein he propounds his cultural theory of the acceleration of communication tools that are presently obliterating geophysical space, is his increasing concern with the fields of television studies, urban theory and tele-action technologies such as the Internet, which 'delocalise' human activities on a global scale (*OS*, 82). Virilio's (2000d [1998]) concept of *The Information Bomb*, by which the dogmas of modern technoscience were analysed, and, later, radicalised as a *Strategy of Deception* (2000b [1999]), has been appreciated both within and without Virilio studies as a theoretical model of a new sort of critique of the art of technology needed to respond to the *Unknown Quantity* (2003b [2002]), and to the transformed aesthetics and technoculture of fear at work in the global *City of Panic* (2005b [2004]). Such a theory must, needless to say, be reflexively critical and unsettling of the suppositions of the very projects of art and technology, of the university, of our theories of catastrophe and of the future, of instantaneity, and of acceleration (see, for instance, Virilio 2010a [2007]; 2010b [2009]; and 2012 [2010]). As Virilio (Virilio and Richard 2012: 80) appropriately and succinctly puts it in *The Administration of Fear*: 'Technology's time is not past, but it can no longer continue *like this*.'

See also: *Aesthetics of Disappearance; City; Military Space; Propaganda of Progress; Speed*

TENDENCY

Mark Featherstone

Virilio discusses the idea of the tendency in *Pure War* (Virilio and Lotringer 2008: 52–3) where he develops a politics of writing in relation to the progress and decline of Western society. Noting that speed and violence are perpetually interlaced, he argues that every invention associated with progress is also the invention of an accident, intimating the continual breakdown of contemporary culture and civilisation (for example, the invention of the train is the simultaneous invention of the train wreck). However, he also observes that the persistence and inevitability of the accident has been censored by those hegemonic forms of thought linked to Western modernity, such as its conceptions of progress, development and modernisation. He proposes that there is no room in these forms of thought for the notion of the inevitable catastrophe, which is why the meaning of the word 'accident' implies uncertainty and indeterminism. In other words, while the accident does not have to happen, after it does, it is only then that people come to believe that things could have been otherwise.

Against this dominant standpoint, Virilio suggests that we should build a museum of accidents with a view to recuperating the notion of the accident within modernity. His estimation is that people have to understand the accidents, interruptions and events that repeatedly disrupt modern 'progress'. For example, he suggests that the striker's barricade is the materialisation of an interruption in space, whereas Sunday, the vacation or death are interruptions in time. He contends that we now occupy a world defined by the struggle between the 'connect' and the 'disconnect', simply by virtue of the fact that the more important the connection becomes in the globalised network society, the more pervasive the disconnect also becomes. And disconnection is ubiquitous. Consider, for instance, the fragmentation of war. There is no more unity of war. War is now everywhere and nowhere. It is no longer about two static lines of troops facing each other, but about urban guerrilla warfare, which is always connected (for example, to the Internet and to mobile phones and so on). And it is for these reasons that Virilio believes that traditional modes of writing and explanation cannot capture the fragmented reality of today's world or understand its likely future. Accordingly, his own politics of writing leads him to proceed through a train of thought that is simultaneously connected and disconnected, that emerges through a mode of expression that is characterised by jumps, cuts, breaks and the refusal of logical development:

I work in staircases – some people have realized this. I begin a sentence, I work out an idea, and when I consider it suggestive enough, I jump a step to another idea without bothering with the development. Developments are the episodes. I try to reach the tendency. Tendency is the change of level. (*PW*, 52–3)

This methodology is essential for Virilio because it has the capacity to embrace the fragmented thoughts, events and incidents that he associates with today's dialectic of connectivity and disconnectivity.

TERRITORY

May Ee Wong

For Virilio, territory is generally defined as terrestrial military space, and, as he explicates in his writings, this geographical definition is made problematic by the effects of military technologies regarding shifting paradigms of dromological warfare. In his discussion of dromology, or the study of speed and the logistics of movement, Virilio presents territory as a dynamically organised form of space, because he sees war as the organisation of perception which is effected by movement and acceleration. Territory has been traditionally regarded as a military technology in itself, as a form of fortification, due to the military's constant concern to establish control over the field of action. This desire for control has led to an acceleration in the workings of transportation, info–communications and weapon technologies in managing the proceedings of war. As the speed of vehicles and weapons increases exponentially along with the extension of the geographical reach of these technologies, Virilio proposes that spatial territory becomes less strategically important as space becomes more temporally defined. He sees (2006 [1977]: 149) space as negated by the 'supersonic vector' of the aeroplane or the rocket, and comments that '[t]erritory has lost its significance in favor of the projectile'. Even though the rise of war has always been geopolitically motivated, in this 'war of time' (2005a [1984]: 102), it is the power one has over time that gives rise to power over territorial space.

Virilio's concept of territory as military space is explicitly discussed in *Bunker Archeology* (1994a [1975]), where he relates how the topography of military violence has come to exceed geographical boundaries, especially in the case of Total War. Describing the Second World War German bunkers along the Atlantic Wall as an emblem of strategic defensive military logic which has transformed the littoral space of the French coast, Virilio locates the bunkers within a larger developmental trajectory of military technologies serving an accelerating war which contracts the geographical dimensions of the world, while increasing projectile power by miniaturising energy particles that are employed in nuclear weapons. The use of 'invisible arms', or weapons of info-communications, which enabled the co-ordination between land, sea and air forces during the Second World War through the transmission of signals in an integrated system, initiated an age of automation of warfare which has challenged the primacy of territory. As the Swiss architect Bernard Tschumi suggests in his 'Foreword' to Virilio's *A Landscape of Events* (Virilio 2000c [1996]: ix), for Virilio, territory is no longer relevant to military considerations as 'a political space that can be enclosed by walls'. Instead, what is important is the 'reaction time' (*LE*, ix) taken for the computational calculation of probabilities before the execution of a military decision, or the perception of war as an event.

The impact of teletechnologies on space has led to a perceptual deterritorialisation of space which invites a reconsideration of the nature and significance of territory itself. In his *Open Sky* (1997 [1995]), Virilio discusses the virtualising effect of real-time transmission of telecommunications technologies on real space, what he terms the '*electromagnetic conditioning of the territory*' (*OS*, 12). The ability of these teletechnologies to produce presence at a distance obliterates the difference between the global and the local, as space is produced at a real instant. We now have the creation of virtual spaces that are projected onto screens by the transmission of electromagnetic particles through optoelectronics which bring into effect the mediated transparency of the aesthetics of disappearance. The boundaries of territory are also reconfigured by the extension of these teletechnologies into space in the form of satellites that transmit extraterrestrial orbital space as a controllable frontier.

The deterritorialisation of space gives rise to geopolitical implications when teletechnologies are used in the context of contemporary infowar. Examining the Kosovo War (1998–9) – the war in the region of Kosovo, of the Federal Republic of Yugoslavia, fought between Yugoslav government forces and Albanian separatist forces, and supported by the North Atlantic Treaty Organization (NATO) – in his *Strategy of Deception* (2000b [1999]), Virilio highlights changes in the notions of territory and sovereignty which are underscored by the conceptual shift in warfare undertaken by the military, as indicated by the computation-driven

Revolution in Military Affairs (RMA), the Pentagon's theorisation of the future of information warfare. In using satellites and Global Positioning System (GPS) technologies which allowed for localised control over space during the Kosovo War, the Allied forces were able to fight an aerial war that bypassed territorial space (Virilio and Armitage 2001b). For Virilio, sovereignty no longer resides in the territory itself, but in the control of the territory (Virilio and Armitage 2001b), which can be remotely managed with teletechnologies. However, sovereignty no longer resides in the political power of the statesman, but in the decision-making processes of the computer that human beings are simply unable to match in speed and analytical power. This situation has resulted in the transformation of traditional political institutions, an issue that Virilio relates to his concept of chronopolitics.

Virilio's discussion of territory implicates the city (or the *polis*) and its politics, as he sees the city as a space that is organised for war and by war. In *Speed and Politics* (2006 [1977]), he provides an account of the development of the city as military territory by demonstrating how the logistical mobilities of warfare shape its physical and sociopolitical dimensions. The city itself is territorialised in its governance, as its dimensions are abstracted and projected as logistical space, with its population perceived as a logistical resource for the military. Foregrounding mobility as the connection between revolutions and social movements and preparations of war engaged by the state, Virilio describes the politics of the city as dromocratic, with the state functioning as an entity that continuously asserts power to maintain and increase systemic traffic and circulation.

The politics of the city has been traditionally aligned with territory, as a citizen's rights are grounded upon the establishment of territorial space, which obligates him or her to defend it. However, in the age of speed and chronopolitics, the deterritorialisation of space has unsettled this correlative relationship between political rights and territory. As Virilio articulates in his vision of an omnipolitan world, while the proliferation of real-time teletechnologies has promoted the importance of the global city with the facilitation of trade, financial and communication exchanges, it has also delocalised human activity, creating a disconnection between citizen and place. Just as territory becomes less of a legitimate factor in warfare, citizenship becomes less of a relevant descriptor of political agency.

See also: City; Deterritorialisation; Military Space; Speed-Space; Technology; War

THEORY

Gerry Coulter

Virilio is one of a number of highly interesting and innovative theorists who have contributed to the contemporary theoretical landscape. His work is important for many reasons, not the least of which is that it points to the importance of developing radical new concepts with which to interpret severe and rapidly deepening conditions afflicting the human condition (dromology, the aesthetics of disappearance, pure war and so on). Virilio is a theorist of technoscience and war more than a 'social theorist' as many have tended to understand the term. He has contributed a new vocabulary to help us to see ourselves the way he does, as a creature in need not of more technoscientific propaganda or glib promotionalism but, rather, of an intelligence of technoscience which will better help us to interpret the many dimensions of our hyper-scientific existence we have not yet examined sufficiently.

Virilio has raised the stakes well beyond those of the neo–Marxist conflict theorists who dominated so-called 'critical' thought during the bulk of the latter half of the twentieth century. He does so by supplanting theories of social conflict with his central concept of war. Virilio's understanding, which he has shared in a succession of brilliant books over the past three decades, is the notion that contemporary global culture is characterised by war. His 'war model' speaks to the rise of modern society and the contemporary city. Virilio is primarily an urbanist and theorist of collective if not social space. His work decentres Marxian political economy, replacing it with an emphasis on the militarisation of space, technology, communications technologies and culture. Vital to this theoretical move has been the development of the concept of polar inertia.

Virilio is thus a theorist of the strategy and rationality of technoscience in the military organisation and reorganisation of urban space since the Middle Ages. That said, his work has many ramifications for how his readers may come to interpret the social (see, especially, Virilio and Petit 1999 [1996]). What Virilio cannot fully explain, yet constantly seeks to understand and share, is an awareness of the way in which the rise of technoscience has led to a deepening sense of a real loss of control in the contemporary era. His work points to the multiple intersections between technoscience and war and its impact upon our logistics of perception. For Virilio, we live among a world of screens in which we can no longer believe what we see – a world in which technoscience and war have impacted upon our understanding of the real and our ability to distinguish between technoscience and the better interests of human society. He has attempted, not without success among circles in which contemporary theory is valued and discussed, to contribute an understanding of the importance of the technoscientific and military organisation of both territory and, importantly, how we perceive territory.

To imagine the contemporary theoretical landscape without Virilio is to understand how significant has been his contribution to our consciousness of the architectures of war and their impact upon the rise of modernity and its elaborations into hypermodernity. For him, the aesthetics of hypermodernity is, upon closer inspection, the aesthetics of a technoscientific way of organising culture and as such is his principle contribution to 'theory'. In a nutshell, Virilio's main theoretical development is a heightened attentiveness to war in the organisation of all aspects of contemporary existence. His contribution to theory leaves many readers with a deeper sense that we may, as a species, have passed a point of no return in our love/hate relationship with technology and science. Virilio also increases our awareness that we may already have entered into a cataclysmic phase the outcome of which will be an answer to the question: can the human survive the technoscientific age? Virilio is neither pessimistic nor particularly optimistic about the possible answers to this question. He does, however, feel a deep responsibility to try to increase our conceptual abilities with which to devise an actual technoscientific intelligence that can stand against the roar of slick advertising campaigns in the age of information and the Internet. Virilio is a strange theory optimist who appears to write because he believes we still have time to correct our course.

What results from his efforts is not a 'Virilian theory' per se, but, rather, a 'Virilio effect' (see, for example, Armitage 2012: 117–39). The Virilio effect is dedicated to piercing the protective bubble of technology in which we have been encased in order to heighten our responsiveness to the militarised aesthetics of hypermodern globalising cultures.

THIRD INTERVAL

Richard G. Smith

'The third interval' (1997 [1995]: 9–21) is Virilio's neologism in his *Open Sky* to conceptualise both the topology of globalisation at the speed of light and to signal the consequences of 'the moment we step beyond the transport age into the organization and *electromagnetic conditioning of the territory*' (*OS*, 12). A staple of the Virilian corpus is that speed, and specifically the relativity afforded by the speed of light, is fundamental not just for physics and astrophysics but also for understanding the space-time of daily life. Absolute understandings of time and space *à la* Sir Isaac Newton, which have framed discussions of the transport age, are inadequate, asserts Virilio, because the global telecommunications age operates at the speed of light and so conceptualisations must now, *à la* Albert Einstein, account for relativity: '*[t]ime* (duration) and *space* (extension) are now inconceivable without *light* (limit-speed)' (*OS*, 13).

The contention of the third interval is that 'Speed not only allows us to get around more easily; it enables us above all to see, to hear, to perceive and thus to conceive the present world more intensely' (*OS*, 12) and consequently is analogous to a host of concepts that have been proposed over the last fifty years – for example, the global village (McLuhan 2001 [1964]), time-space convergence (Janelle 1968: 5–10), time-space distanciation (Giddens 1981), time-space compression (Harvey 1989) – which have similarly attempted to capture how globalisation and advances in information and communication technologies affect the qualities of space and time and so alter how the world is represented and experienced.

The third interval grandly proclaims that the urbanisation of real space is being overtaken – because of the 'transmission revolution' – by the urbanisation of 'real time' so that through technological advances in media and communication, societies are becoming more atomised, insular and immobile. Virilio supposes that the instant globalisation of 'real time' has two negative paradoxes. First, a diremption, 'getting closer to the "distant" takes you away proportionally from the "near" (and dear) [. . .] thus making strangers, if not actual enemies, of all who are close at hand' (*OS*, 20). And, second, a stationariness:

where the motorization of transport and information once caused a *general mobilization* of populations [. . .] instantaneous transmission tools cause the reverse: *a growing inertia*; television and especially remote control action no longer requiring people to be mobile, but merely to be mobile on the spot. (*OS*, 20)

As an attempt to portray how the geographies and sociologies of quotidian life are being transformed by those media and telecommunication technologies that operate at the speed of light, the third interval reads like science fiction. Indeed, the factual basis of the negative paradoxes Virilio supposes are so easily refuted – for example, through recourse to the findings of studies such as those by the sociology of technology researcher Sherry Turkle (2011) – that the third interval is perhaps best understood as a gloomy reminder to humanity that the overwhelming acceleration of everything is the end game of capitalism, a system whose goal is to be fast, to reduce the circulation of capital to 'the twinkling of an eye' (Harvey 1989: 106).

TRAJECTORY

Drew S. Burk

Identity was once built upon our relationship to a stable place, marker, territory or dwelling. Today, however, within the acceleration of reality or what Virilio (1997 [1995]) calls the 'dromosphere', identity is no longer established in a particular 'place' but within a continuous, traceable trajectory of human movement.

Indeed, Virilio (2010b [2009]) claims that we no longer reside within a position of objectivity or subjectivity but within a trajectory. Accordingly, as the perspective of real time takes precedence as a means of demarcating our daily landscape within the globally networked 'city-world', we come to realise that perpetual movement has become the sign by which our identity plays itself out. Within the trajectory, though, it is the instantaneity, ubiquity and immediacy of new information and communications technologies that provide the means by which our daily routines are not only captured and documented but also traced and tracked:

What I mean by traceability is that, today, all our gesticulations, our slightest actions, are observed, sensed, and highlighted by the techniques and technologies of computerized tracking. Each and every one of us is now under the controlling gaze of various detectors, of video cameras, of radars, and of other forms of control and detection, such as the electromagnetic waves carrying the messages of our appropriately named 'cell' phones. (Virilio and Armitage 2009: 103–4)

For Virilio, this technological imposition of perpetual movement and inertia within real time also creates a migratory crisis for the sake of mobility itself. As with the enforced migration of almost the entire population of New Orleans in the aftermath of Hurricane Katrina in 2005, with the installation of the real-time perspective, we also find ourselves facing questions of nomadism, sedentariness, population and temporality. For if the nomad becomes the forced position of populations due to catastrophes or to the accelerated demands of the globally networked city-world, where populations must perpetually move so as to obtain work or to simply survive, then 'the sedentary urbanism of the recent past becomes increasingly *nomadic*' (Virilio and Armitage 2009: 109). In other words, when everyone takes up the position of living within the trajectory, there will be some who will be at home anywhere, as long as they have their mobile phones to connect them, and there will be others who will feel nowhere at home. If these two positions are becoming harder to distinguish between, it is because, within the trajectory, populations must learn to cope with dwelling within 'an exurbanism that entails both the end of sedentary urbanism and also *the "resettlement" of the entire world!*', a 'development' that 'amounts to nothing less than the end of geopolitical cities, the end of the rural-urban exodus, at least in the advanced countries, and the beginning of the cities of the beyond' (Virilio and Armitage 2009: 110).

ULTRACITY

Hugh Davies

Virilio's concept of the ultracity, also known as 'Ultraville', was first described as 'Omnipolis' in his *The Art of the Motor* (1995 [1993]) and briefly elaborated upon in *Speed and Politics: An Essay on Dromology* (2006 [1977]), *Open Sky* (1997 [1995]) and *The Information Bomb* (2000d [1998]). However, the term 'ultracity' is fully developed in Virilio's *The Futurism of the Instant*: *Stop-Eject* (2010b [2009]: 32–69), the second chapter of which is titled and devoted to the idea of the ultracity:

> The original town is giving way to the *ultracity* produced by an exurbanism that is not so much metropolitan as omnipolitan, and this anticipates the not far-off colonial exodus to the *ultraworld* of a distant planet [. . .] (*FI*, 37)

For decades, Virilio has discussed the quickening velocity of transportation and communication technologies and its influence on people and spaces. He identifies the ultracity as a radical new urban architecture resulting from communicative instantaneity, perpetual connectivity and a culture in which the 1930s' German far Right author Ernst Jünger's dream of 'total mobilisation' has been normalised (see, for example, Armitage 2003). For Virilio, this new architecture requires a complete overhaul of ideas around notions of location, citizenship and movement.

This is because the ultracity is not accessible through roads and highways but, rather, through digital devices and superhighways: the ultracity is then a virtual city that is simultaneously everywhere and nowhere. Being a citizen of the ultracity is not a geographical experience but a social, technological and psychological condition. People inhabit the city from wherever they are: in high-speed trains, in jets, in lifts, with their mobile phones and their laptops; in short, the ultracity's major defining characteristic is the movement and interconnectedness of its occupants. Their movement is not concerned with reaching a destination but with achieving a trajectory, a perspective that has the effect of 'relocating' those buildings once on the periphery of the city – airports, train stations, harbours and so on – to the 'centre' of the ultracity. The ultracitizens' connectedness, and, in turn, citizenship is thus guaranteed through their technological tools, their addiction to them, and through their increasing intolerance of older modalities of non-virtual presence. Yet the traceability of such technologies creates claustrophobia. Consequently, for all the speed and movement that these technologies offer, they also prevent our escape from the ultracity's limits, from the demands of work and the proximity of others.

This ubiquitous metropolis whose architecture is not concrete and steel but digital information systems and networks has its own species of commerce. The department stores and skyscrapers of this city – Facebook, Amazon, Google and eBay – are simultaneously monolithic and ethereal. Nevertheless, while the ultracity is not a physical location, it does have significant effects on actual geography, displacing both the physical community and the local identity of the historical city and its rulers. Once a place of election, the city is now a place of ejection. Such ejections occur not only to those travelling in planes and trains but also to a growing nomadic underclass, the latter of which stems from factors such as the forced migration of refugees escaping political conflict and the exodus of populations owing to the disappearance of actual geographic space through rising sea levels. In contrast to the sedentary travellers of the ultracity, who are at home/work everywhere, the nomadic underclass is at home/work nowhere, except, perhaps, in the 'provisional accommodation offered by a now pointless transhumance' and distinguished by dislocation, refugee camps and an 'exoticism of misery' (*FI*, 3).

UNKNOWN QUANTITY

John Armitage

As one of the leading and perceptive contemporary critics of technology and its ethical, political and cultural repercussions, Virilio in his *Unknown Quantity* (2003b [2002]) catalogue, published to supplement the exhibition he created at the Fondation Cartier pour l'Art Contemporain in Paris, considers the philosophical questions provoked by our confrontation with breathtaking accidents and their appalling and unsettling influence on our world. Exposing 'something' about ourselves and the technological systems we erect, Virilio's catalogue not only presents illustrations and photographs of accidents as well as historical paintings and engravings that represent 'natural' and industrialised accidents but also the work of the artists included in the exhibition, such as Lebbeus Woods and Bruce Conner, Tony Oursler and Jonas Mekas.

However, in the essay 'The Unknown Quantity' (2003b [2002]: 128–34) contained in *Unknown Quantity*, Virilio identifies the unknown quantity as the way in which 'daily life today has become pure chance, a permanent accident, with its multiple twists and turns, the spectacle of which is constantly inflicted on us from our screens' (*UQ*, 129). This he distinguishes from life in the past, which was 'still a theatre, a stage with its changing backdrops' (*UQ*, 129). The unknown quantity is thus chiefly associated with the accident abruptly becoming inhabitable, to the loss of the substance of our communal planet, and his terms are clearly applicable to the integral accident, which unites us worldwide, and which at times even divides us both mentally and bodily. But although he (*UQ*, 129) recognises the link between the unknown quantity and the integral accident, not to mention the latter's importance as 'what remains unexpected, truly surprising', he sees this connection in a broader context: in other words, the unknown quantity and the integral accident take place in a completely exposed terrestrial environment overexposed to everybody's gaze, from which the 'exotic' has unexpectedly vanished for the 'endotic' that is within ourselves and from which we must observe our exterior life. 'The Unknown Quantity' essay is then part of Virilio's (*UQ*, 129) polemic against 'the *temporal compression* of sensations' and its related '*great confinement*', an incarceration or claustrophobia that has been imposed upon the world by a contemporary generation of global technoscientists. Yet he (*UQ*, 129) associates nature's unknown quantity with the night, 'our only window on the cosmos', whose imminent disappearance, due to 'the degree of light pollution created by excessively powerful electric lighting', needs to be recognised in a new critical vocabulary of our historic inheritance. The unknown quantity of the world, of the day and of the night, of sunlight itself, is fading, he argues, through our growing observation of TV, computer and mobile phone screens 'to the point where the *audiovisual continuum* actually supplants the substantial continuum of astronomy', surely the mark of a tragedy in space and temporality in the age of real time (*UQ*, 130). Acknowledging the unknown quantity is therefore a way for us to develop and maintain a clear-sighted attitude towards the world in the midst of its unexpected foreclosure; it is the answer, he (*UQ*, 130) argues, to the question of how to remain unconfined in the epoch of 'the time accident of instantaneous telecommunications'.

Virilio's argument is consequently an aesthetic response to the integral accident, to the arrival of unrestrained globalisation, and to the suffocating blindness these promote and appear to need if they are to extinguish the everyday life of all of the species on planet Earth bestowed with movement as part of their being. His remarks here, particularly his emphasis on the imprisonment implied at the terminus of history, associate him with earlier philosophical commentary by Michel Foucault (1991) and Frances Fukuyama (1993) on a world of discipline, punishment and the end of history. Indeed, as the 'last man', it might be said that Virilio is describing our initial forays into the very culture of *posthistoire*.

UNIVERSITY OF DISASTER

John David Ebert

By *The University of Disaster*, Virilio (2010a [2007]) does not so much mean the foundation and creation of a real university dedicated to studying accidents and catastrophes – he has stated that he is not militant enough for that – as he does the taking up of a point of view regarding the situation of today's sciences and humanities. Such an approach would study not only literal disasters, or accidents of substances, but also other disasters such as accidents of knowledge and epistemology. For example, the disaster of specialisation in the universities, or the disaster of the pollution of distances on the earth by technologies of telepresence and the global tourism industry (which have a tendency to exhaust places by over-exploiting them), or else the disaster of the triumph of real-time technologies, which have brought history to an end by contracting time into an eternal present that eliminates history and replaces it with accidents. Thus, the concept of the university of disaster functions like one of those old memory theatres in Renaissance rhetoric designed as mnemonic devices for organising a specific type of discourse; in this case, one that studies the accident of substances as well as the accidents of knowledge in all their various manifestations.

In *The University of Disaster*, Virilio suggests that, in light of the failure of the 'success' of Big Science, the university could be reformed in such a way as to counter the barbarism of progress, the hubris and arrogance of a science that no longer knows, or respects, any bounds and has led from an accident in knowledge to a mass-produced repetition of accidents in substances. This would also be meant to counter Aristotle's assertion that there is no science of the accident, only a science of substances. But, due to the spectacular success of this science of substances, it has wreaked havoc on all traditional forms of knowledge, threatening to render them obsolete. The problem, then, with Big Science in particular, is that it remains oblivious to all its ravages and sees only its own successes instead of seeing how it perpetuates integral accidents that cause chains of other accidents in the various domains of atomic physics, biology and genetics. The ultimate hubris of Big Science, Virilio further notes, is the global outsourcing of looking for an exo-planet for the human race to colonise while leaving the Earth, now rendered too small by the ever-accelerating pace of progress, behind. Speed, in other words, has miniaturised the Earth and transformed it into a claustrophobic object. Hence, the accident of knowledge of the success of progress has paradoxically accelerated the finitude of the Earth. This is one of the effects of a technology that has estranged us from geophysics.

As Virilio (2009: 42) says in *Grey Ecology*, the university was founded around the year 1000 as an antidote to barbarism, but any sort of university of disaster founded nowadays, either real or imagined, would have to counter and curb the effects of the barbarism of the progress of science by making its various knowledge accidents visible through concrete applications.

VISION MACHINE

Scott McQuire

The vision machine describes a new phase in the relation between visual technologies and human perception. It first implies a profound disconnection between image and human eye. We are now inured to images that are seen from 'outside': not only from outside the frame of reference of our own bodies but also outside what could be seen by any human body. A second aspect of this dislocation is that images seen (recorded) by a machine are often no longer addressed to any human eye but are destined for viewing (analysis) by another machine.

If the photograph was the first modern technological image, the vision machine describes the contemporary merging of the photographic apparatus with the computer to produce a machine capable not only of 'seeing' but also of 'interpreting' what it sees. For Virilio, the advent of the vision machine raises the question of the disappearance of the viewer, and, potentially, of the properly 'human' point of view of embodied sight. As such, the concept belongs to contemporary debates about relations between human and non–human actors in complex socio-technical milieux.

Virilio's analysis of 'machines for seeing with' has been a consistent theme in his work at least since *War and Cinema: The Logistics of Perception* (1989 [1984]). The concept of the vision machine was first developed in Virilio's *The Vision Machine* (1994b [1988]). Tracing a history of the modern image through Impressionist painting, photography and cinema, he describes a progressive industrialisation of perception. This has the function of reversing the fundamental precepts of the phenomenology that he holds dear. Merleau-Ponty (1969 [1964]: 162) famously understood vision as an extension of embodied subjectivity, remarking that: 'Everything that I see is in principle within my reach, at least within reach of my sight, marked on the map of the "I can."' Virilio (*VM*, 7) argues that the new conditions of indirect vision enabled by technological images mean: 'The bulk of what I see is, in fact and in principle, no longer within my reach.'

Virilio's account of the emergence of the vision machine begins with the increasing demand for modern forms of representation to accommodate themselves to a world in motion. Impressionism is a touchstone, first because it registers this new concern for temporality, but also because it participates in the growing 'decentring' of the human viewer. His example is the unusual framing adopted by Edgar Degas in his pictures of ballet dancers. If Degas's more casual and contingent composition bespeaks a growing sensibility attuned to capturing phenomena on the move, it also opens the door on a new multiplicity in points of view – positions from which it is considered legitimate to represent the world.

Photography, which was, of course, integral to Degas's practice, pro-duces the paradoxical confirmation of this transformation. On the one hand, the photograph takes the geometric perspective of quattrocento painting and renders it automatic. To nineteenth-century eyes imbued by positivist logic, this seemed to be the apex of objective evidence. Yet the very ease of taking pictures, and the proliferation of points of view that inevitably results from the generalisation of photography, contradicts this certainty. Instead of confirming the truth of geometric perspective, photography points towards the distinctive modern condition in which it becomes progressively more difficult to believe that truth corresponds to a singular point of view. The very term that comes to be associated with the photograph in the 1920s – 'snapshot' – registers the new emphasis on spatial and temporal contingency. Virilio (*VM*, 21) astutely summarises the dialectic set in motion by the invention of the camera: 'Considered irrefutable proof of the existence of an objective world, the snapshot was, in fact, the bearer of its own future ruin.'

If the snapshot confirms the irreducibility of *point of view* in art, for

Virilio, this corresponds with a decline in belief – in faith – which is instead channelled into the secular faith of science. Drawing a direct link between the unmooring of perception in modern aesthetics and the distinctive narratives of modern science, he (*VM*, 21) argues: 'This drift of over-exposed matter [. . .] found a scientific explanation in Einstein's "theory of viewpoint."' This understanding of the fundamental relationality of perspective is also integral to cinema, which is a machine built around the dynamic manipulation of point of view. He explores the way that the dynamic image of cinema rapidly became central to new protocols for surveillance: in colonial administration, in metropolitan police forces and, finally, in what becomes the prototype of the vision machine – aerial reconnaissance in the First World War. It is in these fields that the sheer quantity of images forces the adoption of new protocols that will ultimately challenge the place of the human eye in the process of visual scrutiny.

Describing the American Expeditionary Force famously overseen by renowned fashion photographer Edward Steichen, Virilio underlines the importance of the shift to organising aerial-intelligence like a factory. In a prescient analysis, he (*VM*, 48) argues: 'It was not a matter of images now, but of an uninterrupted stream of images, millions of negatives madly trying to embrace on a daily basis the statistical trends of the first great military-industrial conflict.'

Here the technological image begins to forsake the traditional logic of the visual for a new logic of data. The contemporary 'perfection' of the vision machine follows this trajectory. It depends on a combination of automated recording devices (such as CCTV cameras), smart-image processing (such as face-recognition software programs) and the capacity to analyse large volume image-archives using metadata.

The concept of the vision machine is applicable not only to surveillance systems, such as London's so-called 'ring of steel' (a 10,000 plus strong network of CCTV cameras overseeing the streets of central London), but also to the data-streams uploaded 'voluntarily' to privately owned databases such as Facebook. The vision machine belongs to a social condition in which the sort of observation techniques and image-flows developed in wartime surveillance are generalised and directed at peacetime society, especially through techniques of marketing and advertising. Increasingly, such techniques depend upon a 'machinic' point of view that is not available to human users, but is constructed through algorithms embedded in software. Equally critically, in the context of the vision machine, the role of the image shifts from retrospective analysis to one of predictive capability.

See also: Body; Cinema; Perception, Perspective; Technology

VIRTUAL REALITY

Ronald E. Purser

Virtual reality is not merely a new technology but represents a fundamental change in collective perception. Indeed, an all-inclusive, global cybernetic matrix is perhaps the final quest of the rational mode of consciousness. The imagery of a global cybernetic matrix was the subject of William Gibson's (1995 [1984]) science fiction novel *Neuromancer* and *The Matrix* film trilogy (Tofts 2007). Michael Heim (1998: 7) defines virtual reality technology as consisting of three interrelated components: immersion, interactivity and information intensity. Immersion is the experience the user has of being situated in a qualitatively different space, which is achieved by devices that isolate the human senses. Interactivity is the feeling that responses made by the users are effected in real time, providing the capability for 'tele-action'. Information intensity refers to the degree to which the virtual reality experience provides a sense of telepresence and vividness.

Digital technologies provide the capability to make Descartes's abstract world a virtual reality. Virtual reality technologies make use of computer graphics – digital images founded on abstract mathematical spaces. Computer graphics programmers strive to create state-of-the-art photo-realistic images, but their art, unlike the Renaissance artists, has evolved into pure mathematical and algorithmic technique. Rather than striving to accurately represent the actual world on canvas, graphics programmers are busy with modelling or simulating reality; the source of their art is not the actual world, but the mathematically constructed image. Their aesthetic motivation is not realism, nor representation, but simulation or hyperrealism.

Virilio predicted how virtual reality substitutes information for direct knowledge and embodied experience. This virtual or, rather, substitution of information for reality will require a duplication, a 'split-perspective reality', or an ability to function in what Virilio (1997 [1995]: 41) calls 'stereo-reality'. The challenge of having to function and operate in two worlds at once is the source of emerging perceptual disorders in society. Virtual reality theorists have noted this trend, referring to it as the Alternate World Syndrome (Heim 1993, 1998). The split-world perceptual disorder seems to erode what Sigmund Freud (2003) referred to as the 'reality principle'. Noting this trend, Virilio (1995 [1993]: 142) warns:

Once this happens, disinformation will no longer be concerned with solely with dressing up the facts. It will also latch on to the reality principle to try to subtly introduce a new type of a universe: *a virtual universe*, the ultimate form of an undermining of reality of cosmic proportions in which Newton's universal attraction will be replaced once and for all by the cybernetic domination of thought.

For example, someone seeking to experience unspoiled nature may, in the future, enter a virtual reality room and 'visit' Yellowstone National Park and its various wilderness areas. Why bother actually going to Yellowstone when nature can be 'appreciated' in a virtual reality simulator? Many people carry on 'intimate relationships' now within Second Life.

Children are being introduced to the virtual reality aesthetic at a very early age. It is not unusual to see pre-school children sitting behind computers, or playing with iPads or iPhones, as part of their daily routine. Instead of exposing children to the sensory richness, messiness and ambiguities of the physical world – the raw, organic nutrients necessary for fertilising the imagination – they are spoon-fed a pre-packaged assortment of information junk food: Internet images, streaming video and other multimedia dazzle. Virtual reality learning requires high impact images in order to compensate for the absence of the real world, but this force-fed stimulation, with all its brilliance and stunning displays, leaves little room for childlike wonder to flourish.

Virilio (1995 [1993]: 147) characterises this as a valuing of the 'digital image over the image of the naked eye', coupled with an accelerated production of more high intensity audiovisual images, which ultimately alters the rapport between the real and the virtual. Virtual reality astonishes the user both through sensory overload and by presenting an array of images that can be explored interactively. However, like recreational drug addiction, as the threshold of excitation shifts after prolonged drug use, higher dosages are required to secure the desired effect or 'high'. Not surprisingly, numerous clinics have emerged over the world to treat those addicted to video games (Wikipedia 2011).

As this new cultural aesthetic becomes normalised over time, we may even question why we should bother caring about the 'real' when it becomes harder to differentiate the realm of *physis*, *bios* and *ecos* from the realm of *techne*. We may, in fact, cross a threshold where a sort of collective amnesia sets in, as traces of our history and origins are imperceptibly erased from our long-term cultural memory.

With anticipated advances in virtual reality technologies that allow for remote action (tele-action), this trend toward behavioural inertia in technological society will increase. Is it any wonder that childhood obesity is at an all-time high? Tele-action reduces the need for movement and mobility.

The dystopian vision of virtual reality put forth by Virilio is one of a radically disembodied, solipsistic and easily manipulated instruction follower. He (*OS*, 21) uses such images as the 'human terminal', the 'citizen-terminal' and the 'terminal citizen' – all in servitude to a growing inertia and automatisation. He aptly builds upon Marshall McLuhan's (2001 [1964]) insight that every technological advance can be seen as a simultaneous gain and loss, but also as a metaphorical amputation. Every technology, for Virilio (*OS*, 40), has a hidden face. So, for example, with the driving of an automobile, the driver no longer uses her or his legs for locomotion. Since virtual reality has the capacity to dominate the human sensory field, it essentially amputates our need to perceive reality. Virilio (*AM*, 145–6) views the emergence of virtual reality as pointing 'to a future revelation of some "psychogeography" that will be based entirely on cybernetic energy'. This movement is totalising, amounting to 'a new imperialism of instrumental thought' (*AM*, 152).

See also: Cybernetic; Perception, Perspective; Polar Inertia; Real Time; Technology

WAR

Chris Hables Gray

War, Virilio often remarks, was his university. Everything, we might say, progressed from there. A child coming of age during the Second World War, Virilio was ten years old when he witnessed the massive bombing of the French city of Nantes by the Allied air forces that destroyed 8,000 buildings. Moreover, after the French Resistance assassinated the Nazi Kommandantur in Nantes, the Germans rounded up hostages and shot them. One hostage was from the street where Virilio lived. In another incident, a Nazi sailor shot a childhood sweetheart in the eye as she looked out from a terrace after curfew. He (Virilio and Richard 2012: 13–14) observes of this period that he was a child of war:

I lived through *the ministry of fear* as a child in Nantes after witnessing the Debacle; the Fifth Column, which had been formed during the Spanish Civil War, was omnipresent in everyone's thoughts and conversations [. . .] We had a first-hand experience of the *Blitzkrieg*, the lightning war. Nantes, 1940: one morning, we were informed that the Germans were in Orleans; at noon, we heard the sound of German trucks rolling through the streets. We had never seen anything like it.

Later, as a conscript, Virilio served in the French Army in Algeria, rising to the rank of sergeant.

Virilio's earliest academic studies were also of military architecture during the Second World War (1994a [1975]), which became, first, an essay in 1958, then a book and a museum exhibition in 1975. His explorations of the spaces of war led him to a close analysis of the role of technology and speed in war (and culture in general). Space (especially urban), technology and speed (often conceptualised in terms of the 'race', as in arms race, and analysed under the heading of dromology), along with information, perception (vision) and the accident have been the major themes he has used to illuminate the contours of contemporary conflict and vice versa. In short, many of his works focus on war and none of them ignores it.

He pursues a strategy of epistemological proliferation to understand the excesses, technological and humanitarian, of contemporary war. In his view, war today cannot really be understood in its complexity and horror, but perhaps enough about it can be explained by generating a wide array of ideas so that we can transcend it. This proliferation of the ways in which we can understand war corresponds to postmodern war's proliferation of weapons and modes (Gray 1997). Virilio, then, deploys, almost tactically, concepts, metaphors, analogies and labels to emphasise what is important, new and dangerous, in the organised violence of war that, thanks to relentless technoscience, has become hyperviolence.

Consider some of the many different terms he has applied to contemporary war: pure war and total war, intestinal war, holy war, technological war, political war, internal war, light-war, lightening war, ecological war, total electronic war, non-conventional war, open war, electronic blitzkrieg war, dirty war in real time, promotional war, stealth war and postmodern war, infowar, web war, secular holy war, nodal war, war of the airwaves, clean war, legalist war, preventative war, accidental war, impure war and international civil war.

His approach has produced a wide range of new ideas (the suicidal state, endo-colonisation, dromology) and a reframing of old ones (speed, vision, technoscience, weapons, information, panic, deterrence, accident) that have proven significant and fruitful. His theorisations are pragmatic; they are supposed to be helpful, to make a difference. The role of specific technologies in transforming wars is a central insight, and he has contributed greatly to our understanding of the importance of fortifications, nuclear weapons, cinema, computers, stealth technologies and drones in war today. He shows how different weapons produced different epochs of war and different types of deterrence.

For example, Virilio takes Albert Einstein's term, the information bomb, and shows how information is deployed as a pure weapon to create panic, to foster new types of aggressive and destabilising deterrence, and to obscure the non-accidental nature of accidents. For Virilio, then, war is not simply about information, news and facts, but, more significantly, about interactivity, logistics and organisation. And accidents such as wars, far from being 'chance events' are the results of a tendency wherein excess triumphs over restraint and unreason over the understanding of nation-states.

Virilio's method has allowed him to discern important developments in contemporary conflict long before most other theorists or practitioners noticed them. Among the most important are how technoscience is transforming war through acceleration and the militarisation of information, which is leading to institutionalising war as spectacle, to the ways weapons of mass destruction generate pure war in opposition to the impure war of low-intensity conflict and terrorism, to the transformation of deterrence into many different state-to-state relationships and to the invention of aggressive preventative war, a dynamic that is currently producing suicidal states and the new type of sustained civil war Virilio calls endo-colonisation.

As a philosopher shaped by the student-led protests in Paris in May 1968, Virilio has looked at revolutionary and insurrectionary violence, most notably in his critique of the Red Brigades and related groups in *Popular Defense & Ecological Struggles* (1990 [1978]). A devout Christian, an activist (against war and for the poor and homeless) and a theorist without hubris, he warns against naïve appropriations of violence and argues for non-violence. Importantly, at the heart of current endo-colonialist struggles around information and for political power, *wikis* (the Hawaiian word for fast) such as *Wikileaks*, and related instantaneous social media, are playing a major role. Here, Virilio has also warned of the militarised Web, of which the Internet is only a side street. This Web that focuses on total battlefield awareness, as the American military terms it, is the battle space now, according to Virilio. As he points out, the coming vital question is whether it is actually possible to democratise ubiquity, instantaneity, omniscience and omnipresence.

Virilio's interviews and writings on military strategy (e.g. Virilio and Armitage 2001b: 167–97; Armitage 2012: 406–12) cite the ancient Chinese philosopher Sun Tzu (2008) as the most important theorist of war. Thus, for Virilio, one of the fundamental errors of the strategists controlling postmodern militarised technological advances is that they are not by choice open to the 'fluid approach' that is expressed in Sun Tzu's military strategy. As Virilio comments, his:

is a post-Clausewitzian concept. This is due to the fact that Sun Tzu has a much more fluid approach to the question of war. It is also a very interesting approach and reflects the profound Chinese way of thinking more generally. For example, the Chinese often describe power in terms of water. And water cannot be stopped from flowing. Thus the Chinese do not compare war with fire since fire can be stopped. But what has happened to war today? In the old days, there were two armies at war. One army lost the war and the other won. There were rules. *Victory or defeat was a given.* Each was definitive. *But, nowadays, there is never a victory.* Everyone loses. There is no definitive result. And this is why Sun Tzu's writings are still relevant. (Virilio and Armitage 2001b: 188)

Virilio's analysis of war is then central to philosophers, cultural studies scholars and activists in Europe and the Americas, including Gilles Deleuze and Félix Guattari (2004 [1980]), and has influenced military practitioners, especially in France and Israel, and, through his press commentaries, the general public.

See also: Accident; Pure War; Speed; Technology

WRITING

Ryan Bishop

Virilio always refers to himself as a child of war, and his theoretical obsessions indicate as much: so does his writing, rhetoric and style. In a discussion with Virilio (Virilio and Lotringer 2005: 13), Sylvère Lotringer summarises Virilio's view that Cubism serves not as an experiment or destruction of perspectival painting but as a kind of 'artistic realism' related to the First World War. The war had exploded reality into pieces that George Braque collected into paintings 'the way people collect pieces of flesh after the explosion of a human bomb' (*AA*, 13). Virilio's writing operates stylistically in the same way as Braque's paintings: a gathering together in a completely realistic manner of the shards of reality, which are then reassembled in an aesthetically pleasing and provocative manner. Virilio worked with Braque with the stained glass at the Chapelle de Varengeville, on the site where a German plane crashed in 1942, destroying the small wooden chapel that stood on the spot where the current chapel stands. The same assemblage technique manifest there operates in Virilio's texts. As a theorist and writer, he uses juxtaposition, association, resemblance and evocation to make his arguments, not linear analysis. The trajectory of art and warfare that he presents tells us about his writing too. The increased destruction and disfiguration of the human body found in the move to abstract painting also disfigures the corpus of traditional analytic writing in his theoretical texts. The form follows the content and indeed shapes it.

As a result of the deep relationship between form and content, speed figures in Virilio's style simply as a matter of course. The 'retinal persistence of written text' (Virilio in Armitage 2001: xi) indicates a means for not only freezing the productive and necessary evanescence of speech but for understanding the influence of speed on thought. The text becomes a site of dromoscopic exploration. In an interview with John Armitage (Virilio and Armitage 2001a: 16–17), he links the speed (and temporality) of music to his writing style, emphasising rhythm, tempo and variations. In the same (oral) utterance, he calls his writing a 'dynamic, cinematic process', connecting his style to another great temporally constrained art form in addition to music. However, he places his writing and philosophy generally under the larger rubric of literature, a decidedly static mode of representation that depends on the spatial representation of a temporal process.

Virilio often maintains a hyperbolic tone, a virtual incantation related to technological development and failure. Although he has been criticised as being anti-technology, even a Luddite, his rhetorical position is a canny and strategic placement within the larger technophilic cheerleading of almost the whole of public discourse. In spite of his desire to unsettle knee-jerk reactions to technology and progress, Virilio capitulates to the emergence of *The Vision Machine* (1994b [1988]) in his writing by working with and creating mental images from the text, playing to the visual biases that have solidified over the past several centuries. So, even though he argues that visual technologies are killing off writing, he still deploys images in his own prose because, he claims, concepts are, in fact, mental images. Along with Gilles Deleuze, whom he (e.g. in Virilio and Armitage 2001a: 15–16) frequently names in relation to the power of the concept as a mental image, he aspires to reassert the ascendancy of the mental image from texts in contrast to those produced by visual technologies, again asserting a persistence of vision from the written word that stands opposed to the evanescence of, for example, the image of the computer screen.

Because he is interested in the accident, and the inevitability of the accident, Virilio allows juxtaposition to result in the accident of surprising thoughts and insights: as the self-reflexive discussion of his writing reveals. It is simultaneously static and dynamic, related to literature, cinema and music – not to mention stained glass work, his first full-scale foray into the arts. If we add the gathering together of shards found in Braque's Cubism, the military's accelerated visualising technologies demand a slow response, a brake, but only a tapping of the brake as Virilio's writing hurtles along. The speed that so occupies Virilio also entices him by its seductive prowess, as his own writing becomes a juggernaut of associative relations bounding from one idea to another with little supporting groundwork and documentation. In fact, skipping the 'development' between ideas to simply leap ahead is a conscious rhetorical strategy on Virilio's part, as he attempts to capture a tendency that relates concepts rather than a clarification of the linkages between them (Virilio and Lotringer 2008: 52–3). He largely eschews the knowledge apparatus of traditional academic writing, relying instead on the accelerating rhythm of his prose to pile up in the form of an accidental argument often about accidents.

The interruption and revelatory power of the accident in thought and writing are elements that he consciously brings forward to create a text reliant on implicit relations, forcing readers to puzzle out relations and connections. In the book-length interview with Lotringer called *Pure War* (Virilio and Lotringer 2008) he addresses this point directly by discussing an earlier work:

In *L'Esthétique de la disparition* [*The Aesthetics of Disappearance* 2009a (1980)], I had the revelation of the importance of interruption, of accident; of things that are stopped as *productive* [. . .] I handle breaks and absences. The fact of stopping and saying, 'let's go somewhere else' is very important for me. (*PW*, 53)

In this manner, he ups the heat on what Marshall McLuhan (2001 [1964]) had already called 'a hot medium': the written text, forcing the readers to make the connections he suggests rather than explains. In the same conversation with Lotringer, he explains his opaque writing and the gaps in his thought processes by contrasting his rhetoric with other modes of production in which he participates. 'Being an urbanist and architect,' he says, 'I am too used to constructing clear systems, machines that work well. I don't believe it's writing's job to do the same thing. I don't like two-and-two-is-four type writing' (*PW*, 52). His sustained interest in technological failure as an inevitable part of invention, one often ignored by narratives of scientific progress, becomes a specific rhetorical tool. He pours sand in the machinery of philosophical discourse to ensure the well-oiled apparatus breaks down. Rather like tapping the brakes on the speeding juggernaut of technology writ large, Virilio finds some hope in failure, a chance for humanity that works even at the level of his writing.

See also: Accident; Speed; Technology; Theory

Bibliography

PAUL VIRILIO: BOOKS IN ENGLISH

This subdivision of the Bibliography is of book-length works obtainable in English at the time of writing by Paul Virilio. It is organised in order of publication in the original French where appropriate. The section offers a key to nearly all references to Virilio's writings in the separate entries. These are standardised in order that any reference to one of Virilio's books is either written out, as in '*Bunker Archeology* (1994a [1975])' (where the first date signifies the publication of the English translation, whereas the second, in square brackets, indicates the original French publication date), or is shortened so that, for instance, '(*BA*)' stands for *Bunker Archeology* and '(*BA*, 1)' denotes a particular page in *Bunker Archeology*. This listing includes works that are not exclusively by Virilio and a number that are originally English-language publications.

[*BA*]   Virilio, P. (1994a [1975]) *Bunker Archeology*, trans. G. Collins. Princeton, NJ: Princeton Architectural Press.

[*SP*]   Virilio, P. (2006 [1977]) *Speed and Politics: An Essay on Dromology*, trans. M. Polizzotti. New York: Semiotext(e).

[*PD*]   Virilio, P. (1990 [1978]) *Popular Defense & Ecological Struggles*, trans. M. Polizzotti. New York: Semiotext(e).

[*AD*]   Virilio, P. (2009a [1980]) *The Aesthetics of Disappearance*, trans. P. Beitchman. New York: Semiotext(e).

[*WC*]   Virilio, P. (1989 [1984]) *War and Cinema: The Logistics of Perception*, trans. P. Camiller. London: Verso.

[*LD*]   Virilio, P. (1991 [1984]) *The Lost Dimension*, trans. D. Moshenberg. New York: Semiotext(e).

[*NH*]   Virilio, P. (2005a [1984]) *Negative Horizon: An Essay in Dromoscopy*, trans. M. Degener. London: Continuum.

[*VM*]   Virilio, P. (1994b [1988]) *The Vision Machine*, trans. J. Rose. London: British Film Institute.

[*PI*]   Virilio, P. (2000a [1990]) *Polar Inertia*, trans. P. Camiller. London: Sage.

[*DS*]   Virilio, P. (2002a [1991]) *Desert Screen: War at the Speed of Light*, trans. M. Degener. London: Continuum.

[*AM*]   Virilio, P. (1995 [1993]) *The Art of the Motor*, trans. J. Rose. Minneapolis: University of Minnesota Press.

[*OS*]   Virilio, P. (1997 [1995]) *Open Sky*, trans. J. Rose. London: Verso.

[*LE*]   Virilio, P. (2000c [1996]) *A Landscape of Events*, trans. J. Rose. Princeton, NJ: Princeton Architectural Press.

[*FO*]   Virilio, P. and Parent, C. (1996) *The Function of the Oblique*, trans. P. Johnson. London: Architectural Association.

[*PVW*] Virilio, P. and Petit, P. (1999 [1996]) *Politics of the Very Worst*, trans. M. Cavaliere and S. Lotringer. New York: Semiotext(e).

[*AP*]   Virilio, P. and Parent, C. (1997) *Architecture Principe 1966 and 1996*, trans. G. Collins. Besançon: Les Éditions de L'Imprimeur.

[*IB*]   Virilio, P. (2000d [1998]) *The Information Bomb*, trans. C. Turner. London: Verso.

[*SD*]   Virilio, P. (2000b [1999]) *Strategy of Deception*, trans. C. Turner. London: Verso.

[*WJ*]   Virilio, P. and Brausch, M. (2011 [1999]) *A Winter's Journey: Four Conversations with Marianne Brausch*, trans. C. Turner. London: Seagull.

[*AF*]   Virilio, P. (2003a [2000]) *Art and Fear*, trans. J. Rose. London: Continuum.

[*GZ*]   Virilio, P. (2002b [2002]) *Ground Zero*, trans. C. Turner. London: Verso.

[*CD*]   Virilio, P. and Lotringer, S. (2002) *Crepuscular Dawn*, trans. M. Taormina. New York: Semiotext(e).

[*UQ*]   Virilio, P. (2003b [2002]) *Unknown Quantity*, trans. C. Turner and Jian-Xing Too. London: Thames and Hudson.

[*CP*]   Virilio, P. (2005b [2004]) *City of Panic*, trans. J. Rose. Oxford: Berg.

[*AA*]   Virilio, P. and Lotringer, S. (2005) *The Accident of Art*, trans. M. Taormina. New York: Semiotext(e).

[*OA*]   Virilio, P. (2007a [2005]) *The Original Accident*, trans. J. Rose. Cambridge: Polity.

[*AFE*]   Virilio, P. (2007b [2005]) *Art as Far as the Eye Can See*, trans. J. Rose. Oxford: Berg.

[*UD*]   Virilio, P. (2010a [2007]) *The University of Disaster*, trans. J. Rose. Cambridge: Polity.

[*NL*]   Virilio, P. and Depardon, R. (2008) *Native Land: Stop Eject*, trans. Various. Paris: Fondation Cartier pour l'art contemporain.

[*PW*]   Virilio, P. and Lotringer, S. (2008) *Pure War*, trans. P. Beitchman, B. O'Keefe and M. Polizzotti. New York: Semiotext(e).

[*GE*]   Virilio, P. (2009) *Grey Ecology*, trans. D. Burk. New York: Atropos.

[*FI*]   Virilio, P. (2010b [2009]) *The Futurism of the Instant: Stop-Eject*, trans. J. Rose. Cambridge: Polity.

[GA]   Virilio, P. (2012 [2010]) *The Great Accelerator*, trans. J. Rose. Cambridge: Polity.

[TAF]   Virilio, P. and Richard, B. (2012) *The Administration of Fear*, trans. A. Hodges. New York: Semiotext(e).

PAUL VIRILIO: SELECTED BOOKS IN FRENCH

Selected books in French that are not available as full free-standing English translations at the time of writing are listed here.

[LV]   Virilio, P. (1991) *La Vitesse*. Paris: Éditions Flammarion.

[LT]   Virilio, P. (1993) *L'insécurité du territoire*. Paris: Galilée.

[KV]   Virilio, P. (1999) *Klasen-Virilio. Impact Inspections*. Paris: Expressions Contemporaines.

[DHA]   Virilio, P. and Baj, E. (2003) *Discours sur l'horreur de l'art*. Lyon: Atelier de Création Libertaire.

[TT]   Virilio, P. and Orlan (2009) *Transgression transfiguration*. Paris: L'Une et l'Autre.

[N]   Virilio, P. and Parent, C. (2010) *Nevers: Architecture principe*. Paris: HYX.

[PE]   Virilio, P. (2012) *La Pensée exposée*. Paris: Galilée.

OTHER VIRILIO CITED

Virilio, P. (1993 [1982]) 'The Primal Accident', in B. Massumi (ed.), *The Politics of Everyday Fear*. Minneapolis: University of Minnesota Press, pp. 211–18.

Virilio, P. (1991 [1984]) 'The Overexposed City', in *The Lost Dimension*. New York: Semiotext(e), pp. 9–28.

Virilio, P. (1991 [1984]) 'Improbable Architecture', in *The Lost Dimension*. New York: Semiotext(e), pp. 69–100.

Virilio, P. (1995) 'Speed and Information: Cyberspace Alarm!', *CTheory*. Online at: http://www.ctheory.net/articles.aspx?id=72

Virilio, P. (1996a) 'Architecture Principe', in C. Parent and P. Virilio, *The Function of the Oblique*. London: Architectural Association, pp. 11–15.

Virilio, P. (1996b) 'The Silence of the Lambs' (interview with C. Oliveira), *CTheory*. Online at: http://www.ctheory.net/articles.aspx?id=38

Virilio, P. (1997a) 'Disorientation', in P. Virilio and C. Parent, *Architecture Principe 1966 and 1996*. Besançon: Les Éditions de l'Imprimeur, pp. 7–13.

Virilio, P. (1997b) 'Habitable Circulation', in P. Virilio and C. Parent, *Architecture Principe 1966 and 1996*. Besançon: Les Éditions de l'Imprimeur, pp. ix–x.

Virilio, P. (1997c) 'The Mediate City', in P. Virilio and C. Parent, *Architecture Principe 1966 and 1996*. Besançon: Les Éditions de l'Imprimeur, pp. xvii–xviii.

Virilio, P. (1997d) 'Optics on a Grand Scale', in *Open Sky*. London: Verso, pp. 35–48.

Virilio, P. and Wilson, L. (1997) 'Cyberwar, God and Television: An Interview with Paul Virilio', in A. Kroker and M. Kroker (eds), *Digital Delirium*. Montreal: New World Perspectives, pp. 41–8.

Virilio, P. (1998a) 'The Suicidal State', in J. Der Derian (ed.), *The Virilio Reader*. Oxford: Blackwell, pp. 29–45.

Virilio, P. (1998b) 'Surfing the Accident' (interview with A. Ruby), in J. Brouwer and A. Mulder (eds), *The Art of the Accident*. Rotterdam: V2_ Institute. Online at: http://www.v2.nl/archive/articles/surfing-the-accident

Virilio, P. (1999) 'Virilio – Cyberesistance Fighter: An Interview with Paul Virilio' (interview with D. Dufresne), trans. J. Houis, *Après Coup*. Online at: http://www.apres-coup.org/mt/archives/title/2005/01/cyberesistance.html

Virilio, P. and Armitage, J. (2000) 'The Kosovo War Took Place in Orbital Space: Paul Virilio in conversation with John Armitage', *CTheory*, 18 October. Online at: http://www.ctheory.net/articles.aspx?id=132

Virilio, P. and Armitage, J. (2001a) 'From Modernism to Hypermodernism and Beyond', in J. Armitage (ed.), *Virilio Live: Selected Interviews*. London: Sage, pp. 15–47.

Virilio, P. and Armitage, J. (2001b) 'The Kosovo W@r Did Take Place', in J. Armitage (ed.), *Virilio Live: Selected Interviews*. London: Sage, pp. 167–97.

Virilio, P. and Dercon, C. (2001) 'Speed-Space: Interview with Chris Dercon', in J. Armitage (ed.), *Virilio Live*, trans. D. Miller, London: Sage, pp. 69–81.

Virilio, P. and Kittler, F. (2001) 'The Information Bomb: A Conversation', trans. P. Riemens, in J. Armitage (ed.), *Virilio Live: Selected Interviews*. London: Sage, pp. 97–109.

Virilio, P. and Ruby, A. (2001) 'The Time of the Trajectory', in J. Armitage (ed.), *Virilio Live: Selected Interviews*. London: Sage, pp. 58–65.

Virilio, P. and Zurbrugg, N. (2001) 'Not Words but Visions!' in J. Armitage (ed.), *Virilio Live: Selected Interviews*. London: Sage, pp. 154–63.

Virilio, P. (2008) 'Le krach actuel représente l'accident intégral par excellence' (interview with G. Courtois and M. Guerrin), *Le Monde*, 18 October. Online at: http://www.lemonde.fr/opinions/article/2008/10/18/le-krach-actuel-represente-l-accident-integral-par-excelle nce_1108473_3232.html; English translation at: http://sites.goo gle.com/site/radicalperspectivesonthecrisis/news/paul-virilio-on-the-crisis

Virilio, P. and Armitage, J. (2009) 'In the Cities of the Beyond: An Interview with Paul Virilio', in J. Seijdel and L. Melis (eds), *Open: Cahier on Art and the Public Domain* (18): 2030: *War Zone Amsterdam: Imagining the Unimaginable*, November. SKOR Foundation for Art and Public Space Amsterdam: NAI Publishers, pp. 100–11.

Virilio, P., Geisler, T. and Doze, P. (2009) 'Rock Around The Bunker: Paul Virilio: Design, War and Society', *DAMn° magazine* 21 (March–April): 92–6. Online at: http://www1.uni-ak.ac.at/designtheory/media/pdf/DAMnVirilio.pdf

Virilio, P. (2011), 'Impact Studies', trans. J. Rose, in J. Armitage (ed.), *Virilio Now: Current Perspectives in Virilio Studies*. Cambridge: Polity, pp. 234–8.

Virilio, P. and Armitage, J. (2011) 'The Third War: Cities, Conflict, and Contemporary Art: Interview with Paul Virilio', in J. Armitage (ed.), *Virilio Now: Current Perspectives in Virilio Studies*. Cambridge: Polity, pp. 29–45.

BOOKS ON VIRILIO IN ENGLISH

Armitage, J. (ed.) (2000) *Paul Virilio: From Modernism to Hypermodernism and Beyond*. London: Sage.

Armitage, J. (ed.) (2001) *Virilio Live: Selected Interviews*. London: Sage.

Armitage, J. (ed.) (2011) *Virilio Now: Current Perspectives in Virilio Studies*. Cambridge: Polity.

Armitage, J. (2012) *Virilio and the Media*. Cambridge: Polity.

Armitage, J. and Bishop, R. (eds) (2013) *Virilio and Visual Culture*. Edinburgh: Edinburgh University Press.

Der Derian, J. (ed.) (1998) *The Virilio Reader*. Oxford: Blackwell.

James, I. (2007) *Paul Virilio*. London: Routledge.

Redhead, S. (2004a) *Paul Virilio: Theorist for an Accelerated Culture*. Edinburgh: Edinburgh University Press.

Redhead, S. (ed.) (2004b) *The Paul Virilio Reader*. Edinburgh: Edinburgh University Press.

OTHER TEXTS CITED

Althusser, L. (2005) *For Marx*. London: Verso.

Antonio, R. (ed.) (2002) *Marx and Modernity: Key Readings and Commentary*. Oxford: Wiley-Blackwell.

Arendt, H. (1973) *The Origins of Totalitarianism*. London: Penguin.

Aristotle (2002) *The Metaphysics*. London: Penguin.

Armitage, J. (2001) 'Project(iles) of Hypermodern(organ)ization', *Ephemera* 1 (2): 131–48. Online at: http://www.ephemeraweb.org/journal/1-2/1-2armitage.pdf

Armitage, J. (2003) 'On Ernst Jünger's "Total Mobilization": A Re-evaluation in the Era of the War on Terrorism', *Body & Society* 9 (4): 191–213.

Armitage, J. (2010) 'Temporary Authoritarian Zone', in *Sarai Reader 08: Fear*, ed. Sarai Collective, Centre for the Study of Developing Societies. New Delhi, India: 18–19.

Armitage, J. (2012) 'Paul Virilio as Twentieth-Century Military Strategist: War, Cinema, and the Logistics of Perception', in A. Piette and M. Rawlinson (eds), *Edinburgh Companion to Twentieth-Century British and American War Literature*. Edinburgh: Edinburgh University Press, pp. 406–12.

Armitage, J. (2013) 'The Face of the Figureless: Aesthetics, Sacred Humanism, and the Accident of Art', in J. Armitage and R. Bishop (eds), *Virilio and Visual Culture*. Edinburgh: Edinburgh University Press, pp. 156–79.

Armitage, J. and Graham, P. (2001) 'Dromoeconomics: Towards a Political Economy of Speed', *Parallax* 7 (1): 111–23.

Armitage, J. and Bishop, R. (eds) (2013) *Virilio and Visual Culture*. Edinburgh: Edinburgh University Press.

Baudrillard, J. (1983) *Simulations*. New York: Semiotext(e).

Baudrillard, J. (1993) *Symbolic Exchange and Death*. London: Sage.

Baudrillard, J. (1996) *The Perfect Crime*. London: Verso.

Baudrillard, J. (2001) *Impossible Exchange*. London: Verso.

Baudrillard, J. (2003) *The Spirit of Terrorism*. London: Verso.

Bauman, Z. (2002) *Society under Siege*. Cambridge: Polity.

Beck, J (2011) 'Concrete Ambivalence: Inside the Bunker Complex', *Cultural Politics* 7 (1): 79–102.

Beckman, K. (2010) *Crash: Cinema and the Politics of Speed and Stasis*. Durham, NC: Duke University Press.

Beiser, F. (2005) *Hegel*. London: Routledge.

Bell, S. (2010) *Fast Feminism*. New York: Autonomedia.

Bellour, R. (1990) *L'entre-images: Photo, cinéma, video*. Paris: La Différence.

Bellour, R. (1999) *L'entre-images 2: Mots, images*. Paris: P.O.L. Trafic.

Berman, M. (2010) *All That is Solid Melts Into Air: The Experience of Modernity*. London: Verso.

Benjamin, A. (1994) 'Time, and Task', in P. Osborne and A. Benjamin (eds), *Walter Benjamin's Philosophy*. London: Routledge, pp. 216–50.

Clausewitz, C. von (1968) *On War*. Harmondsworth: Penguin.

Conley, V. A. (2000) 'The Passenger: Paul Virilio and Feminism', in J. Armitage (ed.), *Paul Virilio: From Modernism to Hypermodernism and Beyond*. London: Sage, pp. 201–14.

Crary, J. (1999) *Suspensions of Perception: Attention, Spectacle and Modern Culture*. Cambridge, MA: MIT Press.

Crosthwaite, P. (2011) 'The Accident of Finance', in J. Armitage (ed.), *Virilio Now: Current Perspectives in Virilio Studies*. Cambridge: Polity, pp. 177–99.

Davis, M. (2006) *City of Quartz: Excavating the Future in Los Angeles*. London: Verso.

Debord, G. (1984) *Society of the Spectacle*. Detroit: Black and Red.

Debray, R. (2004) *Transmitting Culture*. New York: Columbia University Press.

de la Billiere, P. (General) (2008) *Storm Command: A Personal Account of the Gulf War*. London: Harper Collins.

Deleuze, G. (1990) *The Logic of Sense*. London: Athlone.

Deleuze, G. (1995 [1990]) 'Postscript on Control Societies', in *Negotiations*. New York: Columbia University Press, pp. 177–82.

Deleuze, G. (2004 [1968]) *Difference and Repetition*. London: Continuum.

Deleuze, G. and Guattari, F. (2004 [1972]) *Anti-Oedipus: Capitalism and Schizophrenia*. London: Continuum.

Deleuze, G. and Guattari, F. (2004 [1980]) *A Thousand Plateaus: Capitalism and Schizophrenia*. London: Continuum.

Foucault, M. (1991) *Discipline and Punish: The Birth of the Prison*. London: Penguin.

Foucault, M. (2000 [1970]) 'Theatrum Philosophicum', in J. Faubion (ed.), *Aesthetics, Method, and Epistemology*. London: Penguin Books, pp. 343–68.

Foucault, M. (2002) *Power: The Essential Works of Michel Foucault 1954–1984: Volume 3*. London: Penguin.

Foucault, M. (2010) *The Birth of Biopolitics: Lectures at the Collège de France, 1978–1979*. London: Palgrave Macmillan.

Freud, S. (1977) *Inhibitions, Symptoms, and Anxiety*. New York: W. W. Norton and Co.

Freud, S. (2000) *Three Essays on the Theory of Sexuality*. New York: Basic Books.

Freud, S. (2003) *Beyond the Pleasure Principle*. London: Penguin.

Freud, S. (2005) *On Murder, Mourning, and Melancholy*. London: Penguin.

Fukuyama, F. (1993) *The End of History and the Last Man*. London: Penguin.

Gane, M. (2003) *French Social Theory*. London: Sage.

Gibson, W. (1995 [1984]) *Neuromancer*. New York: Voyager Books.

Giddens, A. (1981) *A Contemporary Critique of Historical Materialism, Vol. 1: Power, Property and the State*. London: Macmillan.

Graham, P. (2006) *Hypercapitalism: New Media, Language, and Social Perceptions of Value*. New York: Lang.

Gray, C. H. (1997) *Postmodern War: The New Politics of Conflict*. London: Routledge.

Haraway, D. (1985) 'A Cyborg Manifesto: Science, Technology, and Socialist-Feminism in the Late Twentieth Century', *Socialist Review* 80: 65–108.

Hardt, M. and Negri, A. (2000) *Empire*. Cambridge, MA: Harvard University Press.

Harvey, D. (1989) *The Condition of Postmodernity: An Enquiry into the Origins of Cultural Change*. Oxford: Blackwell.

Harvey, D. (2006) *Spaces of Global Capitalism: Towards a Theory of Uneven Geographical Development*. London: Verso.

Hassan, R. (2003) *The Chronoscopic Society: Globalization, Time and Knowledge in the Network Economy*. New York: Peter Lang.

Hassan, R. and Purser, R. (2007) *24/7: Time and Temporality in the Network Society*. Palo Alto, CA: Stanford University Press.

Heidegger, M. (1977) 'The Question Concerning Technology', in *The Question Concerning Technology and Other Essays*. New York: Harper, pp. 3–35.

Heidegger, M. (1978) 'The Question Concerning Technology', in D. F. Krell (ed.), *Martin Heidegger: Basic Writings*. London: Routledge, pp. 307–42.

Heidegger, M. (1998) 'Only a God Can Save Us: *Der Spiegel*'s Interview with Martin Heidegger', in R. Wolin (ed.), *The Heidegger Controversy*. Cambridge, MA: The MIT Press, pp. 91–116.

Heidegger, M. (2000) *An Introduction to Metaphysics*. New Haven, CT: Yale University Press.

Heidegger, M. (2002) 'The Age of the World Picture', in J. Young and K. Haynes (eds), *Martin Heidegger: Off the Beaten Track*. Cambridge: Cambridge University Press, pp. 57–72.

Heim, M. (1993) *The Metaphysics of Virtual Reality*. New York: Oxford University Press.

Heim, M. (1998) *Virtual Realism*. New York: Oxford University Press.

Held, D., Goldblatt, D, Perraton, J. and McGrew, A. (1999) *Global Transformations: Politics, Economics, Culture*. Cambridge: Polity.

Hitler, A. (2007) *Mein Kampf*. New Delhi: Jaico Publishing House.

Hobbes, T. (2002) *Leviathan*. London: Penguin.

Hoofd, I. M. (2004) 'Dialogues between Paul Virilio and Chela Sandoval: Towards a Better Understanding of Uses and Abuses of New Technologies', *Genders* 39. Online at: http://www.genders.org/g39/g39_hoofd.html

Husserl, E. (1970) *The Crisis of European Sciences and Transcendental Phenomenology*. Evanston, IL: Northwestern University Press.

Husserl, E. (1977) *Cartesian Meditations: An Introduction to Phenomenology*, 5th edn. Amsterdam: Martinus Nijhoff Publishers.

Husserl, E. (1983) *Ideas Pertaining to a Pure Phenomenology and to a Phenomenological Philosophy*, First Book. The Hague: Martin Nijhoff Publishers.

Husserl, E. (1998) *The Paris Lectures*. Dordrecht: Kluwer Academic Publishers.

Husserl, E. (2001) *Logical Investigations Volumes I & II*. London: Routledge.

Innis, H. A. (2008) 'A Plea for Time', in *The Bias of Communication*. Toronto: University of Toronto Press, pp. 61–91.

Jameson, F. (1991) *Postmodernism, Or, the Cultural Logic of Late Capitalism*. London: Verso.

Janelle, D. (1968) 'Central Place Development in a Time-Space Framework', *Professional Geographer* 20: 5–10.

Jünger, E. (1993) 'Total Mobilization', in R. Wolin (ed.), *The Heidegger Controversy*. Cambridge, MA: MIT Press, pp. 119–39.

Kellner, D. (2004) '9/11, Spectacles of Terror, and Media Manipulation: A Critique of Jihadist and Bush Media Politics', *Critical Discourse Studies* 1 (1): 41–64.

Kittler, F. A. (1990) *Discourse Networks 1800/1900*. Stanford, CA: Stanford University Press.

Kittler, F. A. (1999) *Gramophone, Film, Typewriter*. Stanford, CA: Stanford University Press.

Kittler, F. A. (2010) *Optical Media*. Cambridge: Polity Press.

Kittler, F. A. and Armitage, J. (2006) 'From Discourse Networks to Cultural Mathematics: An Interview with Friedrich A. Kittler', *Theory, Culture & Society*, 23 (7–8): 17–38.

Kjøsen, A. M. (2010) 'An Accident of Value: A Marxist–Virilian Analysis of Digital Piracy', MA Thesis, The University of Western Ontario.

Kroker, A. (2002) 'The Image Matrix', *CTheory*, 20 March. Online at: http://www.ctheory.net/articles.aspx?id=331

Kroker, A. (2003) *The Will to Technology and the Culture of Nihilism: Heidegger, Marx, and Nietzsche*. Toronto: University of Toronto Press.

Lacan, J. (2007) *Écrits*. New York: W. W. Norton and Co.

Lucan, J. (1996) 'Introduction', in P. Virilio and C. Parent, *The Function of the Oblique*. London: Architectural Association, pp. 5–10.

Lyotard, J.-F. (1984) *The Postmodern Condition: A Report on Knowledge*. Manchester: Manchester University Press.

Lyotard, J.-F. (2011) *Discourse, Figure*. Minneapolis: Minnesota University Press.

Marcuse, H. (1991 [1964]) *One Dimensional Man*. Boston, MA: Beacon Press.

Marinetti, F. T. (2005) 'The Founding and the Manifesto of Futurism', in L. Rainey (ed.), *Modernism: An Anthology*. Oxford: Blackwell, pp. 3–6.

Martin, P. (2011) 'Two-Speed Economy Now a Two-State Economy', *The Sydney Morning Herald*, 8 December. Online at: http://www.smh.com.au/business/twospeed-economy-now-a-twostate-economy-20111207-1ojby.html

Marx, K. (1987) *The German Ideology: Introduction to a Critique of Political Economy*. London: Lawrence and Wishart.

Marx, K. and Engels, F. (2004 [1848]) *The Communist Manifesto*. London: Penguin.

McKenna, R. (1997) *Real Time*. Boston, MA: Harvard Business School Press.

McLuhan, M. (2001 [1964]) *Understanding Media: The Extensions of Man*. London: Routledge.

McQuire, S. (2010) *The Media City*. London: Sage.

Merleau-Ponty, M. (1964) *The Primacy of Perception*. Evanston, IL: Northwestern University Press.

Merleau-Ponty, M. (1969 [1964]) *The Visible and the Invisible*. Evanston, IL: Northwestern University Press.

Merleau-Ponty, M. (1973 [1955]) *Adventures of the Dialectic*. Evanston, IL: Northwestern University Press.

Merleau-Ponty, M. (1984 [1942]) *The Structure of Behavior*. Pittsburgh, PA: Duquesne University Press.

Merleau-Ponty, M. (2000 [1947]) *Humanism and Terror*. New York: Transaction Publishers.

Merleau-Ponty, M. (2002 [1945]) *Phenomenology of Perception*. London: Routledge.

Mumford, L. (1968) *The City in History: Its Origins, Its Transformations, and Its Prospects*. New York: Harcourt Brace International.

Nicholls, P. (1995) *Modernisms: A Literary Guide*. London: Macmillan.

Norrish, P. J. (1958) *Drama of the Group: A Study of Unanimism in the Plays of Jules Romains*. Cambridge: Cambridge University Press.

Perec, G. (1997) *Species of Spaces and Other Pieces*. London: Penguin.

Prix, W. and Swiczinsky, H. (Coop Himmelb[l]au) (1997) 'The Architecture of Clouds', in P. Virilio and C. Parent, *Architecture Principe 1966 and 1996*. Besançon: Les Éditions de L'Imprimeur, pp. 154–6.

Purser, R. (2000) 'The Coming Crisis in Real-Time Environments: A Dromological Analysis', in S. Havolick (ed.), *Best Paper Proceedings*. Academy of Management (CD-ROM).

Schofield, J. (2005) *Combat Archeology: Material Culture and Modern Conflict*. London: Duckworth.

Simmel, G. (1969) 'The Metropolis and Mental Life', in R. Sennett (ed.), *Classic Essays on the Culture of Cities*. Englewood Cliffs, NJ: Prentice Hall, pp. 47–60.

Sokal, A. and Bricmont, J. (1998) *Intellectual Impostures: Postmodern Philosophers' Abuse of Science*. London: Profile Books.

Sun Tzu (2008) *The Art of War*. London: Penguin.

Thrift, N. (2011) 'Panicsville: Paul Virilio and the Aesthetic of Disaster', in J. Armitage (ed.), *Virilio Now: Current Perspectives in Virilio Studies*. Cambridge: Polity, pp. 145–57.

Tofts, D. (2007) 'Truth at Twelve Thousand Frames Per Second: *The Matrix* and the Time-Image Cinema', in R. Hassan and R. Purser (eds), *24/7: Time and Temporality in the Network Society*. Palo Alto, CA: Stanford University Press, pp. 109–21.

Turkle, S. (2011) *Alone Together*. New York: Basic Books.

Wees, W. C. (2010) 'Representing the Unrepresentable: Bruce Conner's *Crossroads* and the Nuclear Sublime', *Incite: Journal of Experimental Media*, 2 (Spring–Fall). Online at: http://www.incite-online.net/wees2.html

West, D. (2010) *Continental Philosophy*. Cambridge: Polity.

Wikipedia (2011) 'Video Game Addiction'. Online at: http://en.wikipedia.org/wiki/Video_game_addiction

Woodruff-Smith, D. (2009) *Husserl*. London: Routledge.

Wright, S. (2002) *Storming Heaven: Class Composition and Struggle in Italian Autonomist Marxism*. London: Pluto.

Young, J. (2001) *Heidegger's Later Philosophy*. Cambridge: Cambridge University Press.

Notes on Contributors

Jason Adams is Visiting Assistant Professor of Political Science at Williams College, USA.

Olga Alekseyeva is a PhD candidate in International Relations at Lancaster University, UK.

John Armitage is Professor of Media Arts at Winchester School of Art-University of Southampton, UK.

John Beck is Reader in American Literature and Culture at Newcastle University, UK.

Josiane Behmoiras is completing a Creative Writing PhD at the University of Melbourne, Australia.

Shannon Bell is Associate Professor in the Department of Political Science at York University, Toronto, Canada.

Ryan Bishop is Professor of Global Arts and Politics at Winchester School of Art-University of Southampton, UK.

Rob Bullard is Lecturer in Cultural, Contextual and Performance Studies at Teesside and Northumbria Universities, UK.

Drew S. Burk is a cultural theorist and director of Univocal Publishing.

David B. Clarke is Professor of Human Geography at Swansea University, UK.

Felicity Colman is Reader in Screen Media at Manchester Metropolitan University, UK.

Verena Andermatt Conley teaches Comparative Literature and Romance Languages and Literature at Harvard University, USA.

Tom Conley teaches in the Departments of Romance Languages and Visual and Environmental Studies at Harvard University, USA.

Gerry Coulter is Professor of Sociology at Bishop's University, Sherbrooke, Quebec, Canada.

Paul Crosthwaite is a Lecturer in English Literature at the University of Edinburgh, UK.

Sean Cubitt is Professor of Film and Television at Goldsmiths, University of London, UK.

Hugh Davies is Senior Lecturer in Creative Art and Media at La Trobe University, Melbourne, Australia.

Marcus A. Doel is Professor of Human Geography at Swansea University, UK.

John David Ebert is an independent American scholar and author of five books.

Mark Featherstone is Senior Lecturer in Sociology at Keele University, UK.

Brianne Gallagher is a Doctoral Candidate in the Department of Political Science at the University of Hawai'i at Mānoa, USA.

Mike Gane is Professor Emeritus at Loughborough University, UK.

Joy Garnett is an artist and writer in Brooklyn, New York, USA.

Phil Graham is Professor and Head of Music at Queensland University of Technology, Australia.

Chris Hables Gray is a lecturer at the University of California at Santa Cruz and California State University at Monterey Bay, USA.

Bob Hanke teaches Media Studies at York University, Toronto, Canada.

Robert Hassan is Senior Lecturer in the Media and Communications Program at the University of Melbourne, Australia.

Ingrid Hoofd is Assistant Professor in the Department of Communications and New Media at the National University of Singapore.

Ian James is Lecturer in French at the University of Cambridge, UK.

George Katsonis is a PhD candidate at the Department of War Studies, King's College, London, UK.

Scott McQuire is Associate Professor in the School of Culture and Communication at the University of Melbourne, Australia.

Nicholas Michelson is a Teaching Fellow in the Department of War Studies, King's College, London, UK.

Eftychia Mikelli teaches English at BCA College, Athens, Greece.

Nick Prior is Senior Lecturer in Sociology at the University of Edinburgh, UK.

Ronald E. Purser is Professor of Management at San Francisco State University, USA.

Julian Reid is Professor of International Politics at the University of Lapland, Finland.

Stephen Sale is a PhD candidate at the London Consortium, UK.

Gregor Schuner is a Research Associate in Migration at the University of Luxembourg.

Richard G. Smith is Senior Lecturer in Human Geography at Swansea University, UK.

Eric Wilson is Senior Lecturer in the Law Faculty at Monash University, Melbourne, Australia.

J. Macgregor Wise is Associate Dean and Professor of Communication Studies at Arizona State University, USA.

May Ee Wong is a PhD candidate in Cultural Studies at the University of California Davis, USA.

Mark Wright is a PhD candidate in the Department of Politics and Philosophy at Manchester Metropolitan University, UK.